TRUTHS WE CONFESS

Also in the R.C. Sproul Library

TRUTHS WE CONFESS

A Layman's Guide to the Westminster Confession of Faith

IN THREE VOLUMES

VOLUME 3: THE STATE, THE FAMILY, THE CHURCH, AND LAST THINGS
(Chapters 23–33 of the Confession)

R.C. SPROUL

P U B L I S H I N G
P.O. BOX 817 • PHILLIPSBURG • NEW JERSEY 08865-0817

Printed in the United States of America

Library of Congress Control Number: 2007931675

CONTENTS

23

The Civil Magistrate

The Westminster Confession of Faith
Chapter 23: Of the Civil Magistrate

Sec. 1. God, the supreme Lord and King of all the world, hath ordained civil magistrates, to be, under Him, over the people, for His own glory, and the public good: and, to this end, hath armed them with the power of the sword, for the defence and encouragement of them that are good, and for the punishment of evil doers.

Sec. 2. It is lawful for Christians to accept and execute the office of a magistrate, when called thereunto: in the managing whereof, as they ought especially to maintain piety, justice, and peace, according to the wholesome laws of each commonwealth; so, for that end, they may lawfully, now under the new testament, wage war, upon just and necessary occasion.

Sec. 3. Civil magistrates may not assume to themselves the administration of the Word and sacraments; or the power of the keys of the kingdom of heaven; or, in the least, interfere in matters of faith. Yet, as nursing fathers, it is the duty of civil magistrates to protect the Church of our common Lord, without giving the preference to any denomination of Christians above the rest, in such a manner that all ecclesiastical persons whatever shall enjoy the full, free, and unquestioned liberty of discharging every part of their sacred functions, without violence or danger. And, as Jesus Christ hath appointed a regular government and discipline in His Church, no law of any commonwealth should interfere with, let, or hinder, the due exercise thereof, among the voluntary members of any denomination of Christians, according to their own profession and belief. It is the duty of civil magistrates to protect the person and good name of all their people, in such an effectual manner as that no person be suffered, either upon pretense of religion or of infidelity, to offer any indignity, violence, abuse, or injury to any other person whatsoever: and to take order, that all religious and ecclesiastical assemblies be held without molestation or disturbance.

Sec. 4. It is the duty of people to pray for magistrates, to honour their persons, to pay them tribute or other dues, to obey their lawful commands, and to be subject to their authority, for conscience' sake. Infidelity, or difference in religion, doth not make void the magistrates' just and legal authority, nor free the people from their due obedience to them: from which ecclesiastical persons are not exempted, much less hath the Pope any power and jurisdiction over them in their dominions, or over any of their people; and, least of all, to deprive them of their dominions, or lives, if he shall judge them to be heretics, or upon any other pretense whatsoever.

Why we have government, what its purpose and role are, and how governmental authority relates to the sovereign authority of God himself are important considerations in this chapter on the civil magistrate.

Sec. 1. God, the supreme Lord and King of all the world, hath ordained civil magistrates, to be, under Him, over the people, for His own glory, and the public good: and, to this end, hath armed them with the power of the sword, for the defence and encouragement of them that are good, and for the punishment of evil doers.

Chapter 23 of the confession begins with the words **God, the supreme Lord and King of all the world, hath ordained civil magistrates, to be, under Him, over the people, for His own glory, and the public good.** Virtually every aspect of this opening statement is on a collision course with the assumptions that hold sway in our culture with respect to civil government. There was a crisis in the role of government in the first half of the twentieth century, which produced the greatest level of international conflict, violence, and warfare in recorded history. The level of armed conflict each century was calculated several years ago by a professor at Harvard University. The greatest era of peace was the first century. The second most peaceful century was the nineteenth century. The most violent century was also the most recent, the twentieth century. There is, therefore, a tendency on our part to assume that international conflict is normal.

Adolf Hitler and his Third Reich and Joseph Stalin and his Soviet Union illustrate what happens when government goes berserk and declares its independence from God. Increasingly, we hear rhetoric from people in the government and in the press about the separation of church and state. What they mean is the separation of the state from God. Their idea is that the civil government is not under God, but independent of him. It has its own autonomous authority. Hitler, Stalin, and Chairman Mao in Red China all held that same assumption. It is a fearful thing to see governments declaring independence from God himself.

Some people say that the longest word in the dictionary is *antidisestablishmentarianism*. That word is awkward because it includes a double negative. Antidisestablishmentarianism is the same thing as

3

establishmentarianism, which is a political philosophy that argues that the state should have an established church, such as the Church of England. In many European and Asian nations, a particular faith is supported financially by government taxation and politically by the power of the sword.

Pilgrims from many nations came to the shores of the New World to flee persecution because they were not in concert with the established church. Among the most significant of those groups were the English Puritans, who were Nonconformists. They found themselves under severe persecution in England, not only from the Roman Catholic Church during the reign of Bloody Mary, but also from her successor, Queen Elizabeth, whose rigorous persecution of the Puritans caused them to flee. Various colonies in America had established churches, and they could not agree on an established church for the new nation. Instead, the principle of freedom of religion was enshrined in the first amendment to the United States Constitution. This meant that the civil magistrate could not establish a particular church. Those who were against an established church were disestablishmentarian, and those who favored it were antidisestablishmentarian in their outlook—giving us that long and cumbersome word.

The first amendment does not express the idea that our nation is independent of God or that it was founded on atheism. It was actually self-consciously theistic in its origin, but refused to grant any particular theistic group favored status under the law. Having said that, let us get back to the confession.

First of all, the Westminster divines describe God as **the supreme Lord and King of all the world**. It is significant that in the discussion of the role of the civil magistrate, they begin with an affirmation of the supremacy of God in his lordship and kingship over the world.

In the Old Testament, two of the most important titles given to Yahweh (which is his name) are *adonai* and the title *melek*. *Adonai* means "the one who is absolutely sovereign." It is translated in our

English Bibles as "Lord." *Melek* is translated as "king." To the Jew in Israel, God was viewed as both the sovereign Lord and the King of the nation of Israel, the supreme King over all of the world. The earth is the Lord's and the fullness thereof, and all of those that dwell therein. He is the Creator of all things; therefore, his realm and reign extend beyond the borders of Israel. He is the Most High God, and the theater of his operation is universal.

When the people of Israel clamored for a king, God spoke to them through the prophet Samuel and told them that because they rejected him as their king, he would let them have a king. But their king would be like everybody else's kings. He would conscript their young people into the army, tax their property and income, and do other objectionable things. God let them have a king, but he was never autonomous. He was always held accountable to the King's law.

When David sinned so egregiously in his affair with Bathsheba, Nathan rebuked and confronted him. It was then that David penned his penitential psalm, Psalm 51. One of the statements that he made in that psalm was, "Do not take your Holy Spirit from me." He was not worried that God would take away the regenerating power of the Holy Spirit, because God never does that. What concerned him was that God might rescind his anointing of him as king. There, at least, David recognized God's authority over him. This became a major crisis in the history of Israel, when the wicked kings, such as Ahab, ruled as if the Lord could be ignored. They sought to be independent from the reign of God.

The central motif in the tapestry woven through the Old and New Testaments is that of the kingdom of God. The New Testament work of Christ is couched in the language of the breaking through of the messianic kingdom. Almost every parable that Jesus told was a parable of the kingdom: "The kingdom of God is like . . ." The gospel that Jesus preached, which was previously declared by John the Baptist, was a gospel of the kingdom: "The kingdom of God is at hand. Repent, and believe in the gospel" (Mark 1:15). The culmination of

5

the ministry of Christ was not the resurrection, but the ascension, when he was elevated and escorted on the clouds of glory into heaven. There he received the throne of his Father, where he is and will be our King and Priest forever.

The Old Testament passage most frequently quoted in the New Testament is Psalm 110:1: "The LORD said to my Lord, 'Sit at My right hand.'" At the center of God's work of redemption is a political consideration. It is the city of God, the reign of God. The person who holds the highest political office in the universe is the Lord Jesus Christ. To him we are to give our supreme allegiance and devotion. We are not Americans first and Christians second. Our highest loyalty, our first allegiance, is to the King of Kings and the Lord of Lords. That concept is seldom mentioned even within devout Christian circles.

John Guest came to the United States from Liverpool, England, as an evangelist in the 1960s. He spent most of his first week in Philadelphia, visiting all the historic sights. He went to antique stores that specialized in Revolutionary War memorabilia. He saw placards that said, "Don't tread on me" and "No taxation without representation," as well as an earlier one that declared, "We serve no sovereign here." John said to me, "That's in your blood as an American. How can I preach the kingdom of God to a people who have a built-in cultural allergy to monarchy?" That is a problem we have as we seek to understand the Bible. The kingdom of God does not exist by referendum. It is not a democracy. It is rooted and grounded in a principle of absolute monarchy, absolute sovereignty, where the Lord God Almighty reigns. Americans resist that.

Before we talk about government, we must understand that God is the supreme Lord and King of all the world. It is he who has ordained civil magistrates. In Romans 13, Paul says: "Let every soul"— or every person—"be subject to the governing authorities. For there is no authority except from God, and the authorities that exist are appointed by God." Another way to translate that last clause is, "The powers that be are appointed by God." We may struggle to think that

God cast the deciding ballot in our national elections or that he appointed Adolf Hitler to be the chancellor of Germany and Joseph Stalin to rule over Russia. What Paul is saying, of course, is that all government is under God's authority. The Scriptures say, "The Most High rules in the kingdom of men, and gives it to whomever He chooses" (Dan. 4:25). If, in his sovereign government of the earth, he installs a despicable person, that does not mean that God therefore sanctions everything the corrupt official does. He used Nebuchadnezzar, Belshazzar, and others to chasten his own people. He uses evil powers to achieve his own righteous goals. When Paul said that the governing powers are appointed by God, he was writing to the Roman Christians, who were on the threshold of living under the oppressive tyranny of Nero. Under Nero's decree, the apostle Paul was executed.

What is government? The simplest, most basic definition is this: government is legal force. Governments are agencies that have the power and the legal right to coerce people to obey their dictates. Their laws are not simply suggestions, but requirements. Laws are backed up by the law enforcement agencies that are established to ensure that the law be maintained. Every law that is passed restricts somebody's freedom and exposes people to the violence of law enforcement if they fail to submit to that law. Governments must have legal force. If they don't, they are no more than advisory committees.

Where did government start? Earthly government started in the garden of Eden after the fall, when God sent Adam and Eve out of the garden and prohibited them from returning. He put a "No Trespassing" sign up in front of the gates to Paradise. He put an angel there with a flaming sword, which was an instrument of force. Had Adam and Eve tried to return, they would have been stopped by force.

Government is necessary because of evil. Augustine said that civil government is a necessary evil made necessary because of evil. We are sinners, and we have a propensity to violate other human beings, to commit injustices or cause bodily harm. We may take property or threaten life. People need to be protected by the civil magistrate, who is instituted and ordained by God to bear the sword. The magistrate has legitimate power and authority to protect us from one another.

The hierarchical structure of the universe, as God has ordained it, finds God himself at the top. Immediately under God is Christ, to whom he has given all authority in heaven and on earth. Under Christ are the civil magistrates, such as kings, senators, presidents, governors, parents, employers, teachers. There is an order of authority and of law. The definition for sin, given by the Shorter Catechism, is "any want of conformity unto, or transgression of, the law of God." Where there is no law, there is no sin. God has delegated the right and authority to enact laws to lesser magistrates. He has not delegated to them the right to enact unjust laws. He never gives anybody the right to do wrong or to do evil. Authorities are there biblically, but the basic structure of government is to be under God and over the people.

Is vengeance bad? No, if vengeance were a bad thing, then God would have no part of it, because God cannot sin. But private vengeance—personal, vigilante vengeance—is bad, for God tells us, "Vengeance is Mine, I will repay" (Rom. 12:19, quoting Deut. 32:35). He prohibits us from being the avengers of the wrongs that are done to us, because he knows that we are never interested in getting even; we want to get one up. If vengeance is left to us, we will commit an injustice by seeking our vindication. However, God does delegate vengeance to the civil magistrate. In the Old Testament, those who were wronged could go to the court for justice and for satisfaction. The same principle operates in the New Testament. The session of the church is a court, and if one person in the congregation violates another person in the congregation, the victim has the right to appeal to the session for justice. The victim does not have the right to take matters into his own hands and inflict punishment on the other person. Government is under God and over the people. However, our culture increasingly understands government to be over the people and independent of God.

I once asked Francis Schaeffer what his biggest concern for America was at that time. He said his biggest concern for the church and for the people was statism, the increasing encroachment and dominion of the federal government in the lives of people: in the school, in the community, in the church, in all areas. One could not turn around without bumping into the federal government. That was his major concern, and since then the intrusion of the federal government in the lives of people has greatly increased.

God has ordained government **for His own glory, and the public good**. I once received a letter which said, "I've talked to many teachers and many ministers about why God would create a universe where he knew people would fall into sin and come under his judgment for eternity. Why would God do such a thing, knowing what the consequences of his act of creation would be?" My response was three words: "For his glory." God did not create us for our glory. He created us for his glory, and God is glorified in his grace. When he saves a fallen sinner who does not deserve to be saved and so manifests his grace, that glorifies God. When he withholds his grace from a willful sinner, and punishes with judgment, he manifests his justice, which glorifies God. There are two places where God is given all glory: heaven and hell. The sinner gets no glory in hell, but God does. Perfect righteousness is vindicated by divine punishment.

God ordains government, first of all, **for His own glory**. Nothing is more insulting to God's glory than our sin. God refuses to let insults to his glory go unpunished. Therefore, he established government to uphold righteousness and to punish wickedness and evil. That is why a sword guarded the gate of Eden. Why must we obey the civil magistrate? The apostle Peter tells us to obey the civil magistrate for Christ's sake. How can my civil obedience glorify Christ? When I am a law-abiding citizen, I am submitting to a magistrate who is under the authority of Christ. If Christ delegates authority to that lesser authority, my submission to the lesser authority redounds to the honor of the One who delegated it. That is the principle that Paul sets forth

9

in Romans 13. The main reason that we are called to be obedient to civil magistrates is to glorify God and honor Christ.

God has also ordained government for **the public good.** He has established government to protect you and me. There may be times when we think the best of all possible worlds would be a world without human government, but anarchy is absolute lawlessness. That is why, historically, political theorists have said that the most corrupt government is preferable to anarchy. That is why our forefathers tried to establish a system of government with checks and balances, so that there would be a division of power at the top to put restraints and restrictions on those in government to guard against moving toward oppressive dictatorship. Government exists both for God's glory and for our good, so that we can be protected from ourselves. It is to this end that God has armed government **with the power of the sword.**

> Sec. 2. It is lawful for Christians to accept and execute the office of a magistrate, when called thereunto: in the managing whereof, as they ought especially to maintain piety, justice, and peace, according to the wholesome laws of each commonwealth; so, for that end, they may lawfully, now under the new testament, wage war, upon just and necessary occasion.

Section 2 of chapter 23, begins, **It is lawful for Christians to accept and execute the office of a magistrate, when called thereunto: in the managing whereof, as they ought especially to maintain piety, justice, and peace, according to the wholesome laws of each commonwealth.** It may seem strange that the Westminster divines took the time to include in the confession an affirmation that it is legitimate for Christians to serve in offices of the state and to serve in the government as representatives, governors, or presidents. Throughout our country's history, we have assumed the lawful right of Christians so to serve, and we are accustomed to Christian believers running for elected office and being elected.

The confession was written, however, in the seventeenth century. The Reformation in the sixteenth century had opened up broad and spirited debate about the relationship between church and state. The particular nuances of this debate became exceedingly complex. We can, for simplicity's sake, reduce the views that arose at that time to three. One is what we call *the unity of church and state*. In this view, the church is subsumed under the state, or vice versa. The civil magistrate is also the ecclesiastical magistrate, or the ecclesiastical magistrate is also the civil magistrate. For much of church history, the papacy controlled political territories as well as exercising ecclesiastical jurisdiction. In this approach, there is a merging or confusing of church and state, with the tendency for the two to be grouped as one. There are those who believe that the goal of the Christian church, the earthly kingdom, is to manifest the heavenly kingdom, with the kingdoms of this world under the authority of the church. That would be a kind of theocracy, such as existed in the Old Testament.

In the theocratic state of Israel, there was a clear division of responsibility between the king and the priesthood. It was not the king's responsibility to offer sacrifices on behalf of the people; that was done by the priests. One of the five greatest kings in the Old Testament, who reigned for over fifty years, was named Uzziah. He ranked alongside David, Solomon, Hezekiah, and Josiah. For most of his reign, Uzziah was a godly and able ruler. His economic policies and military strength were assets to the nation. However, he provoked a crisis late in his life when he went into the temple and assumed the right to offer sacrifices. The priests were horrified that the king would do such a thing. God punished Uzziah with leprosy, making him incapable of finishing out his reign. Before he died, his son ascended to the throne. Even in Israel's theocracy, with a union between church and state, there was a division of labor.

The second view is *the separation of church and state*. In certain Anabaptist groups of the Reformation, there was such a radical separation of church and state, that Christians were not permitted to be involved in the ministry of the state at all. Some of the Anabaptists believed that a Christian could not serve in secular government because that would involve compromise with his commitment to Christ. They declared that church and state are not only two different spheres, but spheres that are not to have any kind of joint activity. Some Anabaptists refused to take oaths in the civil courts. They would not serve in the army or in the government. They would have nothing to do with the evil in the secular state.

The third view is that of *the two kingdoms*, or the two spheres, which was set forth in antiquity by Augustine in his work on the city of God. Luther also talked about the two kingdoms, the kingdom of the government and the kingdom of the church. Calvin embraced this idea of the distinction between the two kingdoms. There were nuanced differences between Luther and Calvin. The idea was that both the state and the church are ordained by God, and when the state is carrying out its God-given mandate, a Christian certainly may be involved in the fulfilling of that mandate.

Part of this has to do with the Reformation concept of vocation, which has been largely obscured in our culture today. The idea of vocation is that God calls people to their life's work in many different spheres. God gifts people in different ways, and it is not only church-related jobs that are to be considered a calling or a vocation. Just as God calls people to the gospel ministry, so he also calls the ministers of the state to perform their tasks. He calls farmers to farming, businessmen to business, and artists to art. The first people said to be filled with the Holy Spirit were the artisans whom God called to fashion the holy vessels and the furniture for the tabernacle in the Old Testament. The Spirit did not come upon them to preach the gospel or to minister as priests or prophets. The Spirit gifted them to produce works of art, to be musicians, and to be sculptors.

As Christians, we should think of our careers as vocations. We should be a banker because God calls us to be a banker. If banking is a legitimate enterprise and contributes to the general welfare of human beings, then it is a legitimate sphere of labor in which a Christian may be engaged. God will and does call people to that and to other vocations.

The Reformation concept of vocation was that God's calling is not limited to the isolated realm of the church. His calling can involve tasks outside the church and can include government service. We have two kingdoms with different job descriptions and responsibilities, but God can call people to be engaged in either one. He calls people to the gospel ministry; he also calls people to be civil magistrates.

That does not mean that every job is something that a Christian can, in good conscience, do. God does not call people to be prostitutes, because that business is forbidden by the Word of God. We have to be careful not to assume that any job we want is sanctioned by God.

So, for that end, they may lawfully, now under the new testament, wage war, upon just and necessary occasion. This was written to refute the Anabaptists, who developed the theory of pacifism, arguing that Christians are not permitted to participate in warfare. They cannot serve in the military. They must be pacifists, and should exercise, wherever possible, the right of conscientious objection. Even if the state does not give them the right of conscientious objection, they must still refuse to be involved in the military or in law enforcement. They must refuse submission to the civil magistrate, even to the point of death. Contrary to that position, the Westminster Confession affirms the classic Christian "just war" theory, which accepts the "just involvement" of Christians in warfare.

This can be a complicated matter. The just war theory goes back again to Augustine, and was given fuller exposition by Thomas Aquinas in the Middle Ages. This theory states that all wars are evil. People are not to take up arms to harm and to kill each other. But not everyone's involvement in war is evil. For example, God has given the civil magistrate the power of the sword, and that gives the magistrate not only the *right* to use the sword, but also the *obligation* to use it under certain circumstances. The magistrates in Israel were rebuked by God for failing to execute criminals convicted of capital crimes. The law in Israel for premeditated murder required capital punishment. If the civil magistrate failed to follow through, God would call him to task for his failure to carry out the punishment.

If the civil magistrate has the sword, and his domain or jurisdiction is invaded by a hostile force, it is not only the right of that nation to defend its borders, but the obligation of the civil magistrate to protect his citizens from harm or death by the invader. A war of aggression, where one nation invades another nation's territorial boundaries, is basically murder on a grand scale.

In a war, is there always one side that can claim justice? There have been wars in history where neither side had a justifiable basis for engaging in armed conflict. There have also been wars where one side was clearly the aggressor. When Hitler marched into Poland and into the Low Countries, it was a classic example of unprovoked aggression, though he claimed to be justified in his action. What the confession teaches is that a Christian in Germany should not have participated in Hitler's aggressive war. One may participate in war, but only when the cause is just. We cannot hide behind the axiom, "My country, right or wrong, my country," because that assumes that our country is always right. History is replete with examples of nations engaging in military activities that are morally unjustifiable. When our government is so involved, we cannot and must not participate.

In this age of sophistication, it is often difficult to know who is right and who is wrong. In the Civil War, Christians stood staunchly on both sides of the conflict. Christians in the South believed that their states' rights were being violated by an aggressor, and the states in the South did not want to wage war. They wanted peace and the freedom to withdraw from an alliance with the North into which they had freely entered. Many Christians in the South believed that since they

14

had been invaded by a hostile foe, they had the right and the obligation to defend themselves.

In the meantime, there were people in the North who believed that the Confederate rebellion was an ungodly, unjustified disruption of the union. They believed that the action of the Northern government was proper and just, and that their involvement in this war was legitimate. At least one side in that war was wrong, even though Christians on both sides fought in good conscience.

Christians who believed that it is never right to rebel against an established government refused to participate in the American Revolution. Other people who were devout Christians believed that lesser magistrates had the right to overthrow the superior magistrate if the superior magistrate becomes corrupt. They willingly engaged in armed conflict against the king of England. The biblical principle and the confession say that we have the right to wage war if the war is just. If it is not just, we are morally obligated to stay out.

In World War II, the atrocities by the German high command included the organized genocide of eight million people. Think how many people had to be involved in that activity. There were those who engineered the trains and those who herded people into boxcars and carried them off to death camps. There were soldiers who shot these people in the back and put them into mass graves. There were people who herded them into the "showers" to be gassed. Many people were involved. The excuse during the war crimes trial was that they had to follow orders. The United States took the position at the Nuremberg trials that they did not have to follow those orders. They saw their government performing a criminal activity. It was their moral duty to refuse to serve. The government of the United States, at that point, was following the principle of just war and necessary-at-times conscientious objection.

Up until the middle of the Vietnam War, the position of the United States government was that people who had conscientious objections to war had the opportunity to be excused from armed conflict. They might be assigned to some peaceable enterprise, but they could receive conscientious objector status. No war in American history provoked the use of this claim as did the Vietnam War. Never in our history, except for the Civil War, was the populace of America so divided over our government's involvement in a war.

Sec. 3. Civil magistrates may not assume to themselves the administration of the Word and sacraments; or the power of the keys of the kingdom of heaven; or, in the least, interfere in matters of faith. Yet, as nursing fathers, it is the duty of civil magistrates to protect the Church of our common Lord, without giving the preference to any denomination of Christians above the rest, in such a manner that all ecclesiastical persons whatever shall enjoy the full, free, and unquestioned liberty of discharging every part of their sacred functions, without violence or danger. And, as Jesus Christ hath appointed a regular government and discipline in His Church, no law of any commonwealth should interfere with, let, or hinder, the due exercise thereof, among the voluntary members of any denomination of Christians, according to their own profession and belief. It is the duty of civil magistrates to protect the person and good name of all their people, in such an effectual manner as that no person be suffered, either upon pretense of religion or of infidelity, to offer any indignity, violence, abuse, or injury to any other person whatsoever: and to take order, that all religious and ecclesiastical assemblies be held without molestation or disturbance.

There was a man who, in addition to being the minister of a church, was a member of the League of the South. The League of the South encourages state legislators to examine, discuss, and work for the preservation of states' rights against the continued intrusion by the federal government. It is not a subversive or racist group. The minister didn't recruit for the organization from within his church or preach sermons on the League of the South. He had a session member who was fiercely patriotic to the federal government and thought that the minister was being less than faithful to the American government by belonging to the League of the South. He brought charges against his minister before the session and lost, and then he lost again when he appealed to the presbytery.

The elder then took his case to the civil court and filed suit against the minister, charging that he was not fit to be the minister. When the civil magistrate agreed to hear the court case, my son wrote an open letter in which he pleaded with the judge not to hear the case because it was a violation of the first amendment. It didn't fall under the jurisdiction of the civil magistrate because it was an ecclesiastical issue. The judge heard the case, found in favor of the plaintiff, and removed the minister from his pulpit. The presbytery of that denomination did nothing. My son pleaded on the floor of the presbytery, to no avail, for support of one of their own against this egregious violation of ecclesiastical rights by the civil magistrate. We are in a perilous situation when the civil magistrate arrogates to himself authority to decide who is fit to be a pastor in a local church. That is the church's sphere of authority, not the state's.

Had the minister committed murder or robbed a bank, then, for those crimes, he would be rightly under the jurisdiction of the civil magistrate. But there are clearly dividing lines of jurisdiction within the two spheres.

Civil magistrates may not assume to themselves the administration of the Word and sacraments; or the power of the keys of the kingdom of heaven; or, in the least, interfere in matters of faith. We are not examining the Constitution of the United States of America, but a theological confession concerning the proper relationship between the state and the church. Nevertheless, section 3 of chapter 23 is an American revision of the original confessional text. The words quoted here follow the original version in substance from "Civil magistrates may not assume" to "the keys of the kingdom of heaven." After that, the American text goes on to set forth a theory of church-state relations substantially different from that of the seventeenth-century British

Reformers. In their view, it was the responsibility of the state to suppress heresy, to prevent or reform corrupt worship, and so forth. The idea of an institutional church-state separation developed later in the American context.

I previously referred to King Uzziah, and how he arrogated to himself the role of the priesthood, for which God punished him with leprosy. King Uzziah stepped across the line, usurped the role of the priesthood, and violated the distinction between the two orders of church and state. Civil magistrates are not to assume the authority to administer the Word and sacraments or the power of the keys of the kingdom of heaven.

Even though, in our culture, there may be no danger of the state taking to itself the right to administer the sacraments, what about the power of the keys of the kingdom? Historically, in the United States, the so-called wall of separation between church and state became part of the fabric of American tradition. The concept was that the exercise of church discipline is not the state's business, but is a matter for the church in conducting its affairs. According to the Reformation, the third necessary mark of a true church, in addition to the preaching of the gospel and the administration of the sacraments, is the exercise of discipline. It is the church's function to determine who may or may not be members of its body. The state cannot tell the church who must be accepted into membership. We do have the right to discriminate *according to creed* because we are a confessional body, and there is a minimal content of affirmation that a person must embrace in order to become a member of the body of Christ. For example, one who does not believe in the deity of Jesus Christ would not qualify for membership, nor would he be permitted to receive the sacrament of the Lord's Supper. That is discriminating according to creed. It is not done in the secular world, but in the church we not only *may*, but *must*, do so in order to maintain the integrity of the church.

We have seen some incidences in recent years where the civil authorities have encroached on the church's right to discipline by excommunication. The civil government has heard some suits, ruled in favor of the excommunicated person, and ordered churches either to pay damages or to receive the person back into their fellowship. That is not only a gross breach of our traditional wall of separation, but also a violation of this principle in the confession. It is a radical violation of the first amendment, which guarantees the right of the free exercise of religion. Part of the exercise of the Christian religion involves the exercise of church discipline. Church discipline is the "power of the keys." The church has the power to impose moral sanctions for the ungodly behavior of church members, starting with rebuke, followed by censure and then temporary suspension from the sacraments, and concluding with excommunication.

According to the confession, civil magistrates never have the right, **in the least, [to] interfere in matters of faith. Yet, as nursing fathers, it is the duty of civil magistrates to protect the Church of our common Lord, without giving the preference to any denomination of Christians above the rest**—there is the principle of disestablishmentarianism—**in such a manner that all ecclesiastical persons whatever shall enjoy the full, free, and unquestioned liberty of discharging every part of their sacred functions, without violence or danger.**

Let me tell you how that applies in a very practical way. As I preached in a church in Memphis one Sunday, a man who was violently hostile to Christianity stood in the back of the church and hurled radical epithets at me and at the church. I told him he was out of order, asked him to be quiet, and continued my sermon. When he started again, two ushers tried gently to escort him from the building. Finally, they had to call the police, who removed this man because he was disturbing the peace of our rightful worship. He posed a threat of violence to that free assembly for worship. Therefore, the church had the right to call upon the civil magistrate to protect them.

On another occasion, I spoke at a conference where there had been threats against my life. The local church took those threats seriously and had the police escort me everywhere I went between services. We are grateful for the protection offered by the civil magistrate, whose task is to ensure the free exercise of religion, rather than to impede the free exercise of religion by imposing its own will.

What Americans call the separation of church and state would, from a Reformed viewpoint, be described as a "separation of powers and duties." We distinguish between the role of the state and the role of the church, because they are two separate institutions. That does not mean that they cannot support each other. Just as the church has a responsibility to honor the civil magistrates, to pray for them, and to render obedience to them, so, by the same token, the civil magistrate has the responsibility to honor the functions of the church. They are to support, rather than oppose, each other.

And, as Jesus Christ hath appointed a regular government and discipline in His Church, no law of any commonwealth should interfere with, let, or hinder, the due exercise thereof, among the voluntary members of any denomination of Christians, according to their own profession and belief. I know of a man who was involved in a divorce process, and to the best of my knowledge he was the innocent party. However, the session of the church met with his wife and heard her complaints, without ever interviewing him, which is a violation of ecclesiastical law. Why didn't they interview him? The wife's attorney had gotten a court order that prohibited him from coming within so many yards of her or the church, and the church was afraid of civil sanctions if they carried through with the normal due process of ecclesiastical discipline. As far as I'm concerned, it was an outrageous act of cowardice on the part of the church to obey the civil magistrate at that point. They should have said to the civil magistrate, "You are out of order." They should have exercised their duty to give due process to that man in the ecclesiastical court.

Problems arise when authorities collide with one another. For example, in marriage and divorce cases, we understand that the civil magistrate has the right to perform marriages and also the right to dissolve them. Historically, the church also has had the right to perform marriages and dissolve them. So the church and the civil magistrate have overlapping jurisdiction and could come into conflict. In such a situation, the state should only have the right to dissolve a marriage performed by the civil court, and only an ecclesiastical court should render the decision in ecclesiastical cases. Historically, however, the church in America has failed to exercise its duty in hearing cases of divorce. Most churches have to deal at some point with a divorce among its membership. Often the attitude is, "That's none of the church's business," but that is exactly the church's business. It is a matter for the church's spiritual oversight.

When we join a church, we submit ourselves and our conduct to the spiritual oversight of that Christian body. That is what church discipline is all about. Secular thinking has now so infiltrated the church, that even people who are faithful and obedient in their church involvement have the idea that the church should play no role in their spiritual discipline.

Jesus Christ hath appointed a regular government and discipline in His Church. Church government and church discipline were not invented by mean-spirited people, but by Christ himself for his church. The Reformers declared there is no church without church discipline because the church that Jesus Christ established included government and discipline. A cursory reading of the Pastoral Epistles and of 1 Corinthians makes that clear. Paul rebuked the Corinthians for failing to exercise discipline in their community.

Because Christ has set up church government and discipline, **no law of any commonwealth should interfere with, let, or hinder, the due exercise thereof, among the voluntary members of any denomination of Christians, according to their own profession and belief.** A number of years ago, I spoke with Anita Bryant, a well-known entertainer and singer, who was the spokesperson on national commercials for orange juice. She was on the board of a Christian school in Florida that had a policy that prohibited practicing homosexuals from becoming teachers

21

at that institution. The gay community in Miami made headlines as they protested against Anita Bryant and against her employers in the orange juice industry because of her affiliation with the Christian school. Ninety percent of her other singing engagements were cancelled, and her contract for the orange juice commercials was cancelled as well. Her livelihood was destroyed because she was considered a bigot. The school policy was declared unjust because it discriminated against gays. Private organizations and public officials have come under increasing pressure from groups opposed to biblical standards for sexual relationships and the definition of marriage.

It is the duty of civil magistrates to protect the person and good name of all their people, in such an effectual manner as that no person be suffered, either upon pretense of religion or of infidelity, to offer any indignity, violence, abuse, or injury to any other person whatsoever. That puts restraints on Christians. Christians do not have the right to carry the sword, nor do they have the right to slander anybody. Slander and libel are prohibited under civil law.

It is the duty of civil magistrates . . . to take order, that all religious and ecclesiastical assemblies be held without molestation or disturbance. As the church is called to honor the magistrate, the magistrate also has the duty to protect the church from being hindered in carrying out its duties. This touches the American Bill of Rights, specifically the First Amendment, which guarantees the "free exercise" of religion.

Sec. 4. It is the duty of people to pray for magistrates, to honour their persons, to pay them tribute or other dues, to obey their lawful commands, and to be subject to their authority, for conscience' sake. Infidelity, or difference in religion, doth not make void the magistrates' just and legal authority, nor free the people from their due obedience to them: from which ecclesiastical persons are not exempted, much less hath the Pope any power and jurisdiction over them in their dominions, or over any of their people; and, least of all, to deprive them of their dominions, or lives, if he shall judge them to be heretics, or upon any other pretence whatsoever.

It is the duty of people to pray for magistrates. The emphasis is switching to our Christian responsibility toward the civil magistrates. The first duty is to pray. This mandate is given repeatedly in the Scripture, and our prayers are not to be limited to pleas for judgment. We are to pray that God will bless our rulers and give them wisdom and integrity. We are also **to honour their persons, to pay them tribute or other dues, to obey their lawful commands, and to be subject to their authority, for conscience' sake.**

If the magistrate is not a Christian or is a different kind of Christian, that does not excuse us from our responsibility to pray for him and to submit to his authority in the civil sphere.

Infidelity, or difference in religion, doth not make void the magistrates' just and legal authority, nor free the people from their due obedience to them: from which ecclesiastical persons are not exempted, much less hath the Pope any power and jurisdiction over them in their dominions, or over any of their people; and, least of all, to deprive them of their dominions, or lives, if he shall judge them to be heretics, or upon any other pretence whatsoever.

Being a Christian—including an **ecclesiastical person** (that is, a church leader)—does not exempt us from obeying the civil magistrate and the laws of the state. Church leaders are not to interfere in civil matters, just as civil magistrates are not to interfere in the free exercise of religion.

Is there ever a time when a Christian has the right to disobey the law or to disobey the civil magistrates? This question arises because of what the confession reaffirms here and what we read in Romans 13, where Paul emphasizes the need for civil obedience. Peter similarly writes that we are to obey the civil magistrate for the Lord's sake, because Christ is the one who redeems us from lawlessness. When laws are passed and we disobey them, we take our stand on the side of lawlessness, rather than on the side of divinely sanctioned obedience. But that does not mean that every law is just or binding upon the conscience of the Christian.

The fact that a law is unjust does not give us the right to disobey it. Every legal system in our world includes laws that, in the final analysis, are unjust and unrighteous. There are laws that inflict inconvenience, suffering, and pain upon its citizens, but that is not an excuse to disobey the civil magistrate. When is it right to disobey? The answer is easy to articulate, but difficult to apply to real-life situations. The principle is this: whenever any authority (civil magistrate, parent, employer, father in the home, husband in the marriage) commands us to do what God forbids or forbids us to do what God commands, we not only *may* disobey, but *must* disobey.

We see examples in the book of Acts where the Sanhedrin, the legal body that ruled over the Jews, stopped Peter and the apostles from preaching and forbade them to preach Christ. Peter replied, rhetorically, "Shall we obey God or man?" (see Acts 4:19). Christ had commanded the disciples to preach the gospel to every creature. They were fulfilling that mandate in Jerusalem. The civil authorities came and ordered them to stop preaching, and the disciples said that they could not obey the civil authorities. That is one of the reasons why Paul spent so much time in jail. He had to disobey human authorities in order to obey God.

When the human authorities inconvenience or inflict suffering upon us, what are we to do? It wasn't convenient for Joseph and his wife to undergo an arduous journey to Bethlehem because the emperor wanted to take a census, so he could increase his taxes on the Jews. Yet Joseph risked the life of his wife and of their promised child to obey the civil magistrate, through which the Scriptures were fulfilled. "But you, Bethlehem Ephrathah, though you are little among the thousands of Judah, yet out of you shall come forth to Me the One to be Ruler in Israel, whose goings forth are from of old, from everlasting" (Mic. 5:2). Here we have a heroic example of obedience to the civil magistrate. Our emotions say they would have been justified to stay in Nazareth, but God had not commanded Joseph and Mary to stay there. God doesn't command us to be happy or to be wealthy. If we don't like the income tax structure and think the government is unjust, that is no excuse for us to disobey, even though it may inconvenience us and cause us discomfort.

We see examples in the Old Testament where, with the sanction of God, people are disobedient to the magistrates. Hebrew midwives, under the capricious decree of Pharaoh, were to kill all the male children born to the Israelites. The midwives delivered those male babies and hid them, rather than killing them. They even lied to cover up what they had done in order to save the lives of those babies, and they received the blessing of God for their acts of civil disobedience (Ex. 1:15–21). Shadrach, Meshach, and Abed-Nego were in the fiery furnace because they wouldn't serve Nebuchadnezzar's gods or worship the golden image as they were ordered to (Dan. 3:12–18). What about Mordecai in the book of Esther and Daniel in the lion's den? They were being obedient to God, rather than to the magistrates. There are occasions when we not only *may* disobey, but *must*.

The debate continues to this day regarding the Revolutionary War, through which this country became a free nation. One of the ideas advanced during the Reformation was that lesser magistrates may revolt against higher magistrates if the higher magistrates are operating in an unjust and illegal manner. Not all Christians adopted that principle, and not all Christians supported the Revolutionary War. There is no doubt that the magistrates who were in favor of revolution were duly appointed magistrates. It wasn't just a grassroots rebellion, for the lesser magistrates were protesting against Parliament and the king for violating British law and the terms under which the colonies were to be governed.

In the civil rights movement in this country in the 1950s and 1960s, Martin Luther King followed Gandhi's principles of peaceful resistance and intentionally engaged in acts of civil disobedience. The question then was, May Christians participate in civil rights protests with Dr. King?

The justification was that no state has the right to enact a statute that denies a guaranteed right of the Constitution. Every individual in the United States of America has certain constitutional rights that no magistrate and no majority has the right to take away. This country was established as a republic and not as a democracy. In a democracy, the majority rules, and the rights of a minority can be trampled underfoot. Majority rule can become mob rule, where the individual or minority falls victim to the desires of the majority. Because of the Bill of Rights, the citizen has the right to peaceably force a test case in the courts to determine the legitimacy of a statute. That was behind King's strategy. He wanted to test the laws and show that individual states, through their majority, had enacted legislation that discriminated against individuals unconstitutionally. I believe the Reformers would consider that a legitimate form of civil disobedience.

24

MARRIAGE AND DIVORCE

The Westminster Confession of Faith
Chapter 24: Of Marriage and Divorce

Sec. 1. Marriage is to be between one man and one woman: neither is it lawful for any man to have more than one wife, nor for any woman to have more than one husband, at the same time.

Sec. 2. Marriage was ordained for the mutual help of husband and wife, for the increase of mankind with a legitimate issue, and of the Church with an holy seed; and for preventing of uncleanness.

Sec. 3. It is lawful for all sorts of people to marry, who are able with judgment to give their consent. Yet it is the duty of Christians to marry only in the Lord. And therefore such as profess the true reformed religion should not marry with infidels, papists, or other idolaters: neither should such as are godly be unequally yoked, by marrying with such as are notoriously wicked in their life, or maintain damnable heresies.

Sec. 4. Marriage ought not to be within the degrees of consanguinity or affinity forbidden by the Word. Nor can such incestuous marriages ever be made lawful by any law of man or consent of parties, so as those persons may live together as man and wife.

Sec. 5. Adultery or fornication committed after a contract, being detected before marriage, giveth just occasion to the innocent party to dissolve that contract. In the case of adultery after marriage, it is lawful for the innocent party to sue out a divorce: and, after the divorce, to marry another, as if the offending party were dead.

Sec. 6. Although the corruption of man be such as is apt to study arguments unduly to put asunder those whom God hath joined together in marriage: yet, nothing but adultery, or such wilful desertion as can no way be remedied by the Church, or civil magistrate, is cause sufficient of dissolving the bond of marriage: wherein, a public and orderly course of proceeding is to be observed; and the persons concerned in it not left to their own wills, and discretion, in their own case.

Sec. 1. Marriage is to be between one man and one woman: neither is it lawful for any man to have more than one wife, nor for any woman to have more than one husband, at the same time.

The Westminster divines affirmed that saving faith is a direct result of the operation of the Holy Spirit in our hearts, and that the Holy Spirit ordinarily creates faith in our hearts through the ministry of the Word. This study of the Westminster Confession seeks to strengthen our faith through a deeper understanding of the Word of God. Insofar as our faith is strengthened, our Christian lives will be more productive and effective.

The subject of marriage and divorce is important for us to understand from a biblical perspective. In a wedding ceremony, the opening words usually are, "Dearly beloved, we are assembled here today in the presence of God and of these witnesses to unite this man and this woman in the bonds of holy matrimony." We go on to consider other aspects of marriage and acknowledge that it was instituted by God and further consecrated by Christ. Then we add this statement: "Marriage is regulated by God's commandments." Marriage is a gift of God to the human race. It is an institution that he has commanded, ordained, and instituted. He did not simply create the estate of marriage, give it to the human race, and allow us to do with it whatever we want. Rather, God circumscribed the institution of matrimony by his law, and he set forth certain principles to govern it. He determined who may enter into marriage, when one may enter into it, and what constitutes a valid marriage and a valid dissolution of it.

We live in a time when biblical law and God's regulations for marriage are rejected or ignored in a wholesale manner, even by many church members. It is important that we examine once again the biblical principles that regulate marriage.

Marriage is to be between one man and one woman: neither is it lawful for any man to have more than one wife, nor for any woman to have more than one husband, at the same time. Set forth here is the principle of monogamy, that a man has but one wife, and a wife has but one husband, at the same time. Prohibited are bigamy and polygamy, which are shades of the same thing. Polygamy refers to marriage to several wives (or, rarely, several husbands) simultaneously. Bigamy refers to having two wives at the same time, as did Jacob with Leah and Rachel.

To understand this call to monogamy, we start with the creation of the human race. When God created man in his own image, male and female, he provided for the sacred union that we call marriage. He gave a mandate to Adam and Eve to be fruitful and to multiply. One of the reasons for marriage is the propagation of the human race. Originally, marriage was defined as a relationship between one

29

man and one woman: "Therefore a man shall leave his father and mother and be joined to his wife" (Gen. 2:24). The principle of leaving and cleaving was set forth at creation, and it follows throughout Scripture.

The Old Testament record gives many examples of otherwise godly men who had multiple wives—and, in the case of Solomon, many wives and many concubines. David had several wives, and he was called a man after God's own heart. What are we to make of this? It doesn't mean that God sanctioned polygamy in the Old Testament. Polygamy never received God's positive sanction. Rather, we see God's forbearance and longsuffering with his people, despite their flagrant disobedience of him. Jacob's taking of two wives did not nullify the creation mandate that one man and one woman are to enter into the sacred and holy union of marriage.

The New Testament clearly sets forth the practice of monogamy as the biblical principle. In the qualifications for elders, 1 Timothy 3:2 says that an elder must be the husband of one wife. Some have said that this makes it impossible for a man who was once divorced and then remarried ever to be an elder in the church. If that is what the text means, it also prohibits a widower from remarrying and becoming an elder, because he would also have had more than one wife. Most scholars agree that Paul's teaching is a prohibition of polygamy or bigamy of any kind. Monogamy is clearly established in the creation account of the Old Testament and by apostolic teaching in the New Testament.

Polygamy and bigamy are not serious issues in our culture today. However, they are serious matters for missionaries who go into cultures where polygamy is practiced. When a man who has multiple wives becomes a Christian, what is he supposed to do about them and their offspring? Should he divorce all but one of his wives, abandon the others, and cease to fulfill the obligations of his marriage contracts? No. The usual way this situation is handled is for the missionaries to communicate God's laws regarding marriage and to instruct the people that from that day forward they should not take multiple wives. In the meantime, men with more than one wife must carry out their commitment to care for their wives and their offspring. It is a difficult situation, but the church has handled it this way throughout church history.

Although we don't have a glaring problem with polygamy in our culture, we have tension with the principle that marriage is to be contracted between one man and one woman. There is no biblical provision for same-sex unions. This has become a major ecclesiastical issue where various denominations either have or are contemplating producing special marriage services for same-sex unions. Some churches have compromised and said they can have a service of *marriage* only for one man and one woman, but can have a service of *union* for two men or two women. Although they won't call it marriage, they will give the church's blessing to same-sex unions.

Churches approving same-sex unions have an inadequate view of scriptural authority. They may argue that the Bible is historically conditioned and is therefore not binding on us today. However, the clarity of the biblical text with respect to this matter is clear. Any sexual relationship between two men or between two women is clearly prohibited by the Word of God. These relationships are not only prohibited, but grossly sinful, an abomination in God's sight.

Sec. 2. Marriage was ordained for the mutual help of husband and wife, for the increase of mankind with a legitimate issue, and of the Church with an holy seed; and for preventing of uncleanness.

Marriage was ordained for the mutual help of husband and wife. The reasons given for marriage start with it being ordained for the mutual help of husband and wife. There is a clear recognition of the *mutuality* of the marital relationship. Clearly the Reformation church of the seventeenth century held that wives are to be subordinate to their husbands. Nevertheless, the church recognized that there is to

31

be mutual concern, care, and responsibility between husband and wife. The wife is not accorded the role of chattel or slave, but fully shares the image of God.

Eve was created initially to be Adam's helpmate, and God prescribed a deep bond between those first two human beings. With each aspect of his creation, God "saw that it was good" (Gen. 1:25). But it was "not good that man should be alone" (2:18). So God said, "I will make him a helper comparable to him" (2:18).

When Adam saw Eve, he was filled with delight, because God had made the perfect helpmate. God then made both Adam and Eve vicegerents over the entire creation. Eve had joint rule over their household and over all of nature. She was placed in an exalted position, but she was still subordinate to her husband. That doesn't mean that she was inferior. She was equal in dignity, value, and honor with her husband, but was still expected to be submissive to him (Eph. 5:22).

Some men have taken their position of authority in marriage to mean, "If God has placed me in a position of leadership in the household, it must be because I am a superior person." That is an invalid inference from the division of labor that God gave to Adam and Eve. Our doctrine of the Trinity is that the Father, the Son, and the Holy Spirit are equal in dignity, honor, glory, and exaltation. Yet, in the economy of redemption, both the Son and the Spirit are subordinate to the Father. It is the Father who sends the Son into the world; the Son does not send the Father into the world. We see the principle of *submission among equals* in our concept of God in three persons. It would be wrong to assume that because someone is in a subordinate role in the home, in the workplace, or anywhere else, he or she is an inferior person. Such thinking would imply that the Son and the Holy Spirit are inferior to the Father.

Marriage was established **for the mutual help of husband and wife.** Even though Eve was created to be Adam's helpmate, he also had responsibilities to help her. The heaviest burden to provide support and help is given to the man, because he is commanded by God to love his wife as Christ loved the church and to give himself to his wife as Christ gave himself to the church. I've asked Christian women who struggle with the biblical mandate to be submissive to their husbands, "How would you feel if you were married to Christ? Would you have a hard time submitting yourself to his headship?" I've never met a Christian woman who has said, "Yes." A woman in that situation could trust him, knowing that her husband loves her and is prepared to die for her at any moment. He would provide for her all that he has and give her all that he is. That is the burden that God puts upon men in marriage. I would prefer to have the responsibility to be submissive, rather than to be responsible to love my wife as Christ loves the church, because I cannot begin to fulfill that mandate. Marriage is the deepest kind of personal commitment into which any two people can ever enter, and so the first purpose of marriage is to provide mutual help for husband and wife.

Marriage was also established **for the increase of mankind with a legitimate issue.** The context for the bearing of children is marriage. Producing children outside of the sacred bond of marriage is the producing of "illegitimate" children. In our culture, we see the proliferation of childbearing outside of marriage, just as we have seen a wholesale attack on the very institution of marriage. There is a public embracing of fornication, which is totally opposed to the law of God in the Decalogue, to the teaching of Christ, and to the apostolic admonition that we read in the New Testament. "But fornication and all uncleanness or covetousness, let it not even be named among you, as is fitting for saints" (Eph. 5:3). Paul wrote that to people who were living in an immoral, pagan environment. He told them, "You Christians have to live differently from the world around you. You are called to a different standard."

It is amazing how many professing Christians have followed the world in repudiating marriage and embracing sexual relationships outside of it. It was not the Puritans or Queen Victoria who declared a sexual relationship outside of matrimony to be sinful; it was God. This is

33

one of the laws that God writes on the human heart. A Christian must understand that neither we nor society makes the rules. God makes the rules. Christians today too readily take their cue from the culture in which they live. If our culture accepts certain kinds of behavior, then we tell ourselves that it is acceptable, even when we know it isn't.

Children are to be born inside the marriage covenant, into an environment that under normal circumstances includes a mother and a father. That is the most fundamental unit of society as established by God. That is verified, not only by the Word of God, but by the history of civilization. The most basic, foundational unit of society is the family, and it is that very unit that is under such fierce attack in our culture today.

One of the issues behind the scenes during the Reformation was the Roman Catholic Church's view of the superiority of celibacy. They argued that the only justification for sex within marriage is the need to propagate the species. Therefore, all forms of birth control are considered evil, since they prevent that purpose from being realized. The Reformers insisted that the mutual joy and pleasure of the marriage bed is undefiled, and that the husband and the wife have every legitimate reason to enjoy each other's bodies, even though not bearing children.

Marriage was also established **for the increase . . . of the Church with an holy seed.** Many people today look upon children as a burden and on large families as irresponsible. But in the Bible, a large family is viewed as a tremendous blessing of God for the parents. Some argue that this is true only in an agrarian society, where having many children assures cheap labor to work on the farm. But now that we are city dwellers, they say, having more than two children is an economic burden.

Children may indeed be an economic hardship. On the other hand, when I look at my life and consider the human relationships that are the most precious and fulfilling to me, I go to my family—to my wife, to my children, and to our broader family.

It is a great blessing of God to have children. My son and his wife have six. They plan to have as many as the Lord will give them. They see children as persons who are extremely valuable. When I see the time that he spends nurturing those children in the Word of God, I know that one of the ways in which the church is strengthened is through the bearing of children. "Be fruitful and multiply" has not been rescinded in our day.

Finally, marriage was established **for preventing of uncleanness.** When Paul said, "It is better to marry than to burn" (1 Cor. 7:9), he was implying that some of the people to whom he was writing were living in sexual sin. Paul's point is not that it is better to marry than to burn in hell. He is talking about burning with lust. God plants a sexual drive in people because he created them for reproduction. God also says that marriage is the only context in which that drive may properly be exercised. A person may try to be chaste, yet have impulses and desires that control him or her. In that situation, it is better to look for a husband or a wife to alleviate that problem. It is better to marry than to burn.

> Sec. 3. It is lawful for all sorts of people to marry, who are able with judgment to give their consent. Yet it is the duty of Christians to marry only in the Lord. And therefore such as profess the true reformed religion should not marry with infidels, papists, or other idolaters: neither should such as are godly be unequally yoked, by marrying with such as are notoriously wicked in their life, or maintain damnable heresies.

Section 3 affirms the specific and unique requirements that are imposed upon God's people. The restriction placed upon believers from Old Testament times through the New Testament is to **marry only in the Lord,** so as to be equally yoked. Paul's correspondence with the Corinthians indicates that some of them were involved with mixed marriages. There was no provision in the early church for a Christian to marry a non-Christian. Presumably, those mixed marriage arose when one of the spouses was converted. That puts a strain upon the marriage.

Church members who have wanted to marry unbelievers have told me, "In our case, it's not going to be a problem, because we've made a pact that religion will not come between us or be a point of tension in the marriage." I've seen marriages work out where one spouse was a church member and the other one was not, but there is a difference between being a church member and being a believer. If a believer in Christ is yoked in the closest possible way with someone who does not share that deep commitment, there will be trouble. There is a mandate from the apostolic word that Christians are not allowed to marry unbelievers.

Furthermore, the confession prohibits marriage between a person who embraces the Reformed faith and a person who embraces the Roman Catholic faith. The church takes this very seriously. This is a matter of prudence and wisdom, yet we live in a culture where people so often get married on the basis of emotion, rather than the basis of principle.

When marriages were arranged by families, it was rare that young people determined their own marital destiny. The church, after the Reformation, came to the conclusion that parents ought not to impose arranged marriages upon their children without their consent. Part of this confessional statement says that those who marry should be **able with judgment to give their consent.** When marriages were arranged, they tended to be long-lasting. The present system, where young people are allowed to make personal commitments without parental supervision, is not working as well.

I am not saying that we should go back to the matchmaker and arranged marriages. My point is that when parents are opposed to the marriage of a young couple, that couple ought to take seriously the wisdom of their parents when they contemplate marriage.

Sec. 4. Marriage ought not to be within the degrees of consanguinity or affinity forbidden by the Word. Nor can such incestuous marriages ever be made lawful by any law of man or consent of parties, so as those persons may live together as man and wife.

Marriage ought not to be within the degrees of consanguinity or affinity forbidden by the Word. There is a distinction between a relationship of consanguinity and a relationship of affinity. Consanguinity refers to a blood relationship. The confession is saying that we are not allowed to intermarry in incestuous relationships. We are not to marry blood relatives.

A relationship of affinity is created by marriage. For example, if you marry a woman, you gain a relationship of affinity with her family members.

Some people have asked, Whom did the children of Adam and Eve marry? The Bible tells us that they had sons and daughters (Gen. 5:4), but mentions no one else of their generation. The presumption is that their sons married their sisters. In the beginning, then, marriages were necessarily incestuous.

How do we respond to that ethically and theologically? The answer is that the prohibition against intermarriage was not established in creation, but only later in history. We also know that biological problems from intermarriage do not ordinarily arise in the first generation. Only after repeated generations do we begin to see birth defects and other problems resulting from the intermarriage of blood relatives. Initially, the populating of the earth required blood relationships, but God refused to allow that to continue once there were spouses available who were not immediately related by blood.

Nor can such incestuous marriages ever be made lawful by any law of man or consent of parties, so as those persons may live together as man and wife. This means that a son cannot marry his mother, a daughter cannot marry her father, nor can brother and sister enter into marriage.

Sec. 5. Adultery or fornication committed after a contract, being detected before marriage, giveth just occasion to the innocent party to

37

dissolve that contract. In the case of adultery after marriage, it is lawful for the innocent party to sue out a divorce: and, after the divorce, to marry another, as if the offending party were dead.

Adultery or fornication committed after a contract, being detected before marriage, giveth just occasion to the innocent party to dissolve that contract. This refers to an engagement contract prior to marriage. If sexual infidelity with another person occurs during the period of engagement, then that infidelity is grounds for breaking the engagement. In some places, historically, engagements involved more than a simple personal promise. There was a certain legal basis as well. We see that in the case of Joseph and Mary. They were not married when she conceived, but they were betrothed, and so Joseph had legal recourse to sue Mary for adultery during their betrothal. He decided to be gracious enough to her to put her away privately. Then God revealed to him that Mary had conceived supernaturally by the Holy Spirit, and he married her.

In the case of adultery after marriage, it is lawful for the innocent party to sue out a divorce: and, after the divorce, to marry another, as if the offending party were dead. Some churches believe that there are no valid grounds for divorce. This issue depends on how one interprets Jesus' discussion with the Pharisees, recorded in Matthew 19. The Pharisees came to Jesus with a dilemma, saying that Moses, in Deuteronomy 24:1, makes provision for the divorce of a wife on the basis of "some uncleanness in her." At the time, there was an ongoing debate about the interpretation of this "uncleanness" among the rabbinical schools. There was a conservative (narrow) interpretation given by the school of Shammai, and a liberal (wide) interpretation by the school of Hillel. The followers of Hillel said that the uncleanness refers to anything that displeases the husband. For example, if the wife accidentally breaks his favorite dish, the husband could write a bill of divorcement and dissolve the marriage. But the followers of Shammai said that divorce is justified only on the grounds of sexual uncleanliness, that is, adultery. The Hillelites replied that the uncleanness in view couldn't be adultery because the punishment for adultery in the Mosaic law was execution, not divorce.

The debate continued for years among the scholars of Israel, and they brought the question to Jesus. Jesus said that the provision for divorce in the Old Testament was a permission on God's part because of the hardness of people's hearts, and that from the beginning it was not so. Jesus reminded the people that marriage was originally intended to be a lifelong contract without dissolution. He then concluded, "Whoever divorces his wife, except for sexual immorality, and marries another, commits adultery" (Matt. 19:9). Jesus prohibited divorce with an exception. The exceptive clause of that text is "except for sexual immorality."

Added to that is the teaching of Paul in 1 Corinthians, where he allows a believer to be freed from an unbeliever in the case of the desertion by the unbeliever (1 Cor. 7:15). Those churches that seek to be confessional and biblical in the matter of divorce generally reduce the legitimate grounds for divorce to two: adultery and desertion. Some people include physical abuse within the scope of desertion, arguing that the abuser has in effect deserted the spouse. That becomes a matter for church courts to interpret.

The options in the traditional marriage vows, "for better or for worse, for richer, for poorer, in sickness and in health," are illustrative, not exhaustive. Those clauses are supposed to mean, "I'm prepared to make this commitment to you, for better or for worse, on Tuesday, on Saturday, and everyday, in season, out of season. No matter what, I will stand by you, love you, comfort you, pray for you, and remain committed to you, so help me God."

We rarely anticipate that things are going to be worse, rather than better, but the vow we take is to live together ever after. First Corinthians 13 reveals the standard of love that God has given to us. It provides one of the most thorough indictments of human behavior that we will ever see. In 1 Corinthians 13, we meet a standard of love so high, holy, and righteous that it convicts us of sin and sends us running to the Savior. Love is so much more than a warm puppy or a handful of roses and a romantic ballad. It is living out the vows that we take before God.

On many occasions, the church must establish the innocent party and the guilty party in a divorce case. If there is a married couple in the church, and one spouse files for divorce without biblical grounds, the church has a responsibility to step in and say, "You can't do that." If the person persists in divorcing a spouse without just grounds, it is the duty of the church to excommunicate that person. The guilty spouse is to be excommunicated in order to protect the innocent party and to allow the innocent party to remarry according to biblical law. However, since secular law does not require excommunication prior to remarriage, most churches abandon their responsibility at that point.

Sec. 6. Although the corruption of man be such as is apt to study arguments unduly to put asunder those whom God hath joined together in marriage: yet, nothing but adultery, or such wilful desertion as can no way be remedied by the Church, or civil magistrate, is cause sufficient of dissolving the bond of marriage: wherein, a public and orderly course of proceeding is to be observed; and the persons concerned in it not left to their own wills, and discretion, in their own case.

When people's interests aren't compatible, there ensues a conflict of values and a clash of wills, and they heap up a variety of reasons to justify their sinful forms of behavior. The confession teaches that divorce has to be according to the law of God, not according to the will of the participants.

Even if there are just grounds for divorce, be it adultery or desertion, it doesn't mean that a person *must* dissolve the marriage. It simply means that he or she *may* seek a divorce. When God gives the right to a Christian to dissolve a marriage, the person who exercises that right ought not to be criticized by the rest of the community.

If a man commits adultery and then pleads for forgiveness from his wife, it is her Christian duty to forgive him. She has no other option. But that doesn't mean that she must stay married to him. She must forgive him and receive him as a brother in Christ, but she does not have to receive him as a husband in Christ. His behavior radically undermined the trust that is foundational to an intimate marital relationship. If she cannot continue in such a damaged relationship, God gives her the freedom to dissolve it. I have seen the Christian community criticize the innocent party in such circumstances for going ahead with the divorce. But the person has that right, and it is wrong to condemn that Christian for exercising his or her right.

25

The Church

The Westminster Confession of Faith
Chapter 25: Of the Church

Sec. 1. The catholic or universal Church, which is invisible, consists of the whole number of the elect, that have been, are, or shall be gathered into one, under Christ the Head thereof; and is the spouse, the body, the fulness of Him that filleth all in all.

Sec. 2. The visible Church, which is also catholic or universal under the Gospel (not confined to one nation, as before under the law), consists of all those throughout the world that profess the true religion; and of their children: and is the kingdom of the Lord Jesus Christ, the house and family of God, out of which there is no ordinary possibility of salvation.

Sec. 3. Unto this catholic visible Church Christ hath given the ministry, oracles, and ordinances of God, for the gathering and perfecting of the saints, in this life, to the end of the world: and doth, by His own presence and Spirit, according to His promise, make them effectual thereunto.

Sec. 4. This catholic Church hath been sometimes more, sometimes less visible. And particular Churches, which are members thereof, are more or less pure, according as the doctrine of the Gospel is taught and embraced, ordinances administered, and public worship performed more or less purely in them.

Sec. 5. The purest Churches under heaven are subject both to mixture and error; and some have so degenerated, as to become no Churches of Christ, but synagogues of Satan. Nevertheless, there shall be always a Church on earth to worship God according to His will.

Sec. 6. There is no other head of the Church but the Lord Jesus Christ. Nor can the Pope of Rome, in any sense, be head thereof.

Sec. 1. The catholic or universal Church, which is invisible, consists of the whole number of the elect, that have been, are, or shall be gathered into one, under Christ the Head thereof; and is the spouse, the body, the fulness of Him that filleth all in all.

The invisible church is made up of those who truly are in Christ, and it is called invisible because we cannot read the hearts of people. However, those who are God's are known to him perfectly. He can read the heart; we cannot. The invisible church exists substantially within the visible church, but cannot be identified with it. It refers to the elect, to those who make genuine professions of faith. The church, as Augustine taught, is always a "mixed body" in this world. It is made up of wheat and tares. Though the tares are in the visible church, they have no place in the invisible church. It is possible for a true believer to be in the invisible church, while not in the visible church, if providentially hindered or if temporarily blinded by false doctrine. There are four marks of the church as set forth at the Council of Nicaea in the fourth century. The church is one, holy, catholic, and apostolic.

Metaphors used in the Bible to describe the church include the body of Christ, the bride of Christ, and the fullness of Christ.

The word *church* derives ultimately from the Greek word *kyrios*, which means "Lord," the title given to Jesus. The church, then, etymologically, consists of "those who belong to the Lord." The people of God are those who have been purchased by Christ and are owned by him. The Greek word *ekklēsia*, from which we get the word "ecclesiastical," is commonly translated "church," and means, literally, "those who are called out (of the world)," referring specifically to the elect.

> Sec. 2. The visible Church, which is also catholic or universal under the Gospel (not confined to one nation, as before under the law), consists of all those throughout the world that profess the true religion; and of their children: and is the kingdom of the Lord Jesus Christ, the house and family of God, out of which there is no ordinary possibility of salvation.

The visible Church . . . is also catholic or universal under the Gospel. The visible church today is not restricted to one nation, whereas the church in the Old Testament was restricted to the nation of Israel. The apostle Paul says in Colossians 1:27 that the great mystery that was hidden in the old covenant, but is now revealed, is "Christ in you" (that is, in the Gentiles), "the hope of glory." In the book of Acts, we see the gospel taken beyond the borders of Israel to the nations, to the Gentiles. Churches were established in Europe, Africa, Asia, and eventually beyond. The visible church is found in its various manifestations all across the globe today. These churches consist of those **that profess the true religion; and of their children: and is the kingdom of the Lord Jesus Christ.**

This section of the confession calls the church three things. First, it is called the *kingdom* of the Lord Jesus Christ. Second, it is called the *house* of God. And third, it is called the *family* of God. Section 1

45

made reference to the church as the *spouse* (bride) of Christ and the *body* of Christ. The New Testament uses these and other metaphors to describe the church. The one we'll consider first is that the visible church is called a *kingdom*.

Many people have been reared in evangelical churches that embrace a theology called dispensationalism, which was created toward the end of the nineteenth century. This theology was popularized by the Scofield Reference Bible. It carved up the history of the church, going back to creation, into seven distinct time periods, called dispensations. God supposedly judged the world differently in each of those periods. Most people think of dispensationalism as a set of teachings about the second coming of Christ. In fact, it is a complete systematic theology that has gone through many revisions, particularly in this country, at Dallas Theological Seminary, Moody Bible Institute, and elsewhere.

We won't consider the whole scope of dispensational theology, but only one particular aspect of it. The kingdom age, the kingdom of God, according to classic dispensational theology, is something that is completely future. The kingdom has not come yet in any way, shape, or form. Classic Reformed theology, on the other hand, says that the kingdom of God began with the arrival of Christ and with his coronation in heaven as the King of Kings and the Lord of Lords. That kingdom is not yet consummated, and won't be consummated until the final return of Jesus.

John the Baptist prepared the way for Jesus and declared to Israel, "Repent, for the kingdom of God is at hand." The Old Testament prophets said that the kingdom of God was coming someday, but with John there was a sense of urgency about its nearness. In Matthew 3:2, John proclaims: "The kingdom of heaven is at hand!" "And even now the ax is laid to the root of the trees" (3:10). "His winnowing fan is in His hand" (3:12). The time of separation, the time of crisis, has come. John called the people to repentance. When Jesus came on the scene, he also announced the kingdom of God, saying it was "in your midst."

That is consistent with what Jesus taught in Luke 11:20: "But if I cast out demons with the finger of God, surely the kingdom of God has come upon you." At the center of Jesus' teaching was the message of the gospel of the kingdom. Much of his teaching began, "The kingdom of God is like . . ." Toward the end of Jesus' sojourn on this earth, the disciples asked, "Lord, will You at this time restore the kingdom to Israel?" (Acts 1:6). They were asking, "Are you going to do it, now that you are departing? We have looked for this manifestation of the kingdom ever since you were baptized by John." Jesus replied, "You shall receive power when the Holy Spirit has come upon you; and you shall be witnesses to Me in Jerusalem, and in all Judea and Samaria, and to the end of the earth" (Acts 1:8).

The word *witness* in the New Testament is the Greek *martyria*. Our English word *martyr* is related to it. The martyrs were called such because they bore witness to Christ with their deaths. In Christian jargon today, the word *witness* is practically synonymous with *evangelism*. We say, "I witnessed to my neighbor the other day," meaning, "I told him the gospel." There are actually many ways in which the church bears witness to Christ besides preaching the gospel. When we give a cup of cold water to a thirsty person, we bear witness to Christ. When we behave in a just manner in our place of work, we bear witness to Christ. To bear witness is to give testimony, evidence, or a manifestation of something that is not seen. Calvin said that the primary task of the invisible church is to make the invisible kingdom visible. Christ ascended to heaven, to be seated at the right hand of his Father and reign as Lord of Lords and King of Kings, but the people on earth wouldn't know it. They would fight over who would be their ruler, unaware that "all authority has been given to Me in heaven and on earth" (Matt. 28:18). As the psalmist tells us:

> The kings of the earth set themselves . . .
> Against the LORD and against His Anointed, saying,
> "Let us break Their bonds in pieces
> And cast away Their cords from us."

He who sits in the heavens shall laugh;
The LORD shall hold them in derision. (Ps. 2:2–4)

His reign, now, is invisible, but his church is visible. The visible church is to bear witness to the invisible Christ and to the reality that already exists, that he is now the King of Kings and the Lord of Lords.

There have been many problems in the church throughout the years because Christians have wrapped their faith in their national flag. Whether it's the American, the German, or the Russian flag, we must be careful that our ultimate allegiance as Christians is to the kingdom of Christ. That does not mean that we can't be patriotic, or serve and love our nation, but the ultimate authority is Christ. The most powerful political statement that one can ever make is: "My citizenship is in heaven; my number one allegiance is to Christ." Christ calls us to be submissive to the earthly magistrates, to honor the rulers of the land in which we live, and we must do that, rendering unto Caesar the things that are Caesar's—but never giving to Caesar the things that are God's.

Luther said that every Christian is called to be Christ to his neighbor. He didn't suggest that we can bear our neighbor's sins or that we can save our neighbor. He meant that we must demonstrate to our neighbor what Christ is like. We are called to mirror and reflect our King because we are his loyal subjects in a land that doesn't want to be subject to his rule. It is significant that the Westminster Confession includes this metaphor of the visible church as the kingdom of the Lord Jesus Christ. We who are true believers, together with our children, are the subjects of the Lord Jesus Christ.

I've always liked the legend of Robin Hood. King Richard, who was the rightful king of England, left the nation to go on a crusade. While he was gone, wicked Prince John usurped the throne and began to exercise tyranny over the people of the land. Those who were loyal to King Richard were forced into hiding, and they lived in Sherwood Forest. Robin Hood, previously Sir Robin of Loxley, was disenfran-

chised because of his loyalty to King Richard and became the leader
of those people around him in the woods, who called themselves the
Merry Men. The point of my analogy is that they lived as pilgrims in
a strange land that should have been theirs because they were loyal to
the rightful king. Their king's authority had been usurped by an evil
enemy.

When King Richard returned from the Holy Land, he crossed
into England in the disguise of a mendicant friar. As he traveled in disguise to reclaim the throne, he went through Sherwood Forest and
was stopped at the point of Robin Hood's sword. Richard removed
his friar's hood, opened his robe, and the emblem of a lion's heart became visible on his shirt. Robin Hood recognized him and fell to his
knees, saying, "My liege," and submitted to his king who had returned. We are in a similar situation. Our King has gone to a foreign
land. While he is absent from us, we seek to be his loyal subjects,
awaiting his return, when he will vindicate his people who cry unto
him day and night.

The visible church is **the house and family of God**. Many people
think of the church as a building, rather than people. We can be a
church without a building. We are called chosen stones. We are God's
"house." Each Christian is a stone used to build that city whose builder
and maker is God. The foundation of that city consists of the apostles and prophets, and Jesus is the cornerstone. The rest of the edifice
is built stone by stone, person by person, so that Jesus can not only
say to Simon, "You are Peter, the rock," but to all of us, "You are
stones," fit together to form the church.

The church is also called the **family of God**, a metaphor that is
based upon the principle that is so precious to our faith—adoption.
The church is made up of those who are the adopted children of God,
brought into his family to be united with Christ, his true child, the
only begotten of the Father. With the advent of liberalism in nine-
teenth-century Europe, which sought to redefine the mission of the
church and to remove the supernatural from Christianity, people like

Adolf von Harnack spoke of the "essence" of Christianity being the universal fatherhood of God and the universal brotherhood of man. Neither of these notions is taught by the Bible. God is not the father of everyone. He is the Creator of all people, and, in a poetic sense (as Paul quotes words from a pagan poet), all are his offspring. But to have a filial relationship to God, in which he is our Father, is a privilege given only to those who have been reborn by the Holy Spirit and adopted into the family of God. Even though we may have been taught it from childhood, we are not all God's children. We are, by nature, the children of Satan and the enemies of God. It is only through the regeneration of the Holy Spirit and adoption by God that we are welcomed into his family.

Because of the privileged position of adoption, which is at the heart of our salvation, we are not in a universal brotherhood. All men are not my brothers; all men are my neighbors. There is a universal neighborhood, in which God calls us to regard every person in this world as our neighbor. We are to love our neighbor, to be kind, just, fair, and honorable to everyone without distinction. The brotherhood and sisterhood, however, is restricted to those who are adopted into the family of God. Christ is the only begotten child of the Father. That is why John expressed apostolic astonishment when he said, "Behold what manner of love the Father has bestowed on us, that we should be called children of God!" (1 John 3:1). For the New Testament church, it was a radical thought that people like us could be considered members of the family of God, actual brothers and sisters of the Lord Jesus Christ. Today we take it for granted, and we miss the significance of what God has wrought in his mercy and grace by including us in this intimate filial relationship. The church is called to be the visible manifestation of the family of God.

Outside of the church, **there is no ordinary possibility of salvation**. In this confession, the Westminster divines are often responding to issues that have been argued quite thoroughly in church history. There is a long history behind this final phrase of section 2. The early church father, Cyprian, authored the maxim *Extra ecclesiam nulla salus*, which means "Outside of the church, there is no salvation." In Cyprian's formulation of this principle, it was as necessary to be in the visible church in order to be saved, as it was for the people in Noah's day to be physically inside the ark to be saved from the flood.

That concept was embraced by the Roman Catholic Church, and, with certain modifications, it has come down through the centuries. One of the biggest problems that the Roman Catholic Church has had to deal with in the last few hundred years is what to make of the Protestants who left the fold. There was a time when it was taught that those outside the visible Roman Catholic Church could not be saved. But in the nineteenth century that view began to be modified.

By the twentieth century, it was modified to the point that if someone is sincere in worship and has an implicit desire to be in the Roman Church, even though he is an ardent Protestant (or even a fervent Muslim), then he is considered part of the Roman Catholic Church.

That may sound like a very humble position, when, in fact, it is the height of arrogance. It is based upon the belief that the Roman Church has the keys to the kingdom, and thus can say who is saved and who is not. If someone is a Muslim, a Buddhist, or a Hindu, he may be saved if the Roman Church is gracious enough to include him in their body by exercising the power of the keys.

The confession, aware of the traditions relating to Cyprian's formula, says that outside of the visible church **there is no *ordinary* possibility of salvation**. At this point, the framers of the Westminster Confession differ from Cyprian and go back to Augustine's position that salvation is found *substantially* within the church, but *not exclusively* within it. People can come to salvation outside of the church, but that is unusual. The ordinary way in which people are saved is through the ministry of the church of Jesus Christ.

Since the days in which this was written in the seventeenth century, we have seen an explosion of parachurch ministries, such as the Billy Graham Association, Youth for Christ, Young Life, Campus

Crusade, and teaching ministries like Ligonier Ministries. Although Ligonier Ministries is not a ministry of evangelism, there are people who tell us they have come to salvation from outside the church by being exposed to Ligonier's teaching via radio, video, or books. There are many ministries that are basically evangelistic, through which people become Christians outside the pale of the visible church. We hope they are quickly brought into the visible church. Even with all of the parachurch ministries in our day, the focal point and the concentration of the means of grace for salvation are still found ordinarily and chiefly in the visible church, because that is where the means of grace are concentrated.

> Sec. 3. Unto this catholic visible Church Christ hath given the ministry, oracles, and ordinances of God, for the gathering and perfecting of the saints, in this life, to the end of the world: and doth, by His own presence and Spirit, according to His promise, make them effectual thereunto.

This section is pregnant with theological significance. First of all, it mentions that Christ has given to the visible church **the ministry, oracles, and ordinances of God.** As a college student, I knew a retired missionary in his late eighties, who lived near the campus. He was infirm and unable to do any manual labor, but he didn't believe that he could ever retire from ministry. So, for eight hours every day, he engaged in intercessory prayer. As college students, we stood in line to get Dr. Jamison to put us on his prayer list. He viewed it as his vocation to be a minister of prayer.

The ministry of prayer is one that is given to the entire church. When Jesus cleansed the temple, he rebuked the temple officials for turning it into a place of merchandise when it should be "a house of prayer" (Matt. 21:13). Christ established that one of the most important ministries is that of prayer, because God works through the prayers of his people in order to bring his purposes to pass. Jesus invites, encourages, and even commands us to bring our requests before him, even though God already knows about our concerns. He invites us to enter into that intimate relationship where we articulate to our Father those things that concern us deeply. God, knowing the content of our concerns and our prayers, works through those prayers as a means by which he brings his plan to fulfillment. Likewise, he does not need us for evangelism. God could call his saints audibly from heaven. In the final analysis, he doesn't need the preacher or the missionary. Yet he has been pleased to choose the foolishness of preaching as the means through which he saves the world. God not only ordains the ends, but also the means to those ends. The means through which he works include prayer, the ministry of the Word, and the sacraments and ordinances that he has given to his church.

When we gather to worship, read the Scripture, and hear a sermon, we are engaged in an exercise ordained by God to take place in his church. There is to be a ministry of God's Word, and the power to impact people's lives comes in and through that Word. The power is not in the preacher, but in the Word of God. We pray that the Word which God promises to attend with the power of his Holy Spirit cuts into people's souls and hearts to bring healing, encouragement, faith, and godliness. Only God can bring forth the fruit of that Word. We plead with God that he will use the proclaimed Word to change people's lives.

The apostle Paul, in Romans 2, labors the point that both Jew and Greek are exposed and vulnerable to the judgments of God. In chapter 3, he asks what advantage there is to being a Jew. He answers, "Much in every way!" because the Jews have "the oracles of God," the Scriptures (Rom. 3:2). What an advantage it is for any person to be able to hear the Word of God. Church is above all a place where we can hear the Word of God and be comforted by it.

It is to the visible church that Christ has given the ministry, the oracles, and the ordinances of God **for the gathering and perfecting**

of the saints in this life. The function of the church is to gather together the people of God. We have already seen that the Greek word for "church," *ekklēsia*, means "those called out." We are the people called out of the world to solemn assembly.

There is a movement among Christians in the United States that in recent years has picked up a great deal of momentum. People are redoing and rethinking church, according to a new model that is called seeker-sensitive worship. The idea is that to reach the lost, we must do away with the traditional apparatus of church. The fastest growing of these churches, Willow Creek Church in the suburbs of Chicago, self-consciously did away with the chancel and replaced it with a stage. There is no pulpit as such, but simply a portable stand. The idea is to create an ambiance that is comfortable for the unbeliever who is "seeking" the things of God.

Sunday morning is devoted to seekers. The believers' special worship service is in the middle of the week in the evening. The whole focus of Sunday morning is to attract those outside the church, a kind of evangelism. I certainly am delighted that people have this kind of zeal for reaching the lost, but I am not so delighted that they think there are such people as unbelieving seekers. According to the Bible, the only people who seek after God are believers. We do not and cannot begin to seek after God until he has found us and brought us to himself. Our conversion begins a lifelong pursuit, a lifelong quest of seeking after God. As Paul tells us in Romans 3:11, "there is none who seeks after God" in his natural state; rather, people flee from God. If we want to have a seeker-sensitive worship service, we need to be chasing people down in race cars, for they are rushing away from the things of God as fast as they can.

The saints do not gather together for selfish purposes, and we certainly don't bar the doors to unbelievers. But this gathering on a weekly basis is the gathering of the people of God. Our worship is for Christians and should be designed to enhance the growth and the development of the believer. Christ has given to his saints the ministry, the oracles, and the ordinances for their gathering and for their sanctification and for their perfecting **in this life, to the end of the world.**

Section 3 goes on to say that Christ **doth, by His own presence and Spirit, according to His promise, make them effectual thereunto.** Recently, Ligonier Ministries has held some seminars around the country on the doctrines of grace, the doctrine of election, and related doctrines. There is probably no doctrine that people struggle with more deeply or fight against more fiercely than the doctrine of election. I try to communicate not simply the truth of this biblical teaching, but the sweetness of it, the delight of it. Historically, when the people of God come to understand the full measure of the doctrines of grace, it sets their feet to dancing, so to speak. When they see what God has wrought in his mercy and grace, it brings comfort and confidence to believers in this hostile world around us.

The Puritans wrote of their gratitude for the doctrine of election because it focuses not simply on the eternal purposes of the Father, but also upon the efficacy of the ministry of the Son. God's eternal purposes will and must come to pass, but in that eternal purpose of God is his determinate counsel to redeem his people. Our election is always *in* Christ, and it is effective and effected *through* Christ. The average so-called evangelical Christian looks at the ministry of Jesus in this way: Jesus obeyed the Father's summons and willingly went to the cross to atone for people's sins, potentially. That is, he made redemption possible for all of those who will put their trust in his work. But it was theoretically possible that no one would trust in him and that he would therefore die in vain. Isaiah said that the Suffering Servant of the Lord would see the travail of his soul and be satisfied (Isa. 53). In this view, he atoned for every sin except one, the sin of unbelief. If people persist in unbelief, they will perish.

However, if he atoned for the sins of all people, then all people would certainly be saved. God would be unjust to punish a person for whom an atonement of their sin had already been perfectly made. We underestimate the value, the purpose, and the power of the atonement when we think like that. The Puritans believed that God sent his Son into the world not only to make redemption *possible* for his people, but to make it *certain*. Christ's atonement was a perfect atonement that completely satisfied the demands of God's justice for God's people.

That is what the confession affirms: that the Lord gives the ministry, the oracles, and the ordinances to the church. And he gives to the church not only these things, but also himself, his presence. When we come to the Lord's Table, it is not for our own internal fellowship, but to feast upon the presence of Christ in the sacramental redemption that he offers to us. He promises his presence at the Lord's Table. We won't be able to see Jesus, but he promises to be present, and he will be present. He will never miss that engagement, and the power of his presence will not depend upon our faith, but upon his integrity. He did not come merely to help us through the gates of paradise, but to take us into the heavenly kingdom. Like the Puritans, we must gain a deeper understanding of the excellency of Christ.

The Puritans were not excited about the doctrine of election because they enjoyed abstract theology or because it ties everything together so beautifully. They came to see that God had appointed us from the foundation of the world. He was the one who brought us to faith in Christ in the first place, and he would not throw us away after a while. He who has begun a good work in us has determined to bring it to its completion, and he is able to do it (Phil. 1:6). He does it *in* and *through* his Son and through the ministry of the Holy Spirit. Salvation is of the Lord, and the powerful and effective Lord brings his people out of Egypt into the Promised Land. That is my great comfort. My only comfort in life and death is Christ and the power of his name and the power of his redemption.

Sec. 4. This catholic Church hath been sometimes more, sometimes less visible. And particular Churches, which are members thereof, are more or less pure, according as the doctrine of the Gospel is taught and embraced, ordinances administered, and public worship performed more or less purely in them.

At the Council of Nicaea, four marks of the church were set forth: that the church is one, holy, catholic, and apostolic. The church is holy in the sense that it has a holy vocation and has been set apart for a special mission. It has a consecrated task and identity, and it is indwelt by the Holy Spirit. However, that does not mean that the church is perfectly pure. We are always a work in progress. Paul chided the people at Corinth to stop behaving like children. Nevertheless, he addressed them as holy ones (saints) because they had been set apart from the world. The confession talks about the church in its visible manifestation, and **particular Churches** as being **more or less pure,** more or less holy.

The church, according to Augustine, is a *corpus permixtum,* "a mixed body," where there are tares growing along with the wheat. That is why any particular visible church can be more or less pure. We want to be committed to the purity of the church. The church can become impure if it crosses the line into apostasy. Then the believer not only may leave, but must leave. We are not to be visibly identified with an apostate body.

There is a difference between an apostate and a pagan. Both, of course, are under the judgment of God. A pagan is one who has never made an outward profession of faith. An apostate, on the other hand, has made a profession of faith and then repudiated it. If a person or a particular church or even a denomination makes a profession of faith in Christ and then denies the deity of Christ, then that person or institution has become apostate because it has denied an essential truth of the Christian faith.

This is what the Protestant–Roman Catholic controversy in the sixteenth century was about, and what a recent papal encyclical revisited. The Protestant churches of the sixteenth century were condemned by Rome for schism and teaching many false doctrines. In turn, the Protestant churches said that Rome was no longer a church. When Rome condemned the doctrine of justification by faith alone, the Reformers said, she became apostate. Once she denied the gospel, she was no longer a legitimate church, no matter how many other truths she maintained. That was the position of Luther, Calvin, Knox, and the rest of the Reformers. Since the sixteenth century, Catholics and Protestants have not recognized each other as valid churches.

The sixteenth century witnessed not only the Catholic-Protestant split, but also the disintegration of the Protestant movement. People sought to authenticate particular churches and determine whether they were a cult or a sect. The Reformers said there were three criteria that must be met for a group to be a legitimate church.

The first criterion is the gospel. Every true church proclaims the gospel. The essential elements of the gospel are simply the basic creedal formulations of historic Christianity. The essential truths about Jesus are his sinlessness, deity, humanity, atonement, resurrection, and ascension. Not only is the work of Christ essential to the gospel, but also how his benefits are appropriated. As Paul indicates, there is only one gospel and it is the gospel of justification by faith alone. If one believes all the essential truths about Jesus, but denies how the benefits of the objective work of Christ are subjectively appropriated, one does not have the gospel.

A few years ago, I met with some theologians and pled the case that justification by faith alone was essential to the gospel. Luther said it was the article upon which the church stands or falls. Calvin said it was the hinge upon which everything turns. But these Christian leaders would not agree that *sola fide*, or justification by faith alone, was essential to the gospel. They were willing to say it was *central* to the gospel, but they choked on the word *essential*. I asked, "Are you saying that what is at the core of the gospel, that which is at its center, is not essential? That means you can have the gospel without its center." They refused to use the term *essential*. Historically, Protestant theology has always said that *sola fide* is not only part of the gospel, but *essential* to it. Without it, there is no gospel. Without the gospel, there is no church. There can be a religious institution, but without the gospel, it is no church.

Secondly, the administration of the sacraments is essential to a true church. So what do we make of the controversy between Protestant bodies who practice infant baptism and those who restrict baptism to so-called believer's baptism? For the most part, Protestants have agreed that the issue of baptism, as serious as it may be, does not determine whether a church is a genuine church or not. It falls into the category of true churches being **more or less pure.**

The confession does not say that there must be agreement on every aspect of the doctrine of the sacraments before we can recognize the validity of another church. Protestants disagree not only about baptism, but also about the nature of the presence of Christ in the Lord's Supper. Nevertheless, all these groups use baptism as a sign and seal of the promises of God in the new covenant. They all intend to communicate the Lord's death in the Lord's Supper. Some Protestant churches are more pure and others are less pure with respect to the sacraments, but they are sufficiently pure to be true churches of Christ.

The third criterion for a church to be authentic is that it has an organized government by which church discipline can be and is exercised. Without discipline, gross and heinous sin or heresy can fester openly, leading to the apostasy of a church.

Sec. 5. The purest Churches under heaven are subject both to mixture and error; and some have so degenerated, as to become no Churches of Christ, but synagogues of Satan. Nevertheless, there shall be always a Church on earth to worship God according to His will.

Section 4 ends with these words: **according as the doctrine of the Gospel is taught and embraced, ordinances administered, and public worship performed more or less purely in them.** Section 5 continues: **The purest Churches under heaven**—not just the least pure churches, but also the most pure churches—**are subject both to mixture and error.** There is no such thing as a perfect church, nor is there any such thing as an infallible church. **Some have so degenerated, as to become no Churches of Christ, but synagogues of Satan. Nevertheless, there shall be always a Church on earth to worship God according to His will.** A particular church or denomination may pass out of existence or may become apostate, but God will never leave this planet destitute of a visible church that worships him properly.

> Sec. 6. There is no other head of the Church but the Lord Jesus Christ. Nor can the Pope of Rome, in any sense, be head thereof.

Finally, section 6 adds two brief sentences to say that there is no vicar of Christ on earth. There is no basis for the papacy in the New Testament. Christ and only Christ is the head of his church. That is an axiom, of course, of Protestant Christianity.

26

THE COMMUNION
OF SAINTS

The Westminster Confession of Faith
Chapter 26: Of the Communion of Saints

Sec. 1. All saints, that are united to Jesus Christ their Head, by His Spirit, and by faith, have fellowship with Him in His grace, sufferings, death, resurrection, and glory: and, being united to one another in love, they have communion in each other's gifts and graces, and are obliged to the performance of such duties, public and private, as do conduce to their mutual good, both in the inward and outward man.

Sec. 2. Saints by profession are bound to maintain an holy fellowship and communion in the worship of God, and in performing such other spiritual services as tend to their mutual edification; as also in relieving each other in outward things, according to their several abilities and necessities. Which communion, as God offereth opportunity, is to be extended unto all those who, in every place, call upon the name of the Lord Jesus.

Sec. 3. This communion which the saints have with Christ, doth not make them in any wise partakers of the substance of His Godhead; or to be equal with Christ in any respect: either of which to affirm is impious and blasphemous. Nor doth their communion one with another, as saints, take away, or infringe the title or propriety which each man hath in his goods and possessions.

One of the definitions of the church is *the communion of saints*. The communion of saints is such an important element in the life of the Christian and of the church, that the Westminster divines thought it prudent to deal with it separately as a distinct article of faith. In that regard, they followed the ancient fathers of the church, who included the communion of saints as one of the elements in the church's oldest confession, the Apostles' Creed: "I believe in the Holy Ghost, the communion of saints, the forgiveness of sins, the resurrection of the body, and the life everlasting." In Latin, it is the *communio sanctorum*, and it touches one of the richest elements of our Christian experience for two reasons. The communion of saints describes our relationship with Christ and our relationship with each other. There are not many relationships that are as important in our lives as those two.

From the Latin *communio*, we see more clearly the etymology of the word *communion*. The prefix *com* means "with." The root of the word is *unio*, so *communion* means "union with." Why add the prefix *com* to *unio* when *unio* expresses union by itself? Historically, there's an important distinction between *union* and *communion*.

In classic forms of non-Christian mysticism, such as Gnosticism or Neoplatonism, there was the belief that one has to bypass the mind to apprehend the divine. In some of the Greek mystery religions, the disciples of Dionysus, also called Bacchus, the god of the vine, for whom the bacchanalia was named, engaged in orgies of drunkenness and feasting. There was immoral behavior with the temple prostitutes. The rationale for these orgies was the notion that to apprehend deity, one must silence the rational barrier of reason. To gain entrance into the transcendent realm and mystically apprehend the divine, they believed, one has to bypass the mind and the five senses. The Dionysian frenzy with intoxication and dancing was designed to produce an ecstasy in which contact could perhaps be made with the divine. One could lose consciousness of oneself and become one with God.

That is a concept in oriental religion, also. In it, the ultimate goal of religious experience is the loss of personal identity and the experience of losing one's individuality and being swallowed up in "the all" or "the one." It is described as becoming like a drop of water, diffused throughout the entire ocean, losing any sense of particularity or individuation, once merged with the oversoul.

There are mystical elements in New Testament Christianity. Paul talks about being caught up in the third heaven, an incredible experience of transcendence where he had a heightened sense and an awareness of Christ. Throughout church history, an element of mysticism has been associated with Christian faith. The difference between pagan mysticism and Christian mysticism is that Christianity never sees the goal of religious faith to be the annihilation of personal identity or the loss of the self. Rather, the goal is a heightened understanding of the self as it relates to God. It is the redemption of the personal identity, not the destruction of it, that we see as our goal. One of the reasons why non-Christian religious movements seek to escape from the self and to become one with a greater entity is to escape from personal responsibility. One can then live however one wants without being held accountable, because redemption will be the loss of personal identity. But the Christian faith offers not the destruction, but the redemption, of the person. Even death does not destroy personal identity. We believe, as Christians, in the continuity of conscious, personal identity at death. We believe that the body dies, but that the soul goes on with what we call the *continuity of personal existence* at death. The ultimate goal of pagan mysticism is to lose personal identity, and to become one with God—*unio*.

The church has been careful to say that the goal of our redemption is not *unio*, but *communio*. That means that there is a mystical union between Christ and his people. Our identity is not swallowed up in the identity of Christ, so that we become gods; rather, we enter into the blessed condition of intense personal fellowship with God. That is what communion means—being with him, not being absorbed in him. The person who is in communion with Christ does not lose his or her personal identity. That is the difference between union and communion.

Two words in the New Testament that need to be distinguished in this connection are *en* and *eis*. The word *eis* is usually translated "into," and the word *en*, "in." If I am outside a room, I could walk "into" (*eis*) it, whereupon I would be "in" (*en*) it. When Paul says in Acts, "Believe *in* the Lord Jesus, and you will be saved" (16:31 ESV), the Greek word translated "in" is actually *eis*, indicating that we put our faith *into* him. Then, when Paul talks about how Christians are *in* Christ and Christ is *in* them, he uses the word *en*. When we become Christians, we enter by faith into Christ and he enters into us, resulting in a mystical union in which we are in him and he is in us. We have been initiated and invited into this intimate spiritual fellowship by Christ himself. We remain distinct persons, and we each have a relationship with Christ, who is the basis of our unity as the church. Our relationships with other Christians need to be based on our mutual inclusion in Christ.

We can't hate someone for whom Christ died. We can be irritated or offended by them, or we can offend them and have altercations, but there is a limit to that hostility beyond which we can't go without at the same time denying Christ. We are to be patient with one another, understanding that our sanctification is still a work in progress. We forbear and love one another because our fellowship is rooted in Christ, who has sacrificed his love and his life for all of us.

64

We must see each other in Christ. As soon as we consider a Christian in that dimension, a remarkable change in our attitude occurs. Our love for Christ and his love for us overcome our tensions and conflicts with one another.

Our mystical union with Christ is effected by the third person of the Trinity, the Holy Spirit. Remember, it is mainly the work of the Spirit to apply the saving work of Christ to us. The Father initiates salvation, the Son accomplishes it, and the Holy Spirit applies it to us. It is the Spirit who causes us to be reborn, who creates faith in our heart, who indwells us and empowers us for our sanctification, and who effects this mystical union of our spirit with Christ. In Romans 8:16, Paul teaches that the Spirit testifies with our spirit that we are the children of God. The Holy Spirit not only brings us into this relationship, but also bears witness to our human spirit that we are in this relationship.

> Sec. 1. All saints, that are united to Jesus Christ their Head, by His Spirit, and by faith, have fellowship with Him in His grace, sufferings, death, resurrection, and glory: and, being united to one another in love, they have communion in each other's gifts and graces, and are obliged to the performance of such duties, public and private, as do conduce to their mutual good, both in the inward and outward man.

All saints, that are united to Jesus Christ their Head, by His Spirit, and by faith, have fellowship with Him in His grace, sufferings, death, resurrection, and glory. One of my deep concerns about modern forms of evangelism is that we are so zealous to win people to Christ and to communicate the benefits of the gospel that we will say "if you come to Jesus, you can have fellowship with him in his grace, in his resurrection, and in his glory"—omitting the fellowship in his sufferings. So important is that concept, in terms of our union with Christ, that the apostle Paul says that unless we are willing to participate in his suffering and death, we will not enter into his exaltation (2 Tim. 2:11–12). If we do enter into the afflictions of Jesus and embrace his humiliation, we will participate in his exaltation and in his glory.

The sacrament of baptism signifies, among other things, that the person being baptized is identified with the sufferings of Christ. Baptism is the sign of our unity with Christ in his death and resurrection. In Colossians 1:24, Paul testifies that he rejoices in his own persecution: "I now rejoice in my sufferings for you, and fill up in my flesh what is lacking in the afflictions of Christ, for the sake of His body, which is the church." It may sound as if Paul is saying that Jesus did 90 percent of the work of salvation, and we have to do the remaining 10 percent. On the contrary, "what is lacking" refers to the consequences of participation in Christ Jesus. The church is the body of Christ, and thus, in one sense, the continuation of his incarnation. Don't misunderstand; I don't mean that the church is God incarnate. Rather, I am saying that the embodiment of Christ in this world today is his church, and he identifies with his church.

Before the apostle Paul became a Christian, he was on the way to Damascus with authority to drag people out of their homes and throw them into prison. When Jesus stopped him and addressed him from heaven, he said, "Saul, Saul, why are you persecuting Me?" (Acts 9:4). He was afflicting Jesus by imposing suffering on those who were in him and in whom he dwells. By hurting Jesus' body, the church, he was hurting Jesus. In that sense, Paul was filling up what was lacking in the body of Christ by *imposing* the sufferings. After his conversion, he was filling it up by personally *receiving* the sufferings with beatings, stonings, shipwrecks, persecutions, and imprisonment. Jesus said to his people, "In the world you will have tribulation" (John 16:33). "If the world hates you, you know that it hated Me before it hated you. If you were of the world, the world would love its own. Yet because you are not of the world, but I chose you out of the world, therefore the world hates you" (John 15:18–19). We will enter into his sorrows, his pain, his afflictions, and then into his glory. We are "joint heirs with Christ, if indeed we suffer with Him, that we may also be glorified together" (Rom. 8:17).

Paul was referring to that concept, and not to any deficiency in the work of Jesus. Through his redemptive suffering at the hands of the Father and the propitiation that he gave us on the cross, his work is finished; that pain is done. Nevertheless, the world is still heaping afflictions upon Christ by persecuting his body, the church. When we suffer for the gospel's sake, we fill up the full measure of the sufferings of Christ by virtue of our communion with him. The confession echoes Paul when it says that we have fellowship with Christ in his grace, in his sufferings, in his death, in his resurrection, and in his glory.

We are **united to one another in love.** We are in union with Christ as the communion of saints. Anyone who is united with Christ is at the same time united with all others who are united with Christ. **Being united to one another in love, they**—that is, the saints—**have communion in each other's gifts and graces, and are obliged to the performance of such duties, public and private, as do conduce to their mutual good, both in the inward and outward man.** Paul describes the diversity of gifts in the body of Christ by using the metaphor of the body, in which a multitude of diverse parts, like eyes, ears, nose, lungs, hearts, arms, and legs, work together. Similarly, the church consists of many members, working together as one body.

At a restaurant, I saw a man pushing his wife in a wheelchair. This man was being the legs for his wife. He participated in her affliction, and she profited by his legs. That is how the church is supposed to work. Some may have the gift of giving, administration, evangelism, teaching, or preaching. When a member exercises his gift, we participate in that gift, because it is used for the edification of the whole church. All who give financially receive a return that does not just benefit themselves, but benefits the whole body. The spiritual gifts work the same way. The ingredient that makes the communion of the saints cohesive is *agapē*, love.

The discourse on love found in 1 Corinthians 13 is sandwiched between chapter 12 and chapter 14, in which the apostle Paul admonishes the Corinthian congregation about their abuse of the gifts of the Spirit. It is in the middle of this that he tells us how the body of Christ is supposed to look. "Though I speak with the tongues of men and of angels, but have not love, I have become sounding brass or a clanging cymbal" (1 Cor. 13:1). Paul is not describing love in the abstract; he is telling us how love looks in the midst of a community that has been gifted by God. The purpose of our gifts and of our graces is to benefit everyone in the body of Christ. Not one gifted person can say, "Look at me." First Corinthians 13 is an exposition of the communion of the saints.

Being united to one another in love, they have communion in each other's gifts and graces, and are obliged to the performance of such duties, public and private, as do conduce to their mutual good, both in the inward and outward man. That is communion. Paul wrote to the Corinthians, "And I, brethren, when I came to you, did not come with excellence of speech or of wisdom declaring to you the testimony of God. . . . I was with you in weakness, in fear, and in much trembling" (1 Cor. 2:1, 3). Paul was with them in their suffering, and he entered into their suffering. He was part of their community, part of their communion. We weep with those who weep, and we rejoice with those who rejoice (Rom. 12:15). That is communion, and that is the essence of biblical community.

Sec. 2. Saints by profession are bound to maintain an holy fellowship and communion in the worship of God, and in performing such other spiritual services as tend to their mutual edification; as also in relieving each other in outward things, according to their several abilities and necessities. Which communion, as God offereth opportunity, is to be extended unto all those who, in every place, call upon the name of the Lord Jesus.

In sections 2 and 3, we find affirmation and denial; that is, section 2 tells us what the communion of saints does mean, and section 3 tells us what it does not mean. First, the affirmation.

Saints by profession are bound to maintain an holy fellowship and communion in the worship of God. The nature and function of the church have been radically rethought in America. We have seen a major change in what many churches do on Sunday morning, provoked to a large extent by Willow Creek Church, near Chicago. A young man with a great vision for evangelism, Bill Hybels, went into suburban Chicago and surveyed many people who had been members of churches, but had dropped out. He found that the number one reason why people had left their church was that it was boring. The second reason most frequently given was that church seemed irrelevant.

Hybels decided to rethink church and to create an atmosphere, ambiance, and structure that would give people no excuse to be bored or to see the church as antiquated. They changed their style of worship in order to reach out to so-called seekers who were not believers, and they did away with the external trappings of the church. Their building looks more like a concert hall than a sanctuary. They don't call themselves a congregation, but rather, an audience, and they have no pulpit. This was the fastest-growing church in the United States in the latter part of the twentieth century. Literally thousands of pastors flocked to that site to learn how to reach out and to experience church growth.

In addition to the Willow Creek model, there was research that led to the church growth movement. This movement employs certain strategies and methodologies in order to facilitate church growth. It has included serious change in the church's approach to worship.

People say that the main reason they attend church is for fellowship. But the main reason people should come to church is for *worship*. Still, fellowship is important in the Christian community. It is what the New Testament calls *koinonia*, the coming together of the people of God. Here is our most important affinity group, people who share the love of Christ. This is part of the communion of saints. However, if we structure church just for fellowship, we have lost sight of the reason for the church's existence.

Our purpose for assembling together is to worship God, to offer the sacrifices of praise. If people are leaving church because they are bored, that is revealing. The answer is not to put on dramatic presentations on Sunday morning, or to include Christian rock music, or any other form of entertainment. If people are bored, they don't have a sense of coming into the presence of God. No one has ever been confronted with the living God and walked away bored. They may burst into tears, faint, or leap with joy, but they are never bored. There is nothing boring about God.

If people leave church saying, "That was absolutely irrelevant," then there are two possible explanations. Either the preacher hasn't preached the Word of God, or the people haven't listened. There is nothing irrelevant about being in the presence of God and hearing his Word.

Fellowship is important, and that is why the church body has times other than worship to be together. I believe that the church that plays together stays together. It is important to have occasions when we can bond as members of a local congregation. It is amazing how we can edify one another in this way. Luther's principle of "the priesthood of all believers" means that every member of the body of Christ is gifted by the Holy Spirit and is expected to use that gift in the service of Christ and of his kingdom. In that sense, we are all priests and we all participate in the ministry of Christ. The church is an army of gifted people, to be trained, disciplined, and sent into the world for mission. The confession affirms that in the communion of saints we are **bound to maintain an holy fellowship and communion in the worship of God, and in performing such other spiritual services as tend to their mutual edification.**

When we make a profession of faith in Christ and become part of his body, we are indwelt by Christ. He is in us, and we are in him.

70

From that day forth, we ought never to neglect the assembling together of the saints (Heb. 10:25). The rule of thumb in most of today's churches is that on any given Sunday, a minimum of 25 percent of the church members will be absent. That includes people who are out of town, people who are sick, and people who are otherwise providentially hindered. Still, that is a high percentage of members who are not present with the rest of the body in worship on Sunday morning.

We must rid ourselves of the cavalier, casual attitude that we who bear the name of Christ can fail to participate in worship or in the fellowship of the body of Christ. It is our job to support and edify one another by gathering together for worship. We remember the warnings in Hebrews that it is a dreadful thing to neglect so great a salvation. It is our duty to be in church and in fellowship with other Christians, engaged in the worship of God for the mutual edification of the saints.

The saints maintain their communion **also in relieving each other in outward things, according to their several abilities and necessities. Which communion, as God offereth opportunity, is to be extended unto all those who, in every place, call upon the name of the Lord Jesus.** This last section almost sounds like communism. In fact, the proof texts include the passage in Acts 2 where the disciples in the early church had all things in common. Some people have deduced from that text that there is a mandate in the New Testament to divest oneself of all private property and to live together in communes where all property is held in common. That represents a superficial understanding of that passage and ignores the rest of Scripture. The Decalogue in the Old Testament and the teaching of the New Testament support the right of private property.

The confession is developing the principle that when we see a person weeping, we weep with him or her. When someone in our fellowship is going through extreme need or want, it is the duty of the congregation to help that person. Most churches have a special fund from which to support people who are lacking food or other necessities. Many of the so-called welfare programs of the government undertake responsibilities that God gave to the church, not to the state. Our responsibility, in the final analysis, is to make sure that, within the shadow of our church, the outward needs of people are being met.

I talked to an Episcopalian priest several years ago whose first pastorate was in the town where I attended high school. It was a town fueled by the steel industry. When the steel industry collapsed, the whole community also collapsed. The young man said, "I'm having trouble getting the church to grow. We only have twenty-five members in our mission church." In fact, it had been a mission church since 1905. "What can I do to build this church?" he asked. I replied: "If you want to build a church in this oppressed community, go where the pain is. Find the pain and minister to it, and you will have a congregation. The town has an unemployment rate of 30 percent. Two places I'd go every day are the union halls and the bars. That's where the people are and where the pain is. A pastor can't just go down to the corner, open a church, and put a sign up outside reading, 'You all come.' It doesn't work like that in a community that is depressed like this one."

To find a congregation, Jesus went out to seek and to save those who were lost. He gave his time and his attention to sinners, to those who were sick, to those who were in need of a Savior. He looked for them. That is what it means for the church to be the church. A congregation ought to be so mobilized that they are looking for troubled people to minister to. I was on the staff of a church in Cincinnati, where I was the minister of theology and of evangelism. I trained two hundred and fifty people in how to do evangelism. Twice a week we went out into the community to communicate the gospel. One of the most incredible things that came out of that was that the people who were involved in that weekly evangelistic visitation program created new ministries.

People in the church created a prison ministry on their own. They created an "unemployment anonymous" program, helping the unemployed to find jobs. They created a hospital visitation ministry on their own. How did this happen? Our evangelism program got us inside people's homes or apartments and talking with them. We saw the suffering and needs of the people. Some were ill and in need of care. Some were hospitalized and had no one to visit them, and the church members responded. Some had family members in prison. There will always be an opportunity to minister for Christ where the pain is.

> Sec. 3. This communion which the saints have with Christ, doth not make them in any wise partakers of the substance of His Godhead; or to be equal with Christ in any respect: either of which to affirm is impious and blasphemous. Nor doth their communion one with another, as saints, take away, or infringe the title or propriety which each man hath in his goods and possessions.

Section 2 explains what the communion of saints entails; section 3 explains what it does not entail.

This communion which the saints have with Christ, doth not make them in any wise partakers of the substance of His Godhead; or to be equal with Christ in any respect: either of which to affirm is impious and blasphemous. Someone once said, "Every person has a spark of the divine within him." That's not true. All we have is humanity. We may have reborn humanity, but it is humanity in the process of sanctification. We may be indwelt by the Holy Spirit, but we never participate in the substance of deity, even though we are created in the image of God. To be the image of God does not mean that we participate in his essence, his deity. It means that there are aspects which God imparts that are similar to his own being. Augustine explained the image of God in man as man's memory, his understanding, and his will. God is a rational being. He has a mind and he thinks, and he is also a volitional being. He has a will. He makes choices, and in order to make choices, there is a mind. A

73

mindless response or reaction is not a willful, voluntary action; it is involuntary. In that sense, we are like God, who has given to man a measure of intelligence and volition that is not found anywhere else in creation to the degree that it is given to man. Nevertheless, it is still a finite mind and a finite will. We do not have omniscience in our understanding, which is an incommunicable divine attribute. The substance of deity is not transferred to humanity. In fact, not only did God not create us as little gods, but he could not, because the essence of deity is found only in self-existent eternal being. God could not create another self-existent eternal being. By definition, any created being would not be self-existent and eternal, because it would be created.

Once, when I was traveling on a train, a girl sitting across from me bubbled with enthusiasm and excitement as she told an elderly lady that she was returning home after being two years in a training camp for New Age philosophy and religion. The lady asked her what she had learned. The girl responded, "I discovered that I am God." She looked over at me enthusiastically and said, "What do you think of that?" I replied, "I think that this is the first time in my life that I have had the opportunity to sit across from God incarnate." She laughed a little bit. Then I continued, "You don't really believe that you are God, do you?" She giggled and said, "Well, no." To that I commented, "Well, there go two years of training down the drain." We laughed about it, but the serious thing is that there are people who believe that they somehow participate in deity, that they are God.

The view of the confession is that any person who thinks that he partakes of the substance of Christ's Godhead, or is equal with him in any respect, is impious and blasphemous. The highest rung on the spiritual ladder is communion with Christ, but that does not make us divine.

Nor doth their communion one with another, as saints, take away, or infringe the title or propriety which each man hath in his goods and possessions. The confession reaffirms the principle of private ownership. This may seem insignificant, but it isn't simply a statement on economics or political theory. The authors of the confession were concerned about Christian ethics and the Christian faith. They wanted to maintain the right of private ownership as an ethical principle.

The New Testament says, "Let him who stole steal no longer" (Eph. 4:28). The Bible prohibits theft, and in doing so it protects the private possession of those who own things. The Bible condemns the sins of greed, envy, and covetousness. If someone has a better job, more money, or a nicer house, the Christian's response is to rejoice in another's prosperity. We are not to be filled with resentment or hostility toward somebody who is blessed in outward circumstances more than we are. When we are covetous, we not only do violence and injury to our neighbor, but we insult God, who is the author of every good and perfect gift. When I am covetous, I am saying, "God, you haven't given me a square deal. You have blessed other people above and beyond what you have blessed me." We are to be satisfied and content in whatever state we are and to learn with the apostle Paul how to abound and how to be abased.

Some people who are prosperous struggle with enjoying that blessing. One of the beautiful things that God does, related to the handling of private property, is to set down a requirement of giving that is the same for everybody. That was the beauty of the Old Testament principle of the tithe. The widow who was in abject poverty gave the same percentage of her goods as Abraham, who was one of the wealthiest men in the world—10 percent.

There is no graduated income tax or politics of envy with God. Not everybody gives the same, but they all give the same percentage. No one can complain. After they have given what is required, they can enjoy what is left with no guilty feeling.

The first year the pilgrims were in New England, they held everything in common, and they had nothing to show for their toil. Finally William Bradford told them that in the second year, they could keep whatever they produced. The second year and following, the community prospered. The difference was that in the first year everybody did as little as possible, knowing that everything they produced was going to be taken away from them. Biblical faith does not follow that concept. It requires what I call stewardship capitalism. We are to be productive and responsible stewards of what we have. That means giving, and that means supporting the ministry of the kingdom, and that means helping the poor. There is a difference between community and communalism. We are to show love and concern to our neighbors, but that does not require us to divest ourselves of private property.

27

THE SACRAMENTS

The Westminster Confession of Faith
Chapter 27: Of the Sacraments

Sec. 1. Sacraments are holy signs and seals of the covenant of grace, immediately instituted by God, to represent Christ and His benefits; and to confirm our interest in Him: as also, to put a visible difference between those that belong unto the Church and the rest of the world; and solemnly to engage them to the service of God in Christ, according to His Word.

Sec. 2. There is, in every sacrament, a spiritual relation, or sacramental union, between the sign and the thing signified: whence it comes to pass, that the names and effects of the one are attributed to the other.

Sec. 3. The grace which is exhibited in or by the sacraments rightly used, is not conferred by any power in them; neither doth the efficacy of a sacrament depend upon the piety or intention of him that doth administer it: but upon the work of the Spirit, and the word of institution, which contains, together with a precept authorizing the use thereof, a promise of benefit to worthy receivers.

Sec. 4. There be only two sacraments ordained by Christ our Lord in the Gospel; that is to say, Baptism, and the Supper of the Lord: neither of which may be dispensed by any, but by a minister of the Word lawfully ordained.

Sec. 5 . The sacraments of the old testament, in regard of the spiritual things thereby signified and exhibited, were, for substance, the same with those of the new.

The worship experience in the life of the church is usually defined in terms of Word and sacrament, and chapters 27–29 of the Westminster Confession discuss the two sacraments of baptism and the Lord's Supper. Chapter 27 discusses sacraments in general, followed by chapter 28 on baptism and chapter 29 on the Lord's Supper. Historically, churches have understood the sacraments in vastly different ways. Because the sacraments are so important to the life of the church, it is understandable that there has been a lot of controversy. It is good that the debates occur, because it indicates that the people of God are taking these aspects of their worship seriously.

There are controversies about the number of the sacraments, their meaning, origin, mode, and efficacy, as well as who may dispense and who may receive them. The word *sacrament* comes from the Latin *sacramentum*, which translates the Greek *mystērion*, and that's why in some churches the sacraments are referred to as "holy mysteries." The term *mystērion*, in the Bible, does not mean "mystery" as that word is used in our culture. We think of mysteries as secretive, sinister, or eerie, perhaps involving murder. The biblical *mystērion*, however, refers to a mystery that once was hidden, but now is revealed. This differs even from our theological use of the term to denote those things that we do not yet understand. The biblical mysteries are things that were once hidden, particularly in Old Testament days, but are now revealed in the coming of Christ and with the apostolic revelation.

A mystery, in the sense of a sacrament, is not intended to conceal something, but just the opposite. A mystery reveals something, and thus the sacraments are nonverbal forms of communication. In the Old Testament, God verbally communicated his truth to his people by way of his spoken or written word. His verbal communications were often supplemented or corroborated by nonverbal forms of communication. The prophets frequently gave object lessons, in which they would act out certain of their revelations for the people. They would talk in terms of analogies. "I see a plumb line," Amos said, and that indicated God's intent to measure his people to see whether they were obedient to the norms that he had established. Throughout the Old Testament, we see these nonverbal forms of communication.

One of the earliest of these was the sign of the rainbow, by which God signified to Noah that he would never again destroy the world with a flood. That sign reminded the people of God's promise. Also in the Old Testament were circumcision, which became the sign of the old covenant, and the celebratory meal at Passover. There was rich symbolism in the celebration of the Day of Atonement, in which two transactions took place. The priest laid his hands on the scapegoat, dramatically transferring the sins of the people to it. The scapegoat was then sent outside the camp into the wilderness, into the outer darkness. Then an animal was sacrificed on the altar. After an elaborate ritual of purification, the high priest was allowed to go into the Holy of Holies. There he sprinkled the blood of the offering on the mercy seat, which was the lid of the ark of the covenant. In this drama, the promise of God to forgive the sins of his people and to provide an atonement for the people was acted out. Throughout Old Testament history, such ritual is part and parcel of God's communication of his

Word to his people. His Word is fortified and confirmed by visible, external, nonverbal forms of communication.

We do not think of those Old Testament visible manifestations as sacraments in the narrow sense of the word, but they are sacramental in the broad sense of the term. In the New Testament, there are sacraments instituted by Christ, and we see God continuing to confirm his Word with actions or nonverbal forms of communication. Ritual is important to the life of God's people. As human beings, we communicate not only with words, but also by facial expressions and gestures. These are nonverbal aspects of communication. This is one of the problems we have when we read the Scripture. We must imagine the tone and inflection of the speaker's voice and the look on his face. What was Pilate's tone when he said to Jesus, "What is truth?" Did he say it with cynicism dripping from his lips? Was Pilate taken aback by Jesus' statement that his mission was to bear witness to the truth and that all who are of the truth hear his voice? We don't know, and although sometimes the context gives us hints and clues, we can't know for sure. Words that we speak or write can be strengthened or intensified by the nonverbal apparatus with which they are associated.

In the New Testament, dramatic and important actions were instituted by Christ, called baptism and the Lord's Supper. Baptism had been introduced before the ministry of Jesus, by John the Baptist. The rite that John introduced to Israel was not exactly the same thing as New Testament baptism. John's baptism was intended to prepare Israel for the coming of the Messiah, whereas Jesus assigned a whole new set of meanings and content to his baptism. In both cases, baptism symbolized cleansing, among other things. People underwent a ritual of cleansing that communicated in a graphic way that they were dirty. Their dirtiness was not from the dirt of the ground, but from the dirt of their sin. Their baptism symbolized their cleansing from their sinful condition.

Jesus established the Lord's Supper when he gathered his disciples to celebrate the Passover one last time before he died. He went to great lengths to find a place that was suitable for him to meet with his inner circle. In the middle of the celebration, Jesus changed the significance of the meal. Previously, the Passover had memorialized Israel's deliverance from Egypt, beginning with the blood of a lamb being spread on the doorposts of Israelite homes so that the angel of destruction would pass over them when he went through Egypt killing the firstborn sons. Holding up a cup of wine, Jesus said to his disciples, "This is my blood, the blood of a new covenant, the blood that is shed for the remission of your sins." He attached new meaning to that ancient ritual. Virtually from that night forward, it has been celebrated weekly by the Christian community. The bread of the meal represents his body, and the wine represents his shed blood. The Lord's Supper communicates the significance of the Lord's death nonverbally. "For as often as you eat this bread and drink this cup, you proclaim the Lord's death till He comes" (1 Cor. 11:26). It is a visible manifestation of the verbal content of the atonement, acted out dramatically.

Sec. 1. Sacraments are holy signs and seals of the covenant of grace, immediately instituted by God, to represent Christ and His benefits; and to confirm our interest in Him: as also, to put a visible difference between those that belong unto the Church and the rest of the world; and solemnly to engage them to the service of God in Christ, according to His Word.

This is a wonderful definition of sacraments. First of all, they are **holy signs and seals of the covenant of grace**. Sacraments are given in the context of covenant. The sign of the old covenant was circumcision, and the sign of the new covenant is baptism. When the people of God entered into the Mosaic covenant, God made promises to the people, and along with the promises came the stipulations, or commandments, of the covenant. The Old Testament covenant included a preamble, a historical prologue, promises, stipulations, and a rite by which people swore their allegiance to their covenant Lord. The sign of the covenant of Abraham, repeated through Moses, was circumcision, which was a cutting rite administered to males. It symbolized two different elements, or dual sanctions. On the one hand, the subordinate party in the covenant, the person being circumcised, was saying, "May I be cut off from the world, set apart from godlessness, and enter into the holy community of the covenant people of God." The cutting of the foreskin was in a sense the cutting out of the person from ungodly humanity, putting him into the privileged position of being numbered among the people of God. It was a mark of consecration, of his being set apart for a holy purpose. That was the positive symbolism behind circumcision.

Conversely, it had a negative symbolism. The circumcised person said with this action, "If I am not faithful to the terms of the covenant and do not obey the law of God, may I be cut off from all of his blessings, cut off from his presence, cut off from fellowship with him, just as I have had the foreskin of my flesh cut off." This was a dramatic image of the terms of the covenant that marked a Jew.

In Genesis 15, God said to Abraham, "Do not be afraid, Abram. I am your shield, your exceedingly great reward" (v. 1). Abraham staggered at that announcement and said, "Lord GOD, what will You give me, seeing I go childless, and the heir of my house is Eliezer of Damascus?" God replied, "This one shall not be your heir, but one who will come from your own body shall be your heir. . . . Look now toward heaven, and count the stars if you are able to number them. . . . So shall your descendants be." Then we read in verse 6, "And he believed in the LORD, and He accounted it to him for righteousness." This is the first expression of the doctrine of justification by faith alone in the Old Testament.

Moments later, Abraham, who was struggling with his faith, asked, "Lord GOD, how shall I know that I will inherit it?" God ordered Abraham to kill certain animals, cut them in half, and arrange their body parts to form an aisle. Half of the body would be on one side of the aisle, and the other half would be on the other side. God put Abraham into a deep sleep, in which he saw a smoking oven and a burning torch moving between the pieces. By doing this, God was symbolically saying, "Because I cannot swear by anything greater, I swear by myself. I am dramatizing, by walking through these pieces of animals that have been torn asunder, that I will keep my promises. If I don't, may I be torn apart, just as these animals have been torn apart." God put his eternal deity on the line. When we struggle with faith and wonder whether we can trust God, it is good to go back and read Genesis 15, where he swore an oath by himself and put his character and being on the line in dramatic fashion.

This was a sacramental act with a small *s*. It was an outward sign that confirmed a promise. In the Old Testament, the sign of participation in the covenant of grace was circumcision. Abraham, who was called after he was an adult and after he had professed his faith, was circumcised. Whatever else circumcision represented, it represented his faith. In the case of adult converts to Israel, those from the outside could only be circumcised after they had made a profession of faith. Israel practiced believer's circumcision for those who came into Israel from paganism, but the Israelite children received the sign of their faith in infancy, before they had faith. Abraham made his profession of faith as an adult, and then he was circumcised, but God commanded that Isaac be circumcised as an infant. This becomes important when we cross over into the New Testament and see the points of continuity between the Old Testament sign and the New Testament sign. They are not identical, but there are important parallels.

The word *sign* is important. It translates the Greek word *sēmeion*, and is found throughout the New Testament, particularly in the book of John. People debate whether there are miracles today or whether they ceased at the end of the apostolic age. Some say the birth of a baby is a miracle; other people say it is an ordinary event, not an extraordinary one. It all depends on what you mean by "miracle." Some English translations of the Bible use the word *miracle*, but there is no one word in Greek that means "miracle." We extrapolate a concept of miracle from several different words in the New Testament. Some-times they are called powers, sometimes they are called wonders, but the word of choice in John's gospel is *sign*. For example: "This be-ginning of signs Jesus did in Cana of Galilee" (John 2:11). The feed-ing of the five thousand was "the sign that Jesus did" (John 6:14).

This concept runs through the New Testament. A sign points be-yond itself to some higher meaning or significance. Baptism is not re-demption in Christ; the Lord's Supper is not the crucifixion of Christ. These things point to the realities, but they are not the realities. They are nonverbal confirmations of the promises of God.

People ask, "Does baptism automatically, supernaturally regen-erate a person? Does baptism save us?" The Reformation answer is no. If baptism does not convey saving grace, then what good is it? How can it be important if it doesn't do what it is signifying? Some people who are baptized are not saved and never come to salvation. In Romans 2, Paul writes about circumcision of the heart: "But he is a Jew who is one inwardly" (Rom. 2:29). Paul spoke against the idea developed among the Jews that because they were circumcised, they were saved. They thought they had proof of their salvation in their circumcision; they had the sign of the covenant, so they believed they were saved. Paul's argument was that a person can have the external sign and not have the internal reality to which that sign points.

The efficacy of the sacraments was a major point of controversy between the Reformers and the Roman Catholic Church. Does bap-tism automatically, *ex opere operato*, convey the grace of justifica-tion? The Roman Catholic Church said yes; the Reformers said no. Rome charged that the Protestants had reduced the sacraments to a *nuda signa*, a naked sign, devoid of any effect. If baptism doesn't con-vey the grace of salvation, then it is an empty sign. The Reformers' answer was that when God makes a promise and confirms that prom-ise with a sign, there is nothing empty about the sign. That is why we can say, as Luther did, when Satan comes after us to accuse us, "Get away from me; I'm baptized." We can say to Satan, "I don't trust you because you're a liar, and I put my trust in the promise of God, which was signified to me in my baptism. I bear the ineradicable mark and sign of God's promise."

The promises of baptism are fulfilled only in and through faith, but the integrity of God's promise to me does not rest upon my faith. Some people have said to me, "I was baptized when I was a baby, and the man who baptized me quit the ministry, and he was a scoundrel. That makes my baptism invalid. Will you baptize me again?" I decline. The integrity of that sign does not rest with the person who gives it, or the person who receives it, or the parents who were there. The integrity of the sign rests with the one whose promise it is.

I also hear from people, "I was baptized as an infant. I didn't know what was going on, and I didn't become a Christian until recently. I'd like to be baptized again because it didn't mean anything to me the first time. Will you please baptize me a second time?" I reply, "I can't do that." One reason is that the church doesn't allow it, and I agree with the church on this point. I'm not just hiding behind ecclesiastical authority. I've never had somebody come to me and say, "I'd like to be baptized again because God's promise failed, and I want to say to God, 'Run that by me again.'" They have an existential desire to participate in baptism in what they think is a meaningful way. I say, "You may not intend to say, 'God, run that by me again,' but that is in fact just what you are saying. You should rejoice that the promise God signified to you in your baptism many years ago is now fulfilled in all of its glory."

The fact that people make these requests indicates that even though we practice baptism in a variety of ways in all denominations, there is very little understanding of the meaning of baptism. First of all, baptism is a sign. Second, it is a seal. It is more than a sign; it is the seal of God's promise.

That word *seal* (in Greek, *sphragis*) is a rich one in the New Testament. The concept of sealing gets its meaning from kings of the ancient world, who, when negotiating agreements, would sign and seal them with wax and a signet ring. The indentations in that ring were unique to that particular monarch and authenticated his agreement.

When the Holy Spirit seals us inwardly, God puts his stamp of ownership upon us with an indelible mark that indicates that we are his and that nothing can change that ownership. That is the inward sealing, which is then signified outwardly by the seal of baptism. Both baptism and the Lord's Supper are outward signs and outward seals of the truth of God's promises. When we celebrate the Lord's Supper, hear the words of institution, and go through the sacrament, we experience in a nonverbal, external way the sign and the seal of all of God's promises of grace. He says, "Let me show you that this is my word." He gives us the seal of baptism and the seal of the Lord's Supper, which are magnificent things.

This is one of the reasons why it is a rule in the church in which I am ordained that we never celebrate the sacrament without preaching, because the signs are never to be given without the Word. The Word and the sacrament may be distinguished, but not separated. This is to guard against a pagan kind of ritualism or externalism, where people go through the motions with no understanding of what they are doing. The nonverbal is to enhance the verbal; the nonverbal cannot stand alone. It must always be accompanied by the verbal. Sacrament and Word go together.

> Sec. 2. There is, in every sacrament, a spiritual relation, or sacramental union, between the sign and the thing signified: whence it comes to pass, that the names and effects of the one are attributed to the other.

This section reinforces the character of the sacraments as signs and seals of the promises of God. The term *sign* is used because a sign is "significant."

There is, in every sacrament, a spiritual relation, or sacramental union, between the sign and the thing signified. People who use sign language for the benefit of those who cannot hear use two different languages at one and the same time. One is the spoken language of the signer, which he hears and then conveys to the people who cannot hear the spoken word but can comprehend the signer's second language, which is his sign language. The sign helps to communicate the content of the verbal message. Sacraments in their sign character reinforce the content of the written Word.

If the Lord's Prayer is being signed, hand gestures signify the content of the prayer. There is a relationship between the sign, or the word, and the content of the prayer itself. It is interesting that Christ, as the incarnate second person of the Trinity, is introduced in John's gospel as the Logos, or the "Word," who was with God and is God, and who became flesh and dwelt among us. The word *incarnate* indicates the outward expression or the embodied sign of God himself. The Logos does not simply communicate God, but is the God whom he communicates. There is a special relationship between Christ as the living Word and God himself. That, of course, transcends the normal function of language, where words point beyond themselves to realities. The confession affirms that sacraments are not empty signs. There is a spiritual relationship between the sign and that which it signifies. That relationship is established by God, who himself attaches the significance to the sacrament.

Let me try to illustrate this. Years ago in Pittsburgh, I worked regularly with the Value of the Person program, a ministry to the steelworkers in western Pennsylvania, when the steel industry was in the middle of its collapse. There was hostility between owners and managers, and between managers and union workers. At that time, the United Steelworkers had one and a half million members, mostly concentrated in western Pennsylvania. I spoke in the morning at Fortune 500 corporate headquarters and in the afternoon at union halls to the rank and file.

At that time, the steelworkers' union was heavily infiltrated by the American Communist Party, and there were radical members of the union who called themselves the Maoists. They were extremely hostile toward management and also toward anything religious. When I spoke, the Maoists sat in the front row with their tape recorders, hoping to trap me into saying something that they could use against me and against the Value of the Person program.

We always began the seminars the same way, asking, "How many of you are University of Pittsburgh fans?" Half of the audience would put their hands up. Then I asked, "How many of you are Penn State fans?" The other half would cheer. They argued about football, about politics, and about religion, but when I asked, "How many of you want to be treated with dignity?" every person in the room raised his or her hand. That was the one thing upon which they could all agree.

What does this have to do with the sacraments? Let me continue. Everybody wants to be treated with dignity. It may be hard to define, but every person knows when he loses it, when he is not being accorded dignity.

I looked at the atheists and said, "Do you have dignity? From where did it come? You tell me that you're a cosmic accident. The origin of your life is meaningless, and your destiny is meaningless as you move toward annihilation. You say that your work matters because you matter, and at the same time you tell me that you come from nothing and you're going to nothing.

"From a theological perspective," I continued, "I believe you have dignity, and the only reason I can give for your dignity is that God says you have dignity. God assigned you dignity when he made you in his image. If you take God out of the equation, don't forget to take your dignity out with it." This is what Sartre, Camus, and other existentialists understand. Without God in the equation, personal dignity is an illusion. A human being, Jean-Paul Sartre said, is nothing more than a useless passion.

The point of my illustration is that we all want to be treated with dignity. We all cherish our dignity. But we have no inherent significance. We are significant only because God says that we are. It is God

88

who takes a pile of dirt and breathes his own breath of life into it and stamps us with his image. We are, in this sense, a living sacrament; we are the outward *sign* of the very character of God because we bear his image. There is a spiritual relationship between our humanity and the God who declared us significant. Our value as a person ultimately rests in the eternal value of God himself. Take that away, and our aspiration for significance, our hope and our dignity, is a myth.

The humanist is in an untenable position. He lives on borrowed capital, as Francis Schaeffer said, "with both feet planted squarely in midair." Humanists protest around the world for human rights and human dignity, but with no basis for it. They steal it from Christianity, but discard the very foundation, and keep only what they like.

There is a spiritual relationship between the outward sign of the sacraments and what the sign signifies. That does not mean that the sacrament causes what it signifies. Just because we participate in the sacrament of baptism does not mean that we are born again, that we are completely removed from original sin, or that we are indwelt by Christ and participate in his death and resurrection. All of those things are communicated by that sign, and it is spiritually tied to the reality because God says it is so. It is as if God is saying, "This is my promise, based upon faith. If you believe, I will cleanse you from all of your sins. I will raise you from spiritual death to spiritual life. I will bring you into union with Christ. I will baptize you and indwell you with the Holy Spirit. All of these things communicated by the sign of baptism are made real by my word." The sacrament is not just an empty ritual. It has spiritual significance and reality because God assigns that to it. Just as the Word of God does not return to him void, neither does the exercise and administration of his sacrament return to him void.

Sec. 3. The grace which is exhibited in or by the sacraments rightly used, is not conferred by any power in them; neither doth the efficacy of a sacrament depend upon the piety or intention of him that doth administer it: but upon the work of the Spirit, and the word of institution, which contains, together with a precept authorizing the use thereof, a promise of benefit to worthy receivers.

The grace that is exhibited by the sacraments is not conferred by any power in them. *Ex opere operato* is a formula that has been embraced and is still taught by the Roman Catholic Church to explain the efficacy of the sacraments. Literally, the Latin expression means "from the working of the work," which strongly suggests that the sacraments work automatically. It follows that the Catholic Church believes that there is a power inherent in the sacraments, so that those who receive them also receive the reality that is signified by them. If baptism signifies regeneration, then we are regenerated when we are baptized, according to Rome.

It is not quite fair to say that the Roman Catholic Church teaches that the sacraments work automatically, but what is meant by *ex opere operato* is that they work if no hindrance is put forward by the recipient. The person has to receive the sacrament freely—not necessarily in faith, but freely. As long as a person doesn't object to being baptized, he or she will receive all the benefits of the sacrament. However, if there were someone in the crowd who said, "Don't touch me with that water," and some fell on him, it would have no effect.

The Protestant doctrine of justification by faith alone implies that the sacraments themselves do not have the power to save. But the Roman Catholic Church says that we receive justification first by baptism, and then through the sacrament of penance, if we need it a second time. According to Rome, we are justified sacramentally. The Reformers disagreed, insisting that we are justified by faith and faith alone; the sacraments are important, but they do not confer salvation.

I once talked to a man who had been to Rome for the Year of Jubilee, and he was excited beyond measure because, as he told me,

90

"I got all my sins forgiven for my whole life when I went 'through the door' in Rome, and I got a papal indulgence." He was thrilled that he had received salvation without faith. He received it, he believed, through the sacrament of penance, to which the Jubilee was tied.

The confession teaches that grace **is not conferred by any power in them [the sacraments]; neither doth the efficacy of a sacrament depend upon the piety or intention of him that doth administer it: but upon the work of the Spirit.** No power resides in the sacraments, nor does the efficacy of a sacrament depend upon the person who administers it. This became a major controversy early in church history—the Donatist controversy, to which the great Augustine addressed himself. There were those who denied Christ under the threat of persecution and were not willing to die as martyrs, but who returned to the faith when the persecution ended. Could lapsed priests, having returned to the church, still administer the sacraments? What about people who had been baptized by them? Were their baptisms valid?

Augustine answered that the validity of the sacrament rests upon the One whose promise it is—not on the one who administers it, nor on the one who receives it, but on God. This is God's word in sacramental form, and the ministers carry a treasure in earthen vessels. The sin of the minister does not destroy the validity of God's promise to the one to whom the sacrament is administered. The sacrament does not have power in itself, and the power of the sacrament does not rest in the minister or in a priest or anybody else. The power of the sacrament rests in God.

Some have been led to Christ by men who later repudiated the faith. That tells me that God can communicate his grace and his truth through pagans, heretics, apostates, and anyone else. He can even speak through Balaam's ass. The power of preaching is not in the preacher. The power of the Word of God is in the Holy Spirit applying the Word to people's hearts. It comes not through the eloquence or the knowledge of the preacher or from the ignorance of the preacher. That is true, not only for the Word, but also for the sacraments. As the confession goes on to say, the efficacy of the sacraments does not depend upon the one who administers them, but upon the Holy Spirit.

The only power in the ministry is the power of the Holy Spirit. Without the Holy Spirit, we have no power whatsoever; we have empty rituals and vain words. God has decreed to send his Spirit to accompany the ministry of the Word and the ministry of the sacrament. The power is there, as long as we know whose power it is and where it is vested.

The efficacy of a sacrament depends **upon the work of the Spirit, and the word of institution, which contains, together with a precept authorizing the use thereof, a promise of benefit to worthy receivers.** The efficacy of a sacrament does not depend upon the piety or intention of the minister, but upon the actual working of the Spirit and upon the One who instituted the sacraments in the first place. The sacraments are Trinitarian. The Father gives authority to his Son; the Son institutes them; the Holy Spirit applies or empowers them. In redemption, the Father sends the Son, the Son accomplishes our redemption, and the Spirit applies the work of the Son.

Every time we celebrate the Lord's Supper, we repeat the words of institution. That reminds people that this is not something that we have invented in order to be relevant to our culture today. We are carrying out what the Lord himself instituted, made sacred, authorized, and commanded to be done in this manner. When Christ gives authority to the sacraments, he is not merely giving permission for the sacraments to be celebrated, but is giving a mandate that his people must celebrate them.

Calvin had a zeal to celebrate the Lord's Supper every Sunday in Geneva because he believed in its importance to the worship of God's people. But to the day he died, the town council of Geneva never permitted it. They allowed the Supper only once a month because they were concerned that by observing it too frequently, it would become a matter of empty externals. We dare not let it become an empty ritual.

We understand that Christ does not command us to do it every Sunday, but he does command us to celebrate the Lord's Supper. It is given to us for our edification and for our comfort. In a special way, it enhances the word of promise that comes through the Scriptures.

The words of institution contain **a promise of benefit to worthy receivers**. The word "**worthy**" puts a condition upon the reception of benefits. The benefits of the sacraments are not received apart from faith. That is one of the reasons why our Baptist friends oppose infant baptism. They say infants are not capable of having faith, and therefore do not qualify for baptism. It is true that the promises given to a child at baptism are never actualized or realized unless that child comes to faith. But who is worthy to receive any benefit from God? We certainly are not, whether we have faith or not. We have no meritorious worth which requires God to give us a benefit, either through baptism or through the Lord's Supper.

The word "**worthy**" is not meant in the meritorious sense that we receive a benefit from the sacraments only if we earn it. "**Worthy**" has in view the use of that word in 1 Corinthians, where Paul warns the church about eating and drinking unworthily, resulting in judgment against them (1 Cor. 11:29). In Corinth, people turned the Lord's Supper into a gluttonous feast, and they showed no concern for the other people who were present. They did not discern the significance of the Lord's Supper or the reality of the ministry of Christ. In that situation, to be worthy meant to come in a proper spirit of reverence and of repentance to the Lord's Table. To be unworthy meant coming impenitently or in a state of cavalier unbelief and merely going through the motions. Going to the Lord's Table without faith and without repentance desecrates the sacrament. Similarly today, if we make a mockery of the holy sacraments, we participate in them unworthily and will receive no benefit from them.

Sec. 4. There be only two sacraments ordained by Christ our Lord in the Gospel; that is to say, Baptism, and the Supper of the Lord:

93

neither of which may be dispensed by any, but by a minister of the Word lawfully ordained.

There are **only two sacraments ordained by Christ our Lord in the Gospel; that is to say, Baptism, and the Supper of the Lord.** The vast majority of Protestant bodies have held that there are two sacraments. The Roman Catholic Church, however, has seven sacraments. They are baptism, confirmation, the Eucharist (Lord's Supper), penance, holy orders, matrimony, and extreme unction. Both the Reformed communions and Rome agree that baptism and the Lord's Supper are sacraments. However, there is a significant difference in the understanding of those two sacraments.

We saw in our study of justification that the Roman Catholic Church regards baptism as the instrumental cause of justification. That is, baptism confers the grace of justification by infusing the righteousness of Christ into the recipient. The person is cleansed from original sin, regenerated by the Holy Spirit, and made able, by virtue of regeneration, to cooperate and to assent to the grace that has been infused into him or her. People maintain their justification by cooperating with the grace that has been infused into them.

For Rome, this sacrament, as well as the others, operates *ex opere operato*. That means that the grace signified by the sacrament is actually conferred on the recipient, unless he resists it. Thus, everyone who receives baptism also receives regeneration and the infusion of the grace of justification at the same time. That is why baptism is considered the instrumental cause (the means) by which one is brought into a state of saving grace, or justification.

We will consider this philosophically and grammatically. In the ancient world, Aristotle, like most philosophers of that time, tried to explain motion. His inquiry was basically a study of causality— what caused something to move from this place to that place. Aristotle identified various types of causes, using the illustration of the sculptor and the sculpture.

94

We need to go over Aristotle's illustration because the various kinds of causes became an integral part of the language of Christian theology in the Middle Ages and through Protestant theology. It is standard to distinguish between material causes and other kinds of causes. The material cause for a statue, according to Aristotle, is that out of which the statue is made, such as marble or stone.

Aristotle talked about the formal cause: the blueprint, sketch, plan, or idea that the artist has in order to create his statue. The final cause is the purpose for which the statue is made. Perhaps it is to fulfill a commission for a wealthy patron.

The instrumental cause is what the artist uses to bring about the finished work. In the case of a painter, it is his brush; in the case of a literary artist, it is his pen, typewriter, or computer. In the case of the sculptor, the instrumental cause is the chisel and the hammer. But the instruments cannot do it alone. They have to be operated or used by someone (or something) who is the efficient cause, the artist. The Holy Spirit is the efficient cause of a person being cleansed of original sin or reborn, according to the Roman Church. But the means that the Holy Spirit uses to bring that to pass is baptism. The means by which God justifies people, according to Rome, is the instrument of baptism. The Protestant view, however, is that the instrumental cause of justification is faith. Faith is the instrument by which we lay hold of Christ, by whose righteousness we are redeemed. That is the philosophical significance of the term *instrumental cause*.

Grammatically, when we talk about justification, we say that justification is "by faith" or "through faith." The ground of our justification is the righteousness of Christ or the merit of Christ. That is the foundation or the grounds by which God declares us righteous when he transfers the righteousness of Christ to us. God doesn't justify us on the grounds of our inherent righteousness; he justifies us on the grounds of the righteousness of Christ, which is applied to us.

When we say that justification is by faith, we do not mean that faith itself is a merit or is the grounds upon which God declares us just. Rather, the word *by* or *through* expresses means. When we say that justification is "by" faith, we are saying that the instrumental cause of justification is faith. Rome, however, says that justification is by baptism. That is a significant difference. Even though we both agree that baptism is a sacrament, we disagree dramatically on how it works, what it does, and what it signifies.

The second sacrament, according to the Roman Catholic Church, is the sacrament of confirmation. When a child is confirmed, he or she takes "first communion." In this sacrament, more grace is given to the person who is confirming the vows that were taken by his or her parents at baptism. Rome understands that when infants are baptized, they aren't cognizant of what is going on. As children grow older, go through the age of accountability, and take instruction, they can confirm publicly, for themselves, what was done for them in the past, and, in a sense, fulfill and consolidate their own baptism. This is largely a rite of passage into adulthood.

In many churches, the confirmation rite includes the laying on of hands to symbolize being filled with the Spirit, but that act does not impart the Holy Spirit. In classical Protestantism, baptism is a sign of all that accompanies salvation. Although water baptism signifies the baptism of the Holy Spirit, it does not confer Spirit baptism. That which baptism signifies does not occur unless or until faith is present.

The traditional Protestant view is that when a person has saving faith, he is indwelt by the Holy Spirit and receives the baptism of the Holy Spirit. The person already has the regeneration of the Holy Spirit, or he wouldn't have the faith necessary to be saved. So, in classical Protestantism, as well as in classical Roman Catholicism, anyone who is truly regenerate or born of the Holy Spirit is, at the same time, baptized with the Holy Spirit. All Christians have the baptism of the Holy Spirit. The baptism of the Holy Spirit means the empowering of the Christian for ministry. There are not two kinds of Christians, those who possess the power of the Holy Spirit for their Christian life and those who do not. Holiness churches, Pentecostals, and charismatics have challenged that view. They argue for two kinds of Christians, those who have been baptized in the Holy Spirit and those who have not. This is a departure from the classical understanding of Catholic and Protestant baptisms.

The fundamental difference between confirmation in the Roman Catholic Church and in Protestant churches is that the Roman Catholic church regards confirmation as a sacrament, while most Protestant churches do not. The Protestant churches see it as a church rite, or an ecclesiastical ordinance, which falls short of the level of a sacrament. There is debate over what qualifies something to be a sacrament. Protestantism historically teaches that a sacrament has to be directly and immediately instituted by Jesus in the New Testament. There is no doubt that he instituted baptism and the Lord's Supper for all Christians. The rite of confirmation, however, is nowhere set forth by Christ in the New Testament. It was instituted by the church. One of the issues that grew out of the Reformation is whether we find our doctrine in Scripture alone or also in the tradition of the church.

We have a church tradition in Protestantism to which we give great attention. The fact that we pay close attention to tradition is proved by this study of a historic confession of faith. We see the Westminster Confession as an important summary of what is in Scripture, and it has two levels of authority. It has the authority to bind our conscience only insofar as it accurately replicates the Word of God. It also has ecclesiastical authority for ministers and elders, who have to confess its content in order to be in good standing in the church. It is not an infallible source, and it cannot absolutely bind one's conscience. In the Roman Catholic Church, in addition to Scripture, there is ecclesiastical tradition, which has the authority to bind one's conscience. That was, in a measure, what the Reformation was about. One of the things that came out of the debate over authority in the sixteenth century was that, though the Roman Church regards confirmation as a sacrament, it doesn't have the mandate of Scripture to support it.

Therefore, even though Protestant churches for the most part practice confirmation, they do not see it as a sacrament.

The third sacrament on the Roman Catholic list is the Eucharist, which Protestants call the Lord's Supper. There is no question that the Lord's Supper was instituted by Jesus to be observed regularly in the life of the church. There are significant differences, not only between Protestants and Rome, but also among Protestants themselves, over the meaning, the significance, and the observance of this sacrament.

The fourth Roman Catholic sacrament is penance, also called reconciliation or confession. We discussed penance previously because it was at the heart of the controversy that sparked the Reformation. Penance in the Roman Church includes confession, an act of contrition, priestly absolution, and works of satisfaction. Penance is defined as the second plank of justification for those who make shipwreck of their souls. According to the Reformed faith, when we are in a state of grace, justified by the righteousness of Christ through faith, we never lose our salvation. Once we are justified, we are always justified. We may lapse into sin, but we will not ultimately lose all of our faith, and therefore we will not lose our justification.

The Roman Catholic Church teaches that if a person who is in a state of grace through baptism commits mortal sin (i.e., a sin that kills the grace in the soul), that person falls from the state of grace. He or she has killed the saving grace of baptism and must be rejustified. The person doesn't get rebaptized. Instead, there is a restorative sacrament to bring him or her back to a state of repentance. The whole process erupted in the sixteenth century over the practice of selling indulgences, which were linked to the third portion of the sacrament of penance, namely, the works of satisfaction.

Luther kept the confessional because he believed that Christians should regularly confess their sins and be assured of their forgiveness and salvation. We try to retain that in our Protestant churches by having a prayer of confession followed by the assurance of pardon. There is nothing wrong with confessing our sins. The Bible doesn't say that we have to confess our sins to a priest or to a minister, but it does command us to confess our sins to one another. Too many people go through life tormented by their guilt because they haven't had an opportunity to get those painful things out of themselves.

It is true that all we need to do is confess them in secret to God. He will hear us and can confirm us. One of the things that the church and ministers do, through the ministry of the Word, is to communicate the assurance of pardon to those who confess their sins. In the Roman Catholic Church, when the priest hears the act of contrition and the confession, he gives priestly absolution and says, "Te absolvo" (I absolve you).

This upsets some Protestants. They ask, "What right does that priest have to grant the forgiveness of sins?" It is understood historically in the Roman Catholic Church that when the priest grants absolution, he is doing what the Protestant minister does when, from the pulpit, he declares the assurance of pardon to all who genuinely confess their sins. The priest is not forgiving sins by any inherent power that he possesses, but basically as a spokesman for Christ.

The Reformers were concerned with the third part of penance, where one had to do works of satisfaction sufficiently meritorious to make it congruous for God to restore him or her to a state of salvation. Congruous merit is not as high as condign merit, but it is still real merit. One cannot have it without grace, and though it doesn't impose an absolute obligation on God to reward it, it nevertheless makes it congruous and fitting for God to restore that one to justification. Luther said that there can be no mixture of our merit with grace. We are to make restitution wherever possible for our sins, but we are not to think that works we perform after a confession of our sin contribute in any way to the merit of Christ alone, which is the sole ground of our justification. It is through the merit of Christ alone that we are justified.

In support of the sacrament of penance, the Roman Church appeals to the New Testament, where the command is, "Repent and believe; repent for the kingdom of God is at hand." Jesus certainly commanded people to repent, but he still did not establish it as a sacrament. There is no evidence in the New Testament that Christ instituted a rite of repentance to restore one to the state of justification.

The sacrament of holy orders is reserved for those who are going into church vocations, like monks, priests, and nuns. Rome claims that their life as religious persons, so to speak, gives them a special element of grace.

In the seven sacraments, a Roman Catholic is covered from the cradle to the grave. For all of the major transitions in life, he has the assistance of a new sacrament to strengthen him for that occasion. At birth, he receives baptism, and then at the transition to adulthood, he is confirmed. There is the continued infusion of grace through the Eucharist, and penance is there to help when he falls into mortal sin. If one goes into the priesthood or into a religious vocation, he is ordained or set apart and receives grace for that ministry.

In Protestant churches, we also have ordination, and even though Luther taught "the priesthood of all believers," he continued to teach that there is a distinction between laity and clergy. He understood that the New Testament makes such a distinction, and it provides for setting apart people to certain tasks, such as preaching and teaching and ministering. Every Christian is called to participate in the mission of the church. There is a world of lost people, and our mission is to go into the whole world, preach the gospel to every living creature, and to make disciples of them.

The sixth sacrament is matrimony. Both Protestant and Catholic churches recognize civil ceremonies. The rite of matrimony was given by God to Adam and Eve, and, by extension, to the whole world. Matrimony is not a uniquely Christian estate. Protestants don't see marriage as a sacrament that is to be restricted only to Christians. We see it as a creation ordinance, not a sacrament. In the Roman Catholic Church, matrimony is a sacrament by which supernatural grace is infused into the lives of the recipients to equip them for their new estate. Those who get married receive a measure of grace from God that they would not have outside of marriage.

Finally, there is the sacrament of extreme unction, which is given when one faces death, and is therefore also called last rites. Unction involves anointing, and in this case one is anointed with oil. The sacrament of extreme unction began as an application of James 5:14–15, "Is anyone among you sick? Let him call for the elders of the church, and let them pray over him, anointing him with oil in the name of the Lord. And the prayer of faith will save the sick." It began in the Christian church as a healing rite, not as a final rite. It was there to encourage people to recover from illnesses. A person could have this unction, not just once, but as many times as needed to be restored. Over time, it became the final application of the sacrament of penance, so that people would not die with unforgiven mortal sin and thus go to hell. That is why, when people are in their last moments of life, there are priests available at the hospital to see that they receive their last rites. The last rites are pronounced over people who have already expired, because, in Roman Catholic theology, there is a window of time in which to keep the soul out of hell by giving this sacrament.

Those are the seven sacraments of the Roman Catholic Church. Clearly, much more could be said about them. What is affirmed in the Westminster Confession, however, is that we have only two sacraments.

The final clause of section 4 is frequently disputed among Christians: **Neither of which may be dispensed by any, but by a minister of the Word lawfully ordained.**

In the so-called Jesus movement of the 1960s and 1970s, young people reacted against traditional authority structures and created an underground church that dispensed with regularly ordained clergy. People gathered around swimming pools and were baptized by Pat Boone or other celebrities. Church officials were unnerved by that and claimed that the sacraments are only to be administered by duly authorized persons, such as ordained clergy. Over against that was an informal view of the matter that saw little need for ordained clergy.

Added to that was the impact of the charismatic movement, in which people supposedly receive special gifts from the Holy Spirit, which empower them for ministry. Most of the New Testament information that we have about the gifts of the Spirit—*charismata*—comes from Paul's first letter to the Corinthian church. In Corinth, people who received gifts from the Spirit challenged the authority of those who had been, under normal circumstances, set apart and consecrated for ministry. Paul's two epistles to the Corinthian community deal with that internal disruption.

At the end of the first century, Clement, who was then bishop of Rome, wrote an epistle to the Corinthian community because the crisis had actually worsened after the death of the apostle Paul. The Corinthian church was in a state of spiritual and ecclesiastical chaos. Clement told the Christians at Corinth to go back and heed the teaching of the apostle Paul. At the end of the first century, the debate had to do with regular ministers of the church as distinguished from charismatic leaders.

In the Old Testament, the gift of the Holy Spirit was given to people for special tasks at particular times. We read that the Spirit of the Lord came upon Jeremiah or upon Ezekiel. They were set apart by God for the special charismatic office of the prophet. The kings of Israel were anointed by the priest, as a sign of their anointing by the Spirit, to exercise their office in a godly manner. Prior to that, God raised up judges like Samson and Gideon as anointed, charismatically gifted leaders to provide some leadership to the loose federation of the tribes of Israel and especially to lead them against an enemy like the Philistines. Moses was also a charismatic leader who was endowed by the Holy Spirit with special gifts. God then anointed Aaron as the high priest and instituted his male descendants as the priesthood. The entire tribe of Levi was set apart for priestly duties and became part of the regular order of the Old Testament ministry.

In the New Testament, the charismatically endowed leaders of the Christian community were the apostles. They were on the same level, as it were, with the Old Testament prophets. The power of the Holy Spirit came upon them, and they became agents of revelation. When the apostle Paul established a church, he customarily instructed his assistants to set apart elders who were called to the office of ministry. We find this in his epistles to Timothy and Titus, where he delineates the standards for office. The elders and deacons became the regular officers of the church, and the ordinary ministers were given the responsibility to care for the spiritual needs of the flock.

Their ministry was no longer dependent upon a special charismatic gift. In the Old Testament, the Holy Spirit endowed with power only part of the covenant community. At Pentecost, he fell upon everyone assembled, and later he came upon the Gentile converts. The inference drawn by the apostles was that all believers, Jew and Gentile alike, had the same full membership and status within the New Testament body of Christ. The Holy Spirit has now empowered the entire church to participate in the ministry of Christ. That was why Luther held his view of the priesthood of all believers. Luther said that the ministry of the gospel was entrusted to the whole church, not just to a few people. But Luther also understood that the New Testament established regular church offices for the ministry of the Word and sacrament and for the spiritual care of the people.

Neither sacrament **may be dispensed by any, but by a minister of the Word lawfully ordained**. When the resurrected Jesus gave the Great Commission, he told the apostles, the first Christian ministers, "Go therefore and make disciples of all the nations, baptizing them in the name of the Father and of the Son and of the Holy Spirit" (Matt. 28:19). In 1 Corinthians 11:20–23, Paul states that he received from the Lord the words of institution for the Lord's Supper. He says in 1 Corinthians 4:1, "Let a man so consider us, as servants of Christ and stewards of the mysteries of God." The phrase "stewards of the mysteries of God" is critical. Hebrews 5:4 tells us, "No man takes this honor to himself, but he who is called by God, just as Aaron was." We see here a ministry in the church that is instituted by the call of God, and that no one has the right to take it upon himself. Included in this ministry is the responsibility of being stewards of the mysteries of God. Just as Old Testament priests were "stewards" of God's mysteries, so that task is also carried out by New Testament ministers.

The word *stewardship* translates the Greek word *oikonomia*. Our English word *economy* derives from that word. It combines the word *oikos*, meaning "house," and the word *nomos*, meaning "law." So *oikonomia* means "house rule" or "house law." Thus, a steward in the biblical sense is a servant who is responsible to manage the affairs of the household. When we speak of Christian stewardship, we are referring to our responsibility to manage the resources that God has entrusted to us.

The Scriptures teach that God gives to ministers the management or stewardship of the sacred mysteries. The word *sacrament* comes from *sacramentum*, the Latin translation of the Greek word *mystērion*, from which we get the English word *mystery*. When Paul refers to "stewards of the mysteries of God," the church understands that to include being "stewards of the sacraments." Though we must not make an identity between the New Testament use of the word *mystery* and our word *sacrament*, there remains a historic link between the words as the Latin *sacramentum* was used by the church to translate the Greek *mystērion*. One of the pastor's responsibilities in the life of the church is to oversee the sacraments.

There is little biblical basis to establish that only ordained people have the authority to administer the sacraments. I think it does teach that sufficiently, but not with a mountain of supporting evidence. In addition to biblical references and the biblical concept of what it means to be a bishop, and the responsibilities of eldership as set forth in the New Testament, the church, in her own development, rightly came to the conclusion that the sacraments are so holy that they must be guarded from frivolous or cavalier usage. That becomes particularly clear when we consider the warning not to partake of the Lord's Supper unworthily.

Paul warns about eating and drinking unworthily in 1 Corinthians 11:30, "For this reason many are weak and sick among you, and many sleep [die]." The New Testament scholar Oscar Cullmann observed that this is one of the most neglected verses in the entire New Testament. He suggests that Paul was saying to the Corinthians that "some of you people have fallen ill, even unto death, directly as a result of your failure to discern the Lord's body in this most holy event." This need for discernment, along with other concerns, lay behind the church's decision to protect the people from the negative effects of mishandling the sacraments. Therefore, the sacraments must be administered by those who have been set apart for the task of ministry in the church. Not just anyone can administer the sacrament. The responsibility to guard the sacrament is put into the hands of the clergy. That is no guarantee that there will not be abuses, but the situation would otherwise be much worse.

When I was ordained, it was to the teaching ministry of the Presbyterian Church, not to the pastoral ministry. In many churches, if one is ordained to the teaching office, all of the rights and privileges of ordination come along with it. Therefore, I had the authority to perform marriages and to administer the sacraments. I rarely had the opportunity, however, to administer the sacraments because I did not have a pastoral ministry. From time to time, I visited churches as a guest preacher, and when they celebrated the Lord's Supper, I had the privilege to administer it. I sometimes would actually feel a physical ache that I was not the minister of a local congregation with the privilege of administering the sacraments.

I have some understanding of Luther's being paralyzed by fear when he sought to administer the Lord's Supper for the first time. I believe baptism is too important to do at a party in someone's swimming pool. It belongs under the rule and supervision of the church. The confession, following the church practice through the ages, says that the sacraments are to be administered by those who are in positions of ordained authority, the lawfully ordained ministers of the Word.

Sec. 5 . The sacraments of the old testament, in regard of the spiritual things thereby signified and exhibited, were, for substance, the same with those of the new.

The principle that is set forth in section 5 is vital to the Reformation understanding and rationale for infant baptism, among other things. The sacraments of the Old and New Testaments, it says, are **the same** in certain respects. But the Westminster divines are not saying that baptism is the same thing as circumcision (or the baptism in the Red Sea), or that the Lord's Supper is the same thing as the Passover. If there were no difference between them, then it would be meaningless to speak of a "new" covenant.

There is an element of discontinuity from the old to the new, but that discontinuity is not radical. That is, there is no discontinuity at root. The discontinuity is in the leaves of the tree, and not at the trunk or the roots of the tree. The confession is careful to say that the sacraments are the same, not in every respect, but **for substance**, with respect to **the spiritual things thereby signified and exhibited**.

For substance means "in essence." We say of the Trinity that God is one in substance and three in person. The distinction of the persons in the Godhead is real, significant, and necessary, but it does not go to the essence of their being. If it were a distinction in essence or in substance, there would be three gods. The Father, the Son, and the Holy Spirit are all the same essence. There is a real difference between them, but not at the point of essence. Likewise, there is an essential continuity between the Passover and the Lord's Supper, and between circumcision and baptism. They are not identical, but in substance they refer to the same ultimate thing.

To understand that, we must know something about the meaning of Old Testament ceremonies. An insight into this is provided by 1 Corinthians 10:1–4: "Moreover, brethren, I do not want you to be unaware that all our fathers were under the cloud, all passed through the sea, all were baptized into Moses in the cloud and in the sea, all ate the same spiritual food, and all drank the same spiritual drink. For they drank of that spiritual Rock that followed them, and that Rock was Christ." Here Paul teaches that in the crossing of the Red Sea, a baptism took place.

All of the ceremonies in the Old Testament, down to the very building of the tabernacle, were types, symbols, and shadows of what was to come in fullness and in glory in the person of Christ. The Israelites annually celebrated their redemption from the angel of death, who passed over the Israelite homes in Egypt because of the blood of the lamb on their doorposts and lintels. After that redemption and rescue from judgment by the grace of God, God told the people of Israel never to forget it. He wanted them on a regular basis to sit down at a table, enjoy the Passover meal, and celebrate their redemption from the judgment of God through the blood of the lamb.

The blood that preserved the children of Israel was not really the blood of that lamb that was killed, because the New Testament tells us that the blood of bulls and goats and sheep cannot take away sin. Rather, that blood pointed to the ultimate Lamb who would cause the judgment of God to pass over the people of God forever. That was why Jesus, going into the upper room one last time to celebrate the Passover, and seeking to maintain continuity with the Old Testament, said, in effect, "Tonight starts the new covenant in my blood, shed for the remission of your sins." He is our Passover lamb. The substance and essence of what was foreshadowed in the Passover carries over into the New Testament celebration of the Lord's Supper. In the Old Testament, the people survived in the wilderness by eating God-given manna. When Jesus came, he said, "I am the bread of life . . . which comes down from heaven" (John 6:48, 50). The manna pointed to the heavenly manna that was Christ.

Even as circumcision was the sign of God's redemptive promises received by faith, which every Jewish man had in his body, so the same promises of salvation are marked by baptism in the New Testament. There is obviously a physical difference between the rite of circumcision and the rite of baptism, but there is also continuity. Both of them signify God's promise to separate people for eternal salvation, and the promise is given to the elect who are justified by faith. Abraham believed God and was justified and counted as righteous. As a sign of the faith that he confessed, God had him circumcised and commanded him to circumcise his sons, giving them the same sign of the same promise. That promise was also received by faith, even before the children had faith. Often there is a protest against giving the sign of faith before faith is present. But if that argument were valid, it would invalidate circumcision in the Old Testament. Circumcision, among other things, was a sign of faith. God not only permitted the children of believers to be given the sign, but also commanded it to be given to them.

28

BAPTISM

The Westminster Confession of Faith
Chapter 28: Of Baptism

Sec. 1. Baptism is a sacrament of the new testament, ordained by Jesus Christ, not only for the solemn admission of the party baptized into the visible Church; but also to be unto him a sign and seal of the covenant of grace, of his ingrafting into Christ, of regeneration, of remission of sins, and of his giving up unto God, through Jesus Christ, to walk in newness of life. Which sacrament is, by Christ's own appointment, to be continued in His Church until the end of the world.

Sec. 2. The outward element to be used in this sacrament is water, wherewith the party is to be baptized, in the name of the Father, and of the Son, and of the Holy Ghost, by a minister of the Gospel, lawfully called thereunto.

Sec. 3. Dipping of the person into the water is not necessary; but Baptism is rightly administered by pouring, or sprinkling water upon the person.

Sec. 4. Not only those that do actually profess faith in and obedience unto Christ, but also the infants of one, or both, believing parents, are to be baptized.

Sec. 5. Although it be a great sin to contemn or neglect this ordinance, yet grace and salvation are not so inseparably annexed unto it, as that no person can be regenerated, or saved, without it: or, that all that are baptized are undoubtedly regenerated.

Sec. 6. The efficacy of Baptism is not tied to that moment of time wherein it is administered; yet, notwithstanding, by the right use of this ordinance, the grace promised is not only offered, but really exhibited, and conferred, by the Holy Ghost, to such (whether of age or infants) as that grace belongeth unto, according to the counsel of God's own will, in His appointed time.

Sec. 7. The sacrament of Baptism is but once to be administered unto any person.

Sec. 1. Baptism is a sacrament of the new testament, ordained by Jesus Christ, not only for the solemn admission of the party baptized into the visible Church; but also to be unto him a sign and seal of the covenant of grace, of his ingrafting into Christ, of regeneration, of remission of sins, and of his giving up unto God, through Jesus Christ, to walk in newness of life. Which sacrament is, by Christ's own appointment, to be continued in His Church until the end of the world.

This first section gives us a hint of the spiritual riches that are expressed by this sacrament, beginning with the first line: **Baptism is a sacrament of the new testament, ordained by Jesus Christ.**

Baptism is the outward sign of the new covenant, just as circumcision was the external sign of the old covenant. Throughout the history of God's dealings with his people, the making of covenants was serious business, a solemn affair. When the covenants were made between God and Abraham, God and Moses, God and David, and God and Noah, they were consigned by oaths and vows. They always contained stipulations. There was also a ritual, usually a blood ritual, that solemnized the covenant promise.

In the covenant that God made with Noah, the external sign was the rainbow. Even to this day, when we see God's rainbow in the sky, it reminds us of his promise to Noah that he will never again destroy the earth by a flood. In the covenant that God made with Abraham, the sign was circumcision. The new covenant is not divorced from the old covenant; there is continuity between the old and the new. In a very real sense, the new covenant is the fulfillment of the promises that God made to Abraham. In the *Magnificat*, Mary praised God for what he had done, "as He spoke to our fathers, to Abraham and to his seed forever" (Luke 1:55). Mary understood that the announcement from the angel Gabriel showed that God remembered the promise that he had made to Abraham. Jesus spoke to the Pharisees in similar terms about Abraham: "Your father Abraham rejoiced to see My day" (John 8:56). The New Testament people of God understood the connection between God's promises in the Old Testament and their fulfillment in the New Testament. Because of the newness of the New Testament, a new sign was given to the people of God. That new sign was baptism. We are told in the confession that baptism was a sign that Christ commanded be carried to all nations: "Go therefore and make disciples of all the nations, baptizing them in the name of the Father and of the Son and of the Holy Spirit" (Matt. 28:19).

New Testament baptism was instituted by Jesus, not by John the Baptist. However, we first encounter the rite of baptism in the Scriptures as it was practiced by John. He announced to the people, "Repent, for the kingdom of heaven is at hand!" (Matt. 3:2). He called the people of Israel to be baptized, and he baptized them, as well as Jesus, in the Jordan River.

John did not institute New Testament baptism. He did not administer the sign of the new covenant. The ritual he performed actually belonged to the Old Testament economy, because John himself belonged to it. We may read about him in the New Testament, but in redemptive history his place is at the end of the old covenant. The new covenant did not begin until Jesus instituted it at the Lord's Supper, where he gave the Passover rite a new dimension: "For this is My blood of the new covenant, which is shed for many for the remission of sins" (Matt. 26:28). He established the new covenant in the upper room. He ratified it the next day with the blood rite at his death.

Everything that happened from the time of Abraham until the Last Supper belongs to the old covenant. As Jesus said, "The law and the prophets were until John" (Luke 16:16). The Greek word for "until" means "up to and including." Jesus said that the period of the law and the prophets incorporated John the Baptist, and then he added, "There is not a greater prophet than John the Baptist; but he who is least in the kingdom of God is greater than he" (Luke 7:28). Here greatness refers to blessedness. Those who are least in the kingdom enjoy greater redemptive blessedness than even John the Baptist enjoyed. The prophets of the Old Testament looked to the far-off day when the Messiah would come and God would inaugurate the kingdom. Isaiah said that one day the King would come. The Messiah would appear in world history, but no time frame was given. Shortly before Jesus began his public ministry, God sent a forerunner to call the people to get ready, to prepare them for the coming of that promised kingdom.

The prophet selected to make that announcement was John the Baptist. He enjoyed a privilege that no other prophet had ever enjoyed. He didn't simply announce the coming of the King; he ushered in the King. The King had not yet established his kingdom. Even though John was the herald of the King, he was still on the outside of this historical reality, called the kingdom of God, looking in. He had the closest vantage point of anybody in the old covenant, but he was still on that side. He told the people to repent because the kingdom of God was at hand. He said, "The ax is laid to the root of the trees" (Matt. 3:10). The kingdom was about to break through. John's analogy was that the woodsman was cutting down the trees. He was not just chipping away at the outer edge of the bark, but cutting to the very heart of the tree. With one more swing of the ax, the tree would come down. It was the time of crisis and of separation. John warned the people that they were not ready for the coming of the Messiah. He called them to a ritual of baptism to cleanse themselves in preparation for his coming.

The ritual of proselyte baptism emerged in the intertestamental period. If a Gentile desired membership in the household of Israel, he needed to do three things. He had to embrace the truth of Judaism— to make a profession of faith, as it were. Second, he had to undergo the rite of circumcision. Third, being an "unclean" Gentile, he had to go through a ritual of purification, a baptismal cleansing rite. This baptism was only for Gentiles, not for Jews. Many Gentiles (such as Cornelius in the book of Acts) became God-fearers, not full converts. God-fearers were Gentiles who embraced the Jewish faith and underwent the ritual of purification, but did not submit to circumcision. John the Baptist's ritual was radical in that he called Jews to take the ritual bath. He said to them, in effect, "You are as dirty and as unclean in the sight of God as Gentiles, who are strangers to the covenant and to the commonwealth of Israel. If you are going to be ready to meet your King, you need to take a bath."

John saw Jesus and said, "Behold! The Lamb of God who takes away the sin of the world!" (John 1:29). Jesus presented himself to John to be baptized. John protested: "I need to be baptized by You, and are You coming to me?" (Matt. 3:14). Jesus responded, "Permit it to be so now, for thus it is fitting for us to fulfill all righteousness" (Matt. 3:15). That is, "I know you don't understand what is happening, John, but I, the Messiah, must represent Israel and fulfill all of the law which God imposes upon his nation." He not only went to

113

the cross to die for the sins of the people, but also submitted to the law from the time of his birth, because he had to fulfill all of the commandments of God on behalf of the people. God added a new requirement that the people had to submit to this cleansing rite. Jesus was to be their representative and fulfill God's command, so he had to submit to the ritual baptism. Jesus was not baptized because he was a sinner, but because the people were sinners and he was their Redeemer. So John baptized Jesus.

This baptism had many things in common with the baptism that Jesus later commissioned his disciples to perform as a sign of the kingdom and of the new covenant. Though it certainly was influenced by the preparatory work of John, it was not the same. Jesus' rite of baptism marked people's entrance into fellowship and community with him. John's was a cleansing rite in anticipation of the coming of the kingdom. John's baptism was a preparatory baptism for the new covenant; Jesus came and said, "Repent, for the kingdom of heaven is at hand" (Matt. 4:17). Later he said, "But if I cast out demons with the finger of God, surely the kingdom of God has come upon you" (Luke 11:20). He commissioned his disciples to baptize people and to celebrate the breakthrough of the kingdom. New Testament theology does not see the kingdom as something utterly in the future. There remain future elements, but the kingdom of God began with the ministry of Christ and reached a tremendous level of reality at his ascension to the right hand of God, where he now reigns. Baptism, among other things, celebrates the beginning of the kingdom of God as it marks people's entrance into this new covenant community, identifying them as part of the body of Christ.

The section continues: **Baptism is a sacrament of the new testament, ordained by Jesus Christ, not only for the solemn admission of the party baptized into the visible church.**

When we studied the doctrine of the church, we noted the difference between the visible and the invisible church. It is possible to be a member of the invisible church and not be a member of the visible church. And not everybody in the visible church is in the invisible church. People sometimes make insincere professions of faith. Jesus, while on earth, spoke about his church being made up of tares along with the wheat. The visible church will always be what Augustine defined as *corpus permixtum*, a mixed body of believers and nonbelievers. Jesus said that at the last day many people would come to him and say, "Lord, Lord, have we not prophesied in Your name, cast out demons in Your name, and done many wonders in Your name?" (Matt. 7:22). But he will reply, "I never knew you; depart from Me, you who practice lawlessness!" (Matt. 7:23). Jesus understood that people can honor him with their lips while their hearts are far from him. Membership in the visible church does not guarantee membership in the invisible church, the true body of Christ.

Baptism is **a sign and seal of the covenant of grace** and of the promise of redemption. The covenant of grace is God's solemn promise to all who believe that they will be redeemed and will receive all of the benefits won for them by and through the ministry of Christ. In the ministry of the Word, the promises of God and the gospel are preached, guaranteeing salvation to all who believe.

In addition to the verbal proclamation of that promise, God gives to his people a visible sign and seal, a nonverbal corroboration of the Word, and that is the sacrament of baptism. God's promise in the covenant of grace is realized only through faith. That was also true in the case of circumcision, as a sign of the covenant of grace in the Old Testament, and not everyone who received that external sign also received what it represented. Paul said, "He is a Jew who is one inwardly" (Rom. 2:29), meaning that circumcision alone did not save anybody and that the heart had to be circumcised. As in the New Testament, a person in the Old Testament was justified only by faith.

The sign of faith does not communicate faith. The sign of God's promise does not guarantee the fulfillment of the promise. What is guaranteed is God's promise to all who believe. That is why we give the sign to adults and also to the children of believers, just as they did in the Old Testament. In this respect, the covenant community in Israel was no different from the covenant community today. All of the people of God and their children are to receive the sign and seal of the promise of redemption. Baptism is not a sign of the child's faith; it is a sign of what the child will receive by faith. It is a sign of God's promise, which is received by faith.

Baptism is a sign and seal to the party baptized **of his ingrafting into Christ**. I can read God's Word and say, "I have in my own body the sign and seal of the King who promised me the remission of my sins. He promised me that I would be ingrafted into Jesus Christ, that I would participate in his death and in his resurrection by faith, and that, if I believe, I can trust the promise of God because I am baptized." How can we ever despise the significance, the value, and the importance of God's promise to redeem us? Jesus instructed his disciples to preach the gospel to every living creature and baptize those who respond in the name of the Father and of the Son and of the Holy Ghost. The Word is to be confirmed by the sign of the church and the kingdom, which is the sign of baptism.

Baptism is also the sign and seal **of regeneration**. Regeneration is conferred sovereignly and solely by the direct and immediate ministry of the Holy Spirit. I can't cause you to be born again. I can't preach you into regeneration, because it is solely the work of God. Baptism is the external sign of the internal work of regeneration. It is the sign of our cleansing, of our renewal, of our resurrection from spiritual death to spiritual life, from bondage to sin to freedom from sin—a supernatural work performed by God alone. It is a work of monergism, not synergism. God changes the disposition of the soul. It is not a joint venture; it is not a cooperative activity between myself and God. God alone can raise me from spiritual death. Regeneration is an act of re-creation. It is not caused by baptism, but it is signified by baptism.

John Gerstner was once asked to perform the sacrament of baptism in a country parish, and he agreed to do so. He was told by an elder, "We have a tradition in our church. Before we baptize the child, we pin a white rose on the child's garment." Dr. Gerstner inquired as to the significance of the white rose. The elder replied, "It signifies the child's innocence." Then Dr. Gerstner asked, "And what is the significance of the water?" The elder explained that it signifies the child's cleansing. "Cleansing from what?" asked Dr. Gerstner. The church didn't understand the conflict in their symbolism. Jesus did not institute the sacrament of the white rose of innocence. He instituted a sacrament of washing that signifies being cleansed from original sin, and all that is involved in this sign.

Baptism is also a sign **of remission of sins**. In our justification, our sins are remitted, which means that they are removed from us. In our justification, we are declared just, and God redeems us by forgiving our sins. The sign of that justification, or the sign of the gospel itself, is baptism. Part of what is being promised in this sign is that all who believe will have their sins removed from them forever. Baptism is a sign of the remission of sins and of justification through Jesus Christ.

Baptism, finally, is the sign of a commitment **to walk in newness of life.** It is not only a sign of our justification, but also of the whole work of redemption. It signifies our election, our regeneration, our justification, our faith, our sanctification, and our glorification. The scope of our redemption is signed and sealed in the promises of God through this remarkable sacrament. That is why it is a special occasion whenever we see someone receive this blessed promise of God and make their solemn entrance into the visible body of Christ. The means of grace are not exclusively found in his church, but they are heavily concentrated there.

Sec. 2. The outward element to be used in this sacrament is water, wherewith the party is to be baptized, in the name of the Father, and of the Son, and of the Holy Ghost, by a minister of the Gospel, lawfully called thereunto.

Christians have historically agreed that water is to be used in baptism, because it was water that Jesus consecrated in his institution of the sacrament. In the Great Commission, he commanded people to be baptized with a Trinitarian formula. A true baptism, therefore, involves the use of water in the name of the Father, the Son, and the Holy Spirit. The one point that tends to be controversial in section 2 is the last one, namely, the claim that it is not lawful for one who is not ordained to administer the sacrament.

We gave considerable attention to this matter when we studied the introductory chapter on the sacraments. In order to protect these sacred rites from misuse or abuse, they have been entrusted to the ministers of the church for supervision and oversight. The church is given not only the ministry of the Word and the task of discipline, but also the administration of the sacraments. It is under the church's authority that they are to be administered.

Sec. 3. Dipping of the person into the water is not necessary; but Baptism is rightly administered by pouring, or sprinkling water upon the person.

Section 3 indicates that, in the seventeenth century, there was an issue with the Anabaptists. At that time in Protestant history, there were not many adult baptisms. At the present time in America, probably the majority of evangelical Christians practice only believer's baptism. I always remind my Baptist friends that throughout church history the vast majority of Christian bodies have understood baptism to apply to the children of believers as well as to adult believers.

Also, throughout the centuries of church history, it has been the practice of Christendom to use various modes of applying water, besides immersion. It has only been in recent times that people have raised objections to sprinkling, dipping, and pouring. They have argued that immersion is required to have a genuine baptism. The usual

118

argument is that the word for "baptize" in the New Testament (*baptizō*) means "to immerse" and never indicates anything other than immersion.

Let me say in passing that that is simply bad scholarship and bad linguistics. There are numerous places in Greek literature where *baptizō* means something other than "to immerse." For example, in the Septuagint version of the Old Testament, one of the cultic rites calls for the sacrifice of two birds of the same size, where one bird is killed and its blood is drained into a basin. The second bird, which remains alive, is then baptized (*baptizō*) in the blood of the first bird. Manifestly, one cannot get enough blood out of one bird to immerse a second bird in it. There could be dipping or pouring, but not an immersion.

In the New Testament, the Ethiopian eunuch makes a profession of faith to Philip and then asks, "What hinders me from being baptized?" (Acts 8:36). Philip sees "some water" and baptizes him on the spot (vv. 36–38). It is doubtful that in that "desert" between Jerusalem and Gaza (v. 26) there was enough water for an immersion. Apparently a minimal amount of water was not a hindrance to baptism. Dipping, sprinkling, and pouring were widely practiced in church history, particularly in arid lands where water was at a premium. The sacrament was administered by sprinkling or by pouring water on the head.

It is commonly assumed that when Jesus was baptized in the Jordan, he was immersed. However, the earliest known depiction of this event in Christian art (dated in the second century) shows Jesus standing next to John the Baptist in waist-high water. In the picture, John is using a ladle of sorts to pour water over Jesus' head. That is not a written record of how John actually baptized. It is simply the earliest graphic representation, but it raises the question of whether John practiced immersion at all.

Be that as it may, Calvin, a strong advocate of infant baptism, preferred immersion because baptism signifies our participation in the humiliation and exaltation of Christ, our joining with him in his death and resurrection. In a remarkable way, putting a person under water pictures his burial with Christ, and bringing him up out of the water pictures his participation in Christ's resurrection. In the Reformed tradition, those who do not restrict baptism to immersion nevertheless are not opposed to immersion, and some see some very real value in its use.

Sec. 4. Not only those that do actually profess faith in and obedience unto Christ, but also the infants of one, or both, believing parents, are to be baptized.

The biggest issue among Christians with respect to baptism has to do with the baptism of infants. It is a vexing question for many people. Christians who practice infant baptism do so because they believe it is what God wants. People who do not practice infant baptism believe that it is displeasing to God. Both sides are trying to please God, but they cannot both be right.

It is important to understand that nowhere in the New Testament do we find an explicit command to baptize infants, nor do we find an explicit prohibition against the baptizing of infants. The cases for and against infant baptism are both built on inferences drawn from the Scriptures. Such a situation should always give us pause when disagreeing with brothers and sisters in Christ. This is an important question, but we should approach it with a spirit of toleration in light of the absence of an explicit biblical mandate.

The single most important objection to infant baptism is that baptism is a sign of faith, which infants are obviously not capable of professing. Furthermore, the command to baptize in the New Testament is linked to commands to repent and believe. The sequence of admonitions that we find in the New Testament tends to be: repent, believe, and be baptized. So Baptists say that the prerequisites for baptism are repentance and faith.

Infant baptism is nowhere found in the New Testament, and every single record of baptism that we have—there are twelve of them—involves the baptism of adults. Each narrative of a baptism involves one or more adults, and there is no specific reference to infants being included with them. It is not until the middle of the second century that we have any surviving record of an infant's being baptized. The silence of early church history with respect to infant baptism is a telling point.

Baptists do recognize a historical continuity between baptism and the Old Testament practice of circumcision, which did include infants. Nevertheless, circumcision marked, among other things, ethnic separation, which passed away in the new covenant community. The idea of marking a sacred race with the sign of circumcision passed away in the New Testament. There would thus be no point in maintaining continuity with the Old Testament practice of marking infants as part of the Jewish race.

Another big concern that Baptists have at this point is a practical one. Some churches teach baptismal regeneration, which can only give people a false sense of security. Because they have been baptized, they may assume they are saved and therefore miss the call to faith, upon which the New Testament places such a premium. Baptists think that for such practical reasons it is important to delay baptism until a person is of the age of accountability, when he or she can understand the teachings of Christ and the content of the gospel, and can genuinely repent and embrace the truth of God.

Those who do baptize their infants do so for the following reasons. Even though they see some discontinuity between circumcision and baptism, continuity is predominant. Circumcision in the Old Testament was the sign of the old covenant, and baptism is the sign of the new covenant. We know for certain that God commanded the sign of the old covenant to be given both to adults and to their children. This is an important covenantal precedent, which suggests that the sign of the new covenant should also be given to the children of believers.

Another point of continuity is that whatever else circumcision indicated, it was a sign of faith, just as baptism is a sign of faith. The Old Testament clearly teaches that circumcision was to be given to a child before he had any capacity for faith. In the case of adults, faith must be present before the sign is applied; in the case of their children, the sign comes first and then the faith. The point is that the administering of the sign was not tied to the time when faith was exercised. If it is wrong to give the sign of faith to someone before he has faith, then it was wrong for the people in Israel to circumcise infants. But God explicitly commanded them to do so.

In the New Testament church, we see cases of repentance and faith preceding the sign of the covenant, which would have been the sequence for converts to the household of Israel. A Gentile had to make a public profession of faith before he could be circumcised and become a Jew. In the Old Testament, we find both infant circumcision and adult circumcision. Similarly, every church that practices infant baptism also practices adult baptism, and adult baptism is reserved for those who are not children of a believer. They are required to make a credible profession of faith before they can receive the sign of baptism. There is no dispute about that. What is in dispute is whether that is also a requirement for the children of believers.

We go to the examples of baptism in the New Testament, of which there are twelve. There is no reference to infants among them— or is there? It depends on the meaning of the Greek word *oikos*, which is the word for "household." Three of the twelve baptisms refer to adults and their household being baptized. In one quarter of the recorded baptisms in the New Testament, we are told that not only did an adult receive the sacrament, but also the members of his or her household, which may or may not have included infants. Oscar Cullmann, the Swiss New Testament scholar, has argued that the term *oikos* refers specifically to infants. If he is right about that, then the debate is over. That would be a clear indication that the New Testament church baptized infants.

122

Each instance of adults being baptized in the New Testament involves first-generation converts. Even under the Old Testament's pattern for circumcision, they would have been required to make a profession of faith before receiving the sign of the covenant—yet their infant children would also have received the sign. If it could be shown that one of the people who was baptized as an adult was born to a believer, then there would be strong evidence against infant baptism. Since that can't be shown, the narratives of adult baptism in the New Testament have no relevance to the question of infant baptism. They have great relevance to the question of what is necessary for adults to be baptized, but they tell us nothing about what should be done with infants.

The question of whether the infant children of believers are to be included in the new covenant is not so ambiguous. Paul teaches: "For the unbelieving husband is sanctified by the [believing] wife, and the unbelieving wife is sanctified by the [believing] husband; otherwise your children would be unclean, but now they are holy" (1 Cor. 7:14). The sanctification in view here is consecration—being set apart, being deemed holy. The unbelieving spouse is considered holy or set apart so that the believing spouse's children will not be "unclean." To the Jews, to be unclean meant to be a stranger to the covenant. Paul says that the infants of one believing parent, no less than those of two believing parents, are "holy"—members of the covenant community. If infants are members of the new covenant community, why would they not be given the sign of the covenant, just as God gave the sign of the covenant to infants in the old covenant community?

As I mentioned above, there is not a single mention in extant literature of babies being baptized until the middle of the second century. However, very little Christian literature prior to that time has survived. Furthermore, the German scholar Joachim Jeremias has argued that infant baptism was the universal practice of the church by A.D. 200 (at least in North Africa). It is hard to believe that a major departure from apostolic practice could have become so widespread without opposition, yet church history knows of no controversy over infant baptism in the ancient church. This historical evidence is best explained by the assumption that infant baptism was of apostolic origin, as the learned church father Origen declared.

There is no clear mandate for infant baptism in the New Testament, but there is no clear prohibition. For thousands of years previous to that, the sign of the covenant was always given to the infants of believers. If, under the new covenant, the practice of marking the seed of believers with the sign of the covenant suddenly stopped, that would have been perplexing—and would have called for explanation somewhere in the New Testament. But there is no such explanation. It would seem that the reason why the New Testament is silent with respect to infant baptism is that Christians assumed that the sign of the covenant would be placed on their children, just as it had since the days of Abraham, the father of the faithful.

Sec. 5. Although it be a great sin to contemn or neglect this ordinance, yet grace and salvation are not so inseparably annexed unto it, as that no person can be regenerated, or saved, without it: or, that all that are baptized are undoubtedly regenerated.

There are certain truths that are essential to, or of the essence of, the Christian faith. To reject them or to deny them would be to repudiate Christianity. The church has argued historically that the doctrines of the Trinity and the deity of Christ are essential to Christianity. If a person denies the deity of Christ and yet claims to be a Christian, his claim would be invalid, according to orthodox Christianity.

For the most part, throughout church history, whether we sprinkle or dip or pour in baptism has not been considered an essential of the Christian faith. So, although we may differ on that question, we can remain in fellowship and recognize each other as Christians, realizing that the difference is nonessential. It may be important, but it is not essential to the Christian faith. All doctrine is important, but not everything is equally important.

We can distinguish between something that is necessary for salvation and something that is necessary for the health and well-being of the church. Some things may not be necessary for salvation, but may be necessary for one's spiritual health. The confession here affirms that baptism is not essential for salvation. We do not have to be baptized in order to be saved. A few Christian denominations have insisted that baptism is essential for salvation, but, for the most part, Protestants have agreed that baptism is not essential for salvation. The thief on the cross, for example, was not baptized, yet Jesus promised him redemption.

We could infer that if baptism is not essential to salvation, then it is insignificant and unimportant. However, the confession teaches that even though baptism is not essential for salvation, it is nevertheless essential for the spiritual well-being of a Christian. If a Christian does not receive the sacrament of baptism, he is living in disobedience to Christ, who commands all Christians to be baptized. The confession says that it is not only a sin to refuse or neglect to be baptized, but a grievous sin.

In the Old Testament, the sign of the covenant was circumcision, and God required all males of the household of Israel to be circumcised. When Moses neglected to have his own son circumcised, God was angry with him for failing to carry out this responsibility.

We could say that since circumcision is not the same thing as baptism, we can't draw conclusions from that sign of the old covenant. However, the Bible describes the new covenant as a better covenant. It is not less inclusive, but more inclusive. To neglect the means of grace in the new covenant economy is even more serious than to neglect them in the old testament economy. If God was so displeased with Moses for failing to circumcise his son, how much more displeased will he be if we neglect baptism today?

The confession is correct when it says that it is **a great sin to . . . neglect this ordinance**—not a sin that would exclude you from the kingdom of God, but one that would do great damage to the church and

125

your own Christian growth. It is a serious matter, and we must pay close attention to our obligation at this point.

The confession continues: **Although it be a great sin to contemn or neglect this ordinance, yet grace and salvation are not so inseparably annexed unto it, as that no person can be regenerated, or saved, without it.** We do not have to be baptized in order to be regenerated and saved. (Conversely, even if we are baptized, there is no guarantee that we are regenerated or saved.) Baptism is a sign and seal of the works of God's grace, which are not dependent upon baptism. Even though the confession is quick to point out that we can be regenerated and saved without baptism, it also insists that we are not to despise or neglect it.

> Sec. 6. The efficacy of Baptism is not tied to that moment of time wherein it is administered; yet, notwithstanding, by the right use of this ordinance, the grace promised is not only offered, but really exhibited, and conferred, by the Holy Ghost, to such (whether of age or infants) as that grace belongeth unto, according to the counsel of God's own will, in His appointed time.

The efficacy or effectiveness of the sacrament is not tied to the time of its administration. The sacrament is the sign and seal of our ingrafting into Christ, our participation in his death and resurrection, our cleansing from original sin, our regeneration, and our baptism by the Holy Spirit. What baptism signifies may never come to pass because these things are dependent upon faith, and we do not receive any of these benefits of salvation apart from faith. However, that which the sacrament signifies can happen truly in the life of a person, either before or after he or she receives the sign of the sacrament.

In the Old Testament, circumcision is a sign of faith. Abraham believed God as an adult, and then he was circumcised. But Isaac was circumcised as an infant, before he became a believer. Similarly today, adults must make a profession of faith (and therefore be regenerate) before they receive the sacrament of baptism. The thing signified comes before the sign in the case of the adult. But when infants receive the sign, regeneration and faith come later, if at all. What baptism represents is not tied to the moment that it is administered.

Section 6 continues: **yet, notwithstanding, by the right use of this ordinance, the grace promised is not only offered, but really exhibited**—and here comes the difficulty: **and conferred, by the Holy Ghost.** The authors of the Westminster Confession have already said that the grace of regeneration is not automatically conferred by the sacrament, and now they write about the grace of the sacrament being really conferred in and through the sacrament. But finish the sentence: **to such (whether of age or infants) as that grace belongeth unto, according to the counsel of God's own will, in His appointed time.** The grace promised by the sacrament of baptism is conferred by the Holy Spirit at whatever time God has decided to confer them. This is an oblique reference to the doctrine of election. Every person who is numbered among the elect will certainly receive the grace indicated by baptism, and he will do so in God's own time, according to his good pleasure. Most certainly, God will confer the grace and all the benefits of that grace upon those who are baptized if they are numbered among the elect.

I wish that election had been explicitly mentioned in the text. That would have left no ambiguity about the meaning. The Westminster divines were pointing out that this sacrament is no naked sign, empty of any significance. It is full of significance for the elect. God elects them not only to receive salvation, but also to receive all the means to that end. God ordained from the beginning of time that all of his elect would be brought to faith. He ensures that all the conditions for salvation are present through his grace and through the power and operation of the Holy Spirit. Baptism is one of the means of grace by which God brings salvation to his people.

The promised grace is **really exhibited, and conferred, by the Holy Ghost, to such (whether of age or infants) as that grace belongeth**

127

unto. Note the mention of infants. Is it possible for an infant to meet the requirements of justification by faith alone? Saving faith involves a certain level of understanding that, presumably, young infants do not have. However, they can have the grace of regeneration, where their heart's disposition is changed and they are redeemed from the power of original sin. The merit of Christ can also be imputed to them without expressed faith. Though infants are too young to process or articulate it, faith is in the heart of the regenerate at least in seminal form. If they are regenerated, they can have the merit of Christ imputed to them and be saved. Expressed faith is a requirement only for people who have the capacity for cognition. Reformed theologians have generally held that infants who die in infancy, being the children of believers, are numbered among the elect and are saved.

If and when a dying infant is saved, that infant is saved not because of innocence, but because of grace. That grace includes the application of the merit of Christ to the child, without which it would perish. If we believe that infants who die in infancy can be and are saved, we must believe that they receive the benefits of the work of Christ to meet the requirements of God for salvation, and that they are regenerated by the Holy Spirit. The Holy Spirit can certainly change the disposition of the soul of an infant. John the Baptist was presumably sanctified while he was still in the womb of his mother, and Jeremiah had a similar experience.

Normally, we do not expect the regenerative work of the Holy Spirit to occur until we are older, but the Holy Spirit is not restricted to waiting for cognitive faculties to develop before he does his saving work within the human soul. That would apply not only to infants who die in infancy, but also to people who are severely retarded or who do not have the ability to grasp all of the content of the gospel. God can and does graciously impute the righteousness of Christ to those people and change the disposition of their hearts through the regeneration of the Holy Spirit. That is why there is a parenthesis in the confession's statement. It is possible for the Holy Spirit to confer everything that is signified by baptism **to such (whether of age or infants)**. Grace is not only offered, but really exhibited and conferred by the Holy Spirit to infants as well as to those of age, if grace belongs to them, **according to the counsel of God's own will, in His appointed time.** God, in his sovereignty, can bestow the grace of salvation when and where and upon whom he decides, because salvation is of the Lord. It is a divine and supernatural work, which is not restricted to geniuses or to the learned, but can go to infants, to the infirm, to all sorts of people whom God in his grace so determines.

Sec. 7. The sacrament of Baptism is but once to be administered unto any person.

Most of us were probably baptized long before we actually came to faith. In those intervening years, the things of God meant nothing to us, and then we were converted to Christ, and we were raised from spiritual death. The things that were formerly repugnant to us then became matters of pure delight.

People say, "I wasn't a Christian when I was baptized. Now I understand, so I would like to experience that sacrament again from the perspective of someone who embraces what it signifies." I understand why people desire to do that, but what they fail to understand is that in baptism the Lord God has promised them eternal life and adoption into his family, to be joint heirs with Christ and to receive the benefits poured out on Jesus, if they have faith and put their trust in Christ. He sealed that promise with the sacrament of baptism, which they received as infants. Now they have come to faith, have been adopted into the family of God, have had their sins remitted, have been empowered by the Holy Ghost for ministry, have received eternal life, and have been united with Christ. All the things that God promised at their baptism have now been actualized in their life. So why should one go before God and say, "Would you run that by me again?" Nobody intends that, but that is the implication of being rebaptized.

There is a parallel illustration in the New Testament. People who were believers came to Paul, wanting to be circumcised. Early in his ministry, Paul said that people could be circumcised if they wanted to, but that it wasn't necessary anymore because everything circumcision signified in the Old Testament had been fulfilled.

Then along came the Judaizers, who claimed that a person is required to be circumcised and can't be saved unless he is circumcised. The apostle Paul wrote to the Galatians and chided them for foolishly entertaining such ideas. In Galatians 3, Paul asks in effect, "What's the matter with you? You have begun in the faith, and now, so quickly, you want to return to the old ways. You're putting yourself again under the burden of the law and trying to fulfill all of the requirements of the old covenant law that have been fulfilled for you by Jesus. If you are circumcised now, after coming to faith and having experienced what circumcision points to, you are, by implication, repudiating the work of Christ."

This is what the author is talking about in Hebrews 6, where he takes this question to its logical conclusion. He says that it would be impossible to restore a person again to salvation, if he or she repudiates Christ. Certainly circumcision won't save a person. Paul spells out what the inference would be if a person knowingly and willfully submitted to circumcision after having embraced Christ. It would be, by implication, a repudiation of Christ. The same principle would apply to rebaptism. In effect, it would be a repudiation of the validity of the promise that God made in the first place. I am confident that that is not a true believer's intent when he requests rebaptism, but many have indeed been baptized more than once out of such motivations. So the divines affirm that baptism is **but once to be administered unto any person.**

29

The Lord's Supper

**The Westminster Confession of Faith
Chapter 29: Of the Lord's Supper**

Sec. 1. Our Lord Jesus, in the night wherein He was betrayed, instituted the sacrament of His body and blood, called the Lord's Supper, to be observed in His Church, unto the end of the world, for the perpetual remembrance of the sacrifice of Himself in His death; the sealing all benefits thereof unto true believers, their spiritual nourishment and growth in Him, their further engagement in and to all duties which they owe unto Him; and, to be a bond and pledge of their communion with Him, and with each other, as members of His mystical body.

Sec. 2. In this sacrament, Christ is not offered up to His Father; nor any real sacrifice made at all, for remission of sins of the quick or dead; but only a commemoration of that one offering up of Himself, by Himself, upon the cross, once for all: and a spiritual oblation of all possible praise unto God, for the same: so that the popish sacrifice of the mass (as they call it) is most abominably injurious to Christ's one, only sacrifice, the alone propitiation for all the sins of His elect.

131

Sec. 3. The Lord Jesus hath, in this ordinance, appointed His ministers to declare His word of institution to the people; to pray, and bless the elements of bread and wine, and thereby to set them apart from a common to an holy use; and to take and break the bread, to take the cup, and (they communicating also themselves) to give both to the communicants; but to none who are not then present in the congregation.

Sec. 4. Private masses, or receiving this sacrament by a priest, or any other, alone; as likewise, the denial of the cup to the people, worshipping the elements, the lifting them up, or carrying them about, for adoration, and the reserving them for any pretended religious use; are all contrary to the nature of this sacrament, and to the institution of Christ.

Sec. 5. The outward elements in this sacrament, duly set apart to the uses ordained by Christ, have such relation to Him crucified, as that, truly, yet sacramentally only, they are sometimes called by the name of the things they represent, to wit, the body and blood of Christ; albeit, in substance and nature, they still remain truly and only bread and wine, as they were before.

Sec. 6. That doctrine which maintains a change of the substance of bread and wine, into the substance of Christ's body and blood (commonly called transubstantiation) by consecration of a priest, or by any other way, is repugnant, not to Scripture alone, but even to common sense, and reason; overthroweth the nature of the sacrament, and hath been, and is, the cause of manifold superstitions; yea, of gross idolatries.

Sec. 7. Worthy receivers, outwardly partaking of the visible elements, in this sacrament, do then also, inwardly by faith, really and indeed, yet not carnally and corporally but spiritually, receive, and feed upon, Christ crucified, and all benefits of His death: the body and blood of Christ being then, not corporally or carnally, in, with, or under the bread and wine; yet, as really, but spiritually, present to the faith of believers in that ordinance, as the elements themselves are to their outward senses.

Sec. 8. Although ignorant and wicked men receive the outward elements in this sacrament; yet, they receive not the thing signified thereby; but, by their unworthy coming thereunto, are guilty of the body and blood of the Lord, to their own damnation. Wherefore, all ignorant and ungodly persons, as they are unfit to enjoy communion with Him, so are they unworthy of the Lord's table; and cannot, without great sin against Christ, while they remain such, partake of these holy mysteries, or be admitted thereunto.

The meaning of the Lord's Supper continues to be one of the most controversial issues in Christianity. The great tragedy of the sixteenth-century Protestant Reformation was that the Reformers could not maintain unity among themselves. The principal reason was their failure to come to an agreement on the doctrine of the Lord's Supper. The Lutherans and the Calvinists were never able to resolve this issue, and, even within the Reformed community in Switzerland, there was significant disagreement between Ulrich Zwingli and John Calvin. These differences among Protestants, and the greater differences between Protestants and Roman Catholics, continue to this day.

One good thing about theological controversy is that it usually takes place when Christians are taking their faith seriously. People who don't believe anything don't usually argue about what they don't believe. It is when something is important to us that we engage in debate and controversy in order to avoid error or corruption. There has been controversy about the Lord's Supper throughout church history because it has been important to the church through the centuries.

When we examine life in the first-century Christian community, even apart from the pages of the New Testament, it is clear that the celebration of the Lord's Supper was central to the worship of the people of God. It became, in many respects, their identity, because they celebrated the sacrament in direct obedience to the command of Christ to do so until he returned.

In chapter 29 of the confession, we find eight sections devoted to the exposition of the meaning and practice of the Lord's Supper. This shows its importance in the eyes of the Westminster divines.

Sec. 1. Our Lord Jesus, in the night wherein He was betrayed, instituted the sacrament of His body and blood, called the Lord's Supper, to be observed in His Church, unto the end of the world, for the perpetual remembrance of the sacrifice of Himself in His death; the sealing all benefits thereof unto true believers, their spiritual nourishment and growth in Him, their further engagement in and to all duties which they owe unto Him; and, to be a bond and pledge of their communion with Him, and with each other, as members of His mystical body.

Section 1 is both substantive and lengthy. It begins by reiterating the words of institution used in most churches at the celebration of the Lord's Supper. Beginning at 1 Corinthians 11:23, Paul speaks of the institution of the Lord's Supper in the upper room by Jesus, on the night in which he was betrayed. The first affirmation that is made is that the Lord's Supper was indeed instituted by Christ. That is part of the definition of a sacrament. This affirmation reminds us that the Lord's Supper was not invented by the church, but was instituted and observed in the first instance by Jesus himself.

He was entering into his passion, and we are told in Luke 22:15 that he had a strong desire to celebrate the Passover one last time before his death. He gave specific instructions to his disciples to find a place where they could celebrate the Passover. Jesus had no place to lay his head, but he was concerned about having a place for worship, a place to celebrate the Passover with his disciples. There is nothing sacrosanct about a church building. The people of God can meet together outside or even in the catacombs of Rome, which was a terrible place. Persecution, especially in the early centuries, has forced the church to carry on its worship in strange places. The New Testament community, when it was very small, met in people's homes. As long as there has been a people of God, all the way back to Abel, they have needed a place to gather.

As we have previously seen, in the midst of celebrating the Passover, Jesus changed the centuries-old liturgy of the feast and gave it new meaning. Instead of the wine representing the blood on the doorposts on the night of the Passover, it would now represent his blood, which would be shed on the next day for the remission of sins. Jesus did not say, "It is my blood which the wine will represent now, instead of some animal's blood that was posted on the door centuries ago." The blood on the doorposts at the start of the Exodus really represented the blood of Christ. In that sense, Jesus didn't change the meaning of the wine, except in terms of its redemptive-historical significance. That which had been foreshadowed and promised by the Passover was now about to reach its consummation. It was not the blood of the paschal lamb who grazed peacefully in the field, but the supreme Lamb of God, whose blood would be shed for the perfect sacrifice once and for all. All of this Jesus did as he modified the liturgy of the Passover and instituted the new covenant. He commanded at that point that the Lord's Supper be observed in his church until the end of the world, for the perpetual remembrance of his sacrifice.

The first reason for the institution of the sacrament has to do with remembrance. Jesus spent three years as a peripatetic rabbi. A *peri*scope is something that looks around, and a *peri*patetic is someone who walks around. Aristotle was known as a peripatetic philosopher because he walked through groves of trees with his students following behind him. Aristotle lectured while he walked, and his students followed him, trying to write down on their clay tablets what the great teacher was saying. Most rabbis had a particular venue where their students came and sat at their feet to learn. As a rabbi, or teacher, Jesus called people to be his disciples, or learners—students in his school. He called them by saying, "Follow me." He was speaking literally: "Follow behind me, listen to what I am saying." His disciples were to pay close attention.

Memorization played a large role in ancient education, if only because writing materials were expensive. In some respects, that is superior to the method we have today. Our students busily scribble in their notebooks while the professor lectures, and then the notebooks are put on the shelf, where the information remains. I tell my students that their notebooks won't help when they are called to the home of a grieving parent whose child has just died. The knowledge of God must be in their head. Learning doesn't actually occur until it becomes integral to one's thinking, in the mind. That is the way Jesus taught.

Jesus was the incarnation of truth, so he never made a desultory remark or an idle comment. When Jesus lectured and taught, there was no extraneous information. Every word that came from his mouth was supremely important. But even Jesus stopped on occasion to say to his disciples, "*Amen, amen,* I say unto you"—that is, "Truly, truly" or "Verily, verily." He was underlining a particular point and saying, "This is really important."

I took comprehensive notes in college because I knew they would help on examinations. But even at that, I didn't take dictation. I condensed material and made judgments about what was important enough to write down. I never memorized every word spoken by the professor, and neither did the disciples memorize everything said by Jesus. But from time to time Jesus would stop and say, "Verily, verily, I say unto you." In this way he called attention to something that was especially important, because he understood that students forget what they have been taught.

To the Jew, apostasy was closely related to forgetting. Apostasy is literally a falling away from the favor of God, from fellowship with God, and from communion with the people of God. The people of Israel sinned against God when they forgot who he was and what he had done for them. They had constant celebrations, festivals, and covenant renewal to remind them of these things. God has a history with his people. In those days, just as it is today, people's spiritual vitality and commitment to the things of God tended to be only as strong as the memory of their latest blessing. Sometimes our attitude toward God is, "What have you done for me lately?" Forgetting is connected with apostasy. The psalmist declares, "Bless the LORD, O my soul; and forget not all His benefits" (Ps. 103:2).

When Jesus celebrated the Passover in the upper room, he redefined the liturgy and said, "This is my body, broken for you, and this is my blood, shed for you." He then commanded them, "Do this in remembrance of me." In effect, Jesus said, "As I enter into my passion and fulfill the work of redemption promised in the garden of Eden when the curse was placed upon the serpent, I am going to crush the head of the serpent. While I crush the head of the serpent, my heel will be wounded and my blood will be poured out. I will not die to satisfy the penal code of the Roman Empire. I will die to satisfy the justice of God. I will shed my blood for the remission of your sins. Don't ever forget what you will see tomorrow. To make sure you don't forget it, you must repeat it—not once a year, like the Passover, but often. When the children ask about it, the parents will say, 'We are remembering when the Lamb of God redeemed us from an oppressor far worse than Pharaoh. He redeemed us from the hands of the one who had enslaved our souls, from Satan himself. Jesus has reconciled us to God through his sacrifice on the cross.'"

I remember the assassination of President Kennedy. I was in the library at Pittsburgh Theological Seminary when the word came. We all left the library and went to a desk where there was a radio. We listened to the news bulletins until we heard the announcement that the

President had been declared dead. That same day, the same assassin allegedly killed another person in Dallas. He was Officer Tippett, but almost everyone has forgotten his name. We remember John F. Kennedy's name because he was the President of the United States. Not only that, but when he was buried, something unusual took place.

He was interred at Arlington Cemetery, and his family paid for an eternal torch at his grave, a gas light that is never to go out, as a perpetual reminder of the life of this President. What happened in the next six months was extraordinary. Many schools were named or renamed after him. Idlewild Airport became John F. Kennedy International Airport. Cape Canaveral became Cape Kennedy. Boats were named after him. A massive effort was made to insure that no one would ever forget that day in American history. However, the memories have grown dim, and people have forgotten the activities that attended that day.

I once drove from Pittsburgh to Beaver Falls, and on to Geneva College. I had to ride through one depressed steel town after another. As I drove, I looked at the people on the streets. Their faces were etched with defeat. They had lived hard lives, and whatever livelihood they had in the steel industry was being taken from them. Everybody looked burdened, and I thought to myself, "Is there no hope for these people?" Store after store was boarded up, and the grimness of defeat was pervasive. Then I saw a storefront church with a cross in the middle. I thought, "There's the sign of hope, the only hope for these people." I drove another half block and saw another cross. Soon I realized that I couldn't go a city block without seeing a cross, a sign of the hope of the world. The sign of the cross reminds us of the perfect sacrifice of Christ; it is a popular way of remembering his death.

But remembering what Christ did on the cross is not the full significance of the Lord's Supper. It has three dimensions to it with respect to time: past, present, and future. Our Lord commanded his disciples in the upper room not to forget the past (in which his death would soon be). When Scripture is read at the Lord's Supper, it is usually Isaiah 53, the crucifixion narratives from the Gospels, or the celebration of the Lamb who was slain in Revelation 5. The Word and the sacrament are used together, so that the Word calls our attention to what was accomplished by Christ. The Scripture readings focus our thinking as we commune, to make sure that we remember what Jesus did. There aren't too many churches that read Scripture during the distribution of the elements, but that is how John Calvin celebrated the Lord's Supper at his church in Geneva.

There is also a future reference in the Lord's Supper. Jesus said to his disciples, "For as often as you eat this bread and drink this cup, you proclaim the Lord's death till He comes" (1 Cor. 11:26)—a reference to the future consummation of the kingdom. In the celebration of the Lord's Supper, we have a foretaste of the marriage feast of Christ with his bride in heaven. Remembering what he has done for us in the past, we also look ahead to what he has promised to do for us in the future.

The church also believes that Christ is truly present here and now, meeting with his people in a special way at the Lord's Table, so that we are not only looking to the past or hoping for the future. There is a present reality that we experience with him and with each other when we celebrate the Lord's Supper.

Continuing on with the first section of this chapter of the confession, we read that the Lord instituted the Lord's Supper **for the perpetual remembrance of the sacrifice of Himself in His death.** Jesus, as our high priest, did not sacrifice an animal, but rather himself. He is our eternal high priest and also the Lamb of God. In the celebration of the Lord's Supper, we remember the sacrifice that our high priest made of himself.

Only Christ could offer himself as a sacrifice. Only he was worthy to offer that sacrifice, as he made very clear: "No one takes it [My life] from Me" (John 10:18). People mocked him when he was on the cross: "He saved others; Himself He cannot save. . . . He trusted in God; let Him deliver Him now" (Matt. 27:42–43). At any moment, he could have stopped his own execution, for he had more authority

139

and more power than the entire Roman army. He had myriads of angels at his disposal. He suffered voluntarily, so we call that the passive obedience of Christ. He was the Lamb who did not open his mouth, who was silent before his shearers, as Isaiah wrote, and he let it all happen to him. There was no authority over him, except that which was given from above. The Romans merely helped him carry out a mission that he chose to perform for us.

There was no priest there to put him on an altar. It was a voluntary act. That was what Paul celebrated: "He humbled Himself and became obedient to the point of death, even the death of the cross" (Phil. 2:8). By the sacrifice of himself in his death came **the sealing all benefits thereof unto true believers** in the Lord's Supper. Every time we celebrate the Lord's Supper, his death is impressed not just upon our memories, but upon our souls.

Recently, I reread *The Wrath of God*, by Jonathan Edwards. The first chapter is on our wretched condition when we are outside of grace. He talks about the wickedness that is stored up in our hearts. The next day, I heard a radio evangelist say, "If you're not a Christian, I want you to know how much God loves you and wants to have a wonderful relationship with you, and that he wants to forgive all of your sins. He wants to be your companion." I thought, "No, the unconverted person is exposed to the unbridled wrath of a holy and just God, who has indeed provided a sacrifice, but who demands repentance." Unless we come to the foot of the cross, we are more despicable in the sight of God than we can imagine. I have been a Christian for many years, yet if God opened up my heart right now, people would see that evil still lurks in it. When I probe my heart and see those shadows, I want to run to the cross. But in the midst of all that darkness, there is the seal of Christ on our souls. That is what we celebrate when we come together: the sealing of all of his benefits, of everything that he accomplished on the cross. He paid the price for every sin I have ever committed or ever will commit in my life. He has accomplished my redemption. Is it any wonder that he says, "Don't ever forget this"?

The Lord's Supper is to be observed for **the sealing all benefits thereof** [i.e., of his death] **unto true believers, their spiritual nourishment and growth in Him, their further engagement in and to all duties which they owe unto Him; and, to be a bond and pledge of their communion with Him.** We call this sacrament holy communion, because it is **communion with Him, and with each other, as members of His mystical body.** People often think that Reformed theology is all cerebral, all intellectual, with nothing in the heart, nothing in the emotions. The more we understand it with our head, however, the more our heart pulsates with passion over these things. And the more emotional I get, the more I understand. When I was a graduate student, there would be days when, after studying the work of Christ all day, I would try to go to bed at ten or eleven o'clock, but my mind would not shut down. I would find myself pacing the floor at three o'clock in the morning, contemplating what I had learned that day about what Christ had done for me. The more we understand with our minds, the more the heart is inflamed in response to these things.

We come to the Lord's Supper to have communion with him and with each other. That is the mystical element. When he is here and we enter into this relationship with him, there is a real communion with the real Jesus. It is not just that I am having it and that you are having it and that our friend is having it. Rather, while I am communing with Christ, I am also communing with everyone in his body. This is what binds us together.

Sec. 2. In this sacrament, Christ is not offered up to His Father; nor any real sacrifice made at all, for remission of sins of the quick or dead; but only a commemoration of that one offering up of Himself, by Himself, upon the cross, once for all: and a spiritual oblation of all possible praise unto God, for the same: so that the popish sacrifice of the mass (as they call it) is most abominably injurious to Christ's one, only sacrifice, the alone propitiation for all the sins of His elect.

141

In the seventeenth century, when the confession was written, Reformed theology often defined itself vis-à-vis Roman Catholic Church theology. Section 2 has to do with one of the critical disagreements between Rome and Protestantism. That critical issue is how Rome understands the drama of the Mass.

The question is whether the Lord's Supper is an actual repetition of the sacrifice of Christ upon the cross. The Roman Catholic Church teaches that every time the Mass is celebrated, Christ is offered up afresh to the Father in a real sacrifice. Although this sacrifice is considered to be an "unbloody" sacrifice, it is nevertheless a real sacrifice and involves a real repetition. There is no question, historically and theologically, that the Roman Catholic Church teaches that Christ is sacrificed in the Mass. The priest offers him up to remind the Father of the work that Christ accomplished in the past, as if the Father needed any reminder. The disagreement on this matter is irreconcilable unless Rome retreats from her teaching of the sacrificial character of the Mass. There is no hope of reconciliation between the Catholic and the Reformed churches because this is such a major point of controversy.

The confession states: **In this sacrament, Christ is not offered up to His Father; nor any real sacrifice made at all, for the remission of sins of the quick or dead; but only a commemoration of that one offering up of Himself, by Himself, upon the cross, once for all.** I would like to take out the word "**only**" from that statement. The Lord's Supper is indeed a commemoration, but it is more than that. Of course, every member of the Westminster Assembly understood that. What is meant by "**only**" is that the Lord's Supper is a commemoration of that sacrifice that was made **once for all**, and that there is no actual repetition of the sacrifice that Christ made.

There was **one offering up of Himself, by Himself, upon the cross, once for all**. In the English language, we use three words, *once for all*, because we do not have a single word that captures this idea. The closest word we have is *unique*, but there is a difference between *unique* and *once for all*. When Roger Bannister broke the four-minute mile barrier, he was the only person in the world who had done so. Since that time, his mark has been broken many times. The only thing that is "once for all" about Roger Banister is that he was the first one to run that fast. No one can ever replace him for that. But he is no longer unique.

In German, there is a word that captures this concept, *Einmaligkeit*. *Einmal* means "one time," and *igkeit* on the end makes it "one timeness." Christ offered himself at one time for all time. There was no room for repetition of any kind. Because of the perfection of Christ's sacrifice, there is no need to repeat it in any way. Our Lord said on the cross, before he died, "It is finished!" (John 19:30). Christ's work was finished; when he died, our debt was paid in full.

This is tied together with the person and work of Christ and how he has saved us in himself. No priest offered him up for us. He offered himself up for us. When we remember his sacrifice in the Lord's Supper, we offer up only **a spiritual oblation of all possible praise unto God. Thus, the popish sacrifice of the mass (as they call it) is most abominably injurious to Christ's one, only sacrifice, the alone propitiation for all the sins of His elect.** If a person commits mortal sin in the Roman Catholic scheme of things, he loses the grace of his justification and needs to be justified a second time, through the sacrament of penance. The sacrament of penance was objectionable to the Reformers, not because of confession or priestly absolution, but rather because of the demand for works of satisfaction. The sinner has to do enough to satisfy the demands of God's justice that it would be fitting or congruous for God to restore him to a state of grace. But Christ's perfect sacrifice offered perfect propitiation once for all. God's righteousness and justice were satisfied by Christ for us, forever. We cannot add to the propitiatory value of the cross. Our works of satisfaction have neither condign nor congruous merit. God's demand for justice was satisfied once for all on the cross.

When we come to celebrate the Lord's Supper, we come rejoicing in the perfection of the atonement that Christ has already given. We must not try to repeat it or add to it. God says that he requires us to worship him in spirit and in truth. The truth matters in worship, not just whether we feel good. There is good reason for, and content to, what we celebrate in the Lord's Supper.

I recently read Calvin's writings on the reformation of the church because of my concern about so-called contemporary worship. I realize that I'm not immune to the we've-always-done-it-this-way syndrome, and I recognize that every hymn that we love in the church today was at one time new. I also know the difference between contemporary music and contemporary worship. That is a distinction we need to keep in view.

It seems to me that the contemporary worship movement that has swept across America is riding the crest of bad theology. Worship is not an indifferent matter. As early as the sixteenth century, Calvin was concerned that worship had become married to the entertainment principles of the world. And now we are in the most entertainment-saturated age in human history, and people conclude that if the church is to compete, it must entertain.

There is a theology at work here. Our theology dictates that worship, above all else, involves the giving of honor, glory, and praise to the majesty of God. Everything that we do in our worship should serve that end. There should be a sense of transition from the world to the church, from the parking lot to the sanctuary. People should enter his courts with a sense of preparation of the soul. We come to honor God and his Son, who has won salvation for us once for all.

The Westminster divines say, in polemical language, "Here is not only what we believe, but also what we do not believe and why we do not believe it. And unless you understand these things, it really doesn't matter." When people say to me, "Doctrine doesn't matter," they are telling me they are unconverted—if they really understand what they are saying and mean it. If doctrine doesn't matter, then it doesn't matter whether we worship Christ or the Antichrist, whether we're saved by grace or by works, whether we worship Buddha or Jesus. A person who says, "I am a Christian," and then adds,

"Doctrine doesn't matter," publicly betrays Jesus Christ. Christians can do that unwittingly and still be Christians, but we need to realize that it does matter what we believe and how we worship God.

Even if it does not matter to us, it does matter to God. In Leviticus 10, we learn that the sons of Aaron were instantly killed by God for a transgression, when they offered strange fire on the altar, which God had not commanded. They were being innovative and experimental. When Aaron protested to Moses, Moses replied, "This is what the LORD spoke, saying: 'By those who come near Me I must be regarded as holy; and before all the people I must be glorified'" (Lev. 10:3). In our worship, the first thing we want to do is to regard God as holy.

Sec. 3. The Lord Jesus hath, in this ordinance, appointed His ministers to declare His word of institution to the people; to pray, and bless the elements of bread and wine, and thereby to set them apart from a common to an holy use; and to take and break the bread, to take the cup, and (they communicating also themselves) to give both to the communicants; but to none who are not then present in the congregation.

In this corporate celebration, all of the people of God are involved. The confession requires that the words of institution be declared and that the prayer of consecration be said. We do not believe that the prayer of consecration changes the essential structure of the bread and the wine, or that any miracle takes place. We do believe in a prayer of consecration, so that the elements, commonly used for daily nourishment, may now be set apart for a special, holy, and sacred activity. When we pray over the elements, we do not change them into the actual body and blood of Jesus; rather, we ask God, who instituted this sacrament, to "assign" special significance to the elements. There is nothing magical about the elements or the prayer of consecration, but we do ask God to set them apart from their common, everyday usage, to signify for us the atonement of Christ.

Sec. 4. Private masses, or receiving this sacrament by a priest, or any other, alone; as likewise, the denial of the cup to the people, worshipping the elements, the lifting them up, or carrying them about, for adoration, and the reserving them for any pretended religious use; are all contrary to the nature of this sacrament, and to the institution of Christ.

Reformed confessions, such as the Westminster Confession, the Belgic Confession, the Heidelberg Catechism, and the Thirty-Nine Articles, characteristically set themselves over against the Roman Catholic Church in light of the controversies that arose in the sixteenth century. This is nowhere more evident than in this section on the Lord's Supper because of the serious differences between the Reformed view of the Lord's Supper and the Roman view of the Mass. We will look at this with respect to the Roman Catholic understanding of the presence of Christ in and through the sacraments.

Section 4 is a far-reaching condemnation of Roman Catholic practices: **Private masses, or receiving this sacrament by a priest, or any other, alone; as likewise, the denial of the cup to the people, worshipping the elements, the lifting them up, or carrying them about, for adoration, and the reserving them for any pretended religious use; are all contrary to the nature of this sacrament, and to the institution of Christ.** No polemical rhetoric is spared when the Westminster divines repudiate the Roman Catholic understanding of the Lord's Supper here in section 4—or in sections 5 and 6, where there are references to the Roman Catholic doctrine of transubstantiation.

Worshipping the elements is mistaken. The elements are not to be adored. They are exalted and adored in Roman Catholic liturgy and ritual.

In every Roman Catholic church, at the back of the altar, there is a so-called tabernacle. It is usually a gold box of sorts. The tabernacle contains the consecrated element, which means that Christ is truly present at all times in the tabernacle. A Roman Catholic, upon

146

entering the church sanctuary, before being seated, genuflects. The priest, ministering in front of the altar, genuflects repeatedly during the service when he passes the tabernacle. They genuflect because they believe Christ is physically present in the tabernacle. It was in opposition to such a view that section 4 was written.

Sec. 5. The outward elements in this sacrament, duly set apart to the uses ordained by Christ, have such relation to Him crucified, as that, truly, yet sacramentally only, they are sometimes called by the name of the things they represent, to wit, the body and blood of Christ; albeit, in substance and nature, they still remain truly and only bread and wine, as they were before.

Sec. 6. That doctrine which maintains a change of the substance of bread and wine, into the substance of Christ's body and blood (commonly called transubstantiation) by consecration of a priest, or by any other way, is repugnant, not to Scripture alone, but even to common sense, and reason; overthroweth the nature of the sacrament, and hath been, and is, the cause of manifold superstitions; yea, of gross idolatries.

The substance of bread and wine, according to Roman Catholic doctrine, is changed by priestly consecration into **the substance of Christ's body and blood.** This change is called transubstantiation, referring to an alleged change in substance. Ancient philosophers talked about the essence, stuff, or substance by which something is truly and ultimately what it is. Aristotle distinguished between the substance of a thing and its accidents, or external, nonessential qualities. A duck, for example, can lose one of its external qualities, but still remain a duck. If it gets laryngitis and doesn't quack anymore, one of its accidents is removed, but it is still a duck. Various outward manifestations may be changed without destroying the essence of the duck. It is important to understand Aristotle's view because Thomas Aquinas created a synthesis between Christian theology and Aristotelian philosophy. Since the Middle Ages, much of theology has been cast in the language of Aristotle.

For Aristotle, if an object has the accidents of an elephant, then it is certainly an elephant and not a daffodil. There is an inseparable unity between the substance of a thing and its accidents. Now when the priest says the prayer of consecration during the Mass, the bread and wine supposedly change into the body and blood of Jesus. However, they still look, taste, sound, feel, and smell like bread and wine. So Rome says that, in the miracle of transubstantiation, while the substance of the elements is transformed into the substance of the body and blood of Christ, the accidents remain unchanged. Before the miracle, we have the substance of bread and wine and the accidents of bread and wine. After the miracle, we have the substance of Christ's body and blood and still the accidents of bread and wine. There is a double miracle because the substance changes and the new substance does not have its accidents.

Martin Luther wrote a scathing critique of transubstantiation in *The Babylonian Captivity of the Church*. However, Luther still insisted upon the real, corporeal presence of Christ in the Lord's Supper. He asserted that Christ's physical body and blood are truly present in the Lord's Supper. Because of that view, the Lutheran wing of the Reformation and the Reformed wing could not maintain doctrinal agreement. Luther's view is called consubstantiation, although Lutherans reject that designation. According to Luther, the miracle is that Christ, in his human body and blood, becomes present in, under, and through the bread and wine. There is not a change of elements, but an addition to them. Added to the bread and wine are the body and blood of Christ, though the latter are not visible.

Luther insisted on the physical presence of Christ's body and blood because he believed that Christ's words of institution ("This is my body; this is my blood") had to be interpreted literally. However, Jesus also said, "I am the door" and "I am the vine." He frequently used the verb *to be* in a metaphorical or representative sense. It is perfectly natural to interpret "This is my body" as "This represents my body."

Calvin and other Reformers rejected both transubstantiation and consubstantiation on Christological grounds. If the physical body of Christ is in heaven, they asked, how can it also be present wherever on earth the sacrament is being observed—and all at the same time? That would require the human nature of Christ to have the divine attribute of omnipresence.

At one of the most important ecumenical councils, the Council of Chalcedon in 451, the church defined her understanding of the mystery of the incarnation and the dual nature of Christ to stop the mouths of heretics, particularly Eutyches and Nestorius. Rome still holds to the declarations of Chalcedon, as do Protestants and all of Orthodox Christianity. Chalcedon represents the limit of where the mind of theologians can go in seeking to understand the mystery of the incarnation. Chalcedon said that Christ was *vere homo, vere Deus*—truly man, truly God. Chalcedon affirmed the dual nature of Christ, saying that he is one person with two natures, a divine nature and a human nature. The difficulty is to understand how the human nature and the divine nature relate to one another. In the fifth century, a heretical group, the Monophysites, said that in Christ there was only one nature. That single nature was neither human nor divine, but rather a mixture of deity and humanity. Eutyches said that Christ had a single, theanthropic (God-man) nature. That was either a deified humanity or, even worse, a humanized deity. The church responded to the Monophysites by declaring their belief to be heretical.

The church said that the two natures of Christ are united in such a way that they are not confused or mixed. By saying that they are not confused or mixed or blended, the church repudiated the Monophysite heresy. The church also said that the two natures are united without separation or division. This repudiated the Nestorians, who separated the two natures almost to the point of saying that Jesus was two persons.

There are two natures in Christ, a divine nature and a human nature. To explain the connection of relationship between these two natures, the church fathers used the way of negation. They didn't tell us how the two natures are united. Rather, they told us how they are *not* united. They are united without mixture, without confusion, without separation, and without division. We cannot penetrate the mystery of the incarnation. We do not understand how the divine nature and the human nature are united, but we do know how they are not united. They are not to be understood in terms of confusion, mixture, separation, or division.

The Council of Chalcedon established the boundaries within which one must work to try to understand the person of Christ. To step over those boundaries in any direction is to enter into heresy. Whenever one compromises one of the negatives of Chalcedon, one ends up in some Christological heresy.

The Catholic Church affirmed the Council of Chalcedon, as did Luther. But Calvin insisted that both of them forgot the message of Chalcedon when they developed their understanding of the Lord's Supper. After stating the four negatives—without confusion, without mixture, without separation, without division—Chalcedon added: each nature retains its own attributes. In the incarnation, the divine nature does not stop being divine. The second person of the Trinity did not give up his divine nature in the incarnation, nor did God die on the cross. If God had died on the cross, the universe would have disappeared. God not only created the universe, but maintains its existence, moment to moment. In the incarnation, the divine nature did not lose any of its attributes, and the human nature of Christ retained its humanity after the resurrection and ascension. We must neither deify the human nature nor humanize the divine nature.

But the doctrines of transubstantiation and consubstantiation give a divine attribute to the human nature of Christ. In order for Christ's body and blood to be physically present whenever and wherever the Lord's Supper or the Mass is celebrated, his physical body must be ubiquitous or omnipresent—everywhere at the same time. But that is a divine attribute. In the Middle Ages, the Catholic Church explained this as the communication of attributes from the divine to the human nature (*communicatio idiomatum*). On this view, the divine nature, in the incarnation, not only communicated information from the mind of God to the mind of the human nature of Christ, but also communicated or transferred divine powers and attributes, such as omnipresence, to the human nature. This could explain how the physical body and blood of Christ are present in thousands of places at the same time, but it compromises the Chalcedonian view that each nature of Christ retains its own attributes. The divine nature of Christ can be here and there at the same time, but the human nature of Jesus is in heaven, at the right hand of God. This explains how Jesus could tell his disciples that he was departing from them, yet would still be present with them to the end. The Heidelberg Catechism teaches, "Touching his human nature, Jesus is no longer present with us. Touching his divine nature, he is never absent from us." Thus, we do not see the human nature of Jesus when we celebrate the Lord's Supper. Body and blood belong to his humanity, not to his deity.

Christ is present at the Lord's Supper, but he is made present to us by the divine nature. The people who were in Jesus' company when he was on earth in the flesh, and who communed with him, were communing not only with a human being, but also with God, because Christ has two natures. If they communed with the human nature, they communed at the same time with the divine nature, and vice versa. When we commune with the divine nature, we are thereby communing with the whole Christ, even though his human nature is in heaven. We commune with the human nature because wherever the divine nature is, he is. His divine nature is not separated from the human nature. The only difference is that he does not bring his human nature to communion; it remains in heaven. Unfortunately, Luther embraced the concept of the communication of attributes, and that is why Reformed theologians considered the Lutheran view of the

Lord's Supper to be Monophysite. They placed Christ's human nature in different places at the same time. On the other hand, Lutheran theologians accuse Reformed theology of Nestorianism, saying that if Jesus is not present everywhere physically, then the two natures of Christ are divided. But Reformed theology is not Nestorian. It distinguishes between the two natures, but never separates them.

In the sixteenth century, Calvin defended the Reformed view of the Lord's Supper on two fronts. On the one hand, he had to deal with the Roman Catholic and Lutheran views of Christ's physical presence. On the other hand, he had to deal with the so-called spiritualists, who argued that the Lord's Supper is a mere memorial service, where the elements symbolize a past event. They denied the real presence of Christ in any significant way in the Supper. But Calvin insisted that Christ was spiritually present in a special way.

The key word in these debates was *substance*. Calvin's Roman Catholic and Lutheran opponents used the word to refer to the physical or corporeal presence of Christ in the sacrament. But when Calvin debated with the spiritualists, he used the term differently, referring to the "real" presence of Christ in the sacrament, not just a symbolic or intellectual presence. Calvin taught the real presence of Christ, but not his physical presence.

To go further with the controversy, one of Calvin's principles was *Finitum non capax infiniti*, "The finite cannot contain (or grasp) the infinite." Expressions like this are useful because they have a precise meaning, which does not get muddied by overuse. Calvin used it to express the incomprehensibility of God. Our finite minds cannot comprehend the infinite God.

In the incarnation, God took upon himself a human nature, but the nature of God was not thereby confined to the geographical location of the body of Jesus. When Jesus, in his human nature, prayed to the Father, he was not talking to himself. The divine nature was present far beyond the boundaries of his human nature. The fullness of the Godhead dwells in Jesus, but is not limited by human finitude.

The divine nature remained infinite after the incarnation, retaining all of its attributes, including omniscience, omnipotence, eternality, and omnipresence.

The disciples once asked Jesus when he would return. He answered, "Of that day and hour no one knows, not even the angels in heaven, nor the Son, but only the Father" (Mark 13:32). We find that hard to believe. How could Jesus not know? Wasn't he God?

We know from Scripture that Jesus sweated, slept, and ate. We don't generally ask, "How could Jesus be sleeping, eating, or sweating, since God doesn't need to do those things?" We understand that those things refer to his human nature. He had both a divine nature and a human nature, which were perfectly united; nevertheless, we can and must distinguish them. Certain things that Jesus did were clear manifestations of his human nature rather than the divine nature. So we don't get upset when Jesus eats, or sleeps, or sweats. But when he says, "I don't know," we think that cannot be. This is the Jesus who knew Nathaniel before meeting him. This is the Jesus who knew everything about the woman at the well before meeting her. He had supernatural knowledge and insight. He even knew what people were thinking. How could he not have known the day of his return?

Throughout Israel's history God supernaturally revealed information to human beings like the prophets, who then declared the message to the world. We do not conclude from that that Jeremiah or Isaiah knew everything. Similarly, the divine nature of Christ communicated information to the human nature of Christ. His divine nature had all the attributes of deity, including omniscience. The divine nature knew the day and the hour. But the divine nature did not communicate everything to the human nature, including that information, so his human knowledge was limited. Jesus, as a human being, could manifest supernatural knowledge only when his divine nature communicated it to his human nature.

Thomas Aquinas struggled with this and was perplexed by the mystery of the incarnation. He devised what he called an "accommodation" theory to explain Jesus' apparent lack of knowledge. He said that Jesus had to know the time of his return, since his human nature was perfectly united with the divine nature. Therefore, Jesus must have sidestepped his disciples' question by telling them that he did not know the answer, when in fact he did.

Such a theory rescues the omniscience of Christ, but at a very heavy price. Under this system, Jesus, who is the truth incarnate, speaks falsehood. If he ever told a lie, he would have disqualified himself from being our Redeemer. We cannot accept that Jesus ever lied. We must reject this theory of accommodation.

Subsequently, the church developed a doctrine of the *communicatio idiomatum*—the communication of attributes. In this scenario, not only is information communicated from the divine nature to the human nature of Christ, but attributes are also communicated from the divine to the human nature. On this view, the divine nature empowers the human nature, making it possible for the human nature to be everywhere or to know everything. The divine attributes of omniscience and omnipresence are communicated to the human nature. It was at this point that Calvin vehemently disagreed. The Council of Chalcedon said that the two natures are without mixture, and that each nature retains its own attributes. The idea of a transfer of divine attributes to the human nature involves a mixing of the two natures. The human nature no longer retains its attributes of finitude and limited knowledge. Christ is given a deified humanity, which is the very thing the church was trying to prohibit at Chalcedon when it condemned the Monophysite heresy.

In understanding the two natures of Jesus, heresy lurks on both sides of the aisle. Liberals allow the deity of Christ to be swallowed up in his humanity, effectively denying his deity. Conservatives and evangelicals, on the other hand, are zealous to affirm and protect the deity of Christ, but sometimes his humanity is obscured and swallowed up by his deity. We must protect a true union of two natures, one that is truly divine and one that is truly human. Jesus has a true human nature and a true divine nature that exist in perfect unity.

> Sec. 7. Worthy receivers, outwardly partaking of the visible elements, in this sacrament, do then also, inwardly by faith, really and indeed, yet not carnally and corporally but spiritually, receive, and feed upon, Christ crucified, and all benefits of His death: the body and blood of Christ being then, not corporally or carnally, in, with, or under the bread and wine; yet, as really, but spiritually, present to the faith of believers in that ordinance, as the elements themselves are to their outward senses.

This section carefully articulates the Reformed view of the Lord's Supper. It is a summary of Calvin's position. Sometimes we say, "I can't be with you physically, but I will be with you in spirit." But the confession is not talking about Christ being present in his thoughts. Nor is he present merely in our thoughts, as we remember him so vividly that he seems to be with us.

In section 7, Christ's spiritual presence is twice qualified by the word *really*. He is not present just in our thinking or in our imagination, but really in a spiritual way. He is truly present in his divine nature, so that we really feed upon the risen Christ. Christ's human nature is at the right hand of God in heaven; his divine nature is at the Lord's Table, where we meet him. When we meet him, we meet the One who still perfectly unites the human and divine natures. Through his divine nature, we commune with the whole Christ. We meet the whole person of Jesus at the Lord's Table, not because his human nature can be physically present here and all over the world, but because the divine nature that is perfectly united to the human nature does come to visit us. When he comes, he does not come without the whole person.

That is mystical and difficult to grasp. Reformed people, Rome, Lutherans, and Episcopalians believe in the real presence of Christ in the Lord's Supper. But we disagree in how we understand that real presence. The difference has to do with the dual nature of Christ as it was set forth at the Council of Chalcedon.

Sec. 8. Although ignorant and wicked men receive the outward elements in this sacrament; yet, they receive not the thing signified thereby; but, by their unworthy coming thereunto, are guilty of the body and blood of the Lord, to their own damnation. Wherefore, all ignorant and ungodly persons, as they are unfit to enjoy communion with Him, so are they unworthy of the Lord's table; and cannot, without great sin against Christ, while they remain such, partake of these holy mysteries, or be admitted thereunto.

The reference here is to what is known as the *manducatio indigna*—the eating and drinking unworthily. In 1 Corinthians 11:28–29, Paul warns the people of Corinth to examine themselves before they come to the Lord's Supper, because they have been abusing it. He warns that it is not a neutral event to be approached with a casual, cavalier attitude. It is the table of Jesus Christ. One comes into his true presence, and if there is a haughty, arrogant, impenitent spirit or an unbelieving participant, they are trampling on holy ground. They are eating and drinking unto their own damnation because this is the sacrament that is given to those who believe. If one is not a true believer, he mocks the truth of what is signified. The cross is being handled in a blasphemous way.

Paul adds to his warning about eating and drinking unworthily: "For this reason many are weak and sick among you, and many sleep" (1 Cor. 11:30). We take our life into our hands when we come to the Lord's Table. We come to feed upon his spiritual life, that wells up into everlasting life. To come hypocritically in unbelief while we are still at enmity with Christ is heaping up wrath against the day of judgment. That is why the Table is fenced. The idea is not for us to be arrogantly exclusive, but to protect people from the consequences and dangers of improperly participating in the celebration of the Lord's

Supper. We believe that Christ is present in a special way to pour out his tender mercy upon us, to condescend to our weakness, to restore the joy of our salvation, to assist us in our struggle for sanctification. We enter his house, come to his table, and commune with the risen Christ in a real way. We need to be discerning.

30

CHURCH CENSURES

The Westminster Confession of Faith
Chapter 30: Of Church Censures

Sec. 1. The Lord Jesus, as King and Head of His Church, hath therein appointed a government, in the hand of Church officers, distinct from the civil magistrate.

Sec. 2. To these officers the keys of the kingdom of heaven are committed; by virtue whereof, they have power, respectively, to retain, and remit sins; to shut that kingdom against the impenitent, both by the Word, and censures; and to open it unto penitent sinners, by the ministry of the Gospel; and by absolution from censures, as occasion shall require.

Sec. 3. Church censures are necessary, for the reclaiming and gaining of offending brethren, for deterring of others from the like offences, for purging out of that leaven which might infect the whole lump, for vindicating the honour of Christ, and the holy profession of the Gospel, and for preventing the wrath of God, which might justly fall upon the

Church, if they should suffer His covenant, and the seals thereof, to be profaned by notorious and obstinate offenders.

Sec. 4. For the better attaining of these ends, the officers of the Church are to proceed by admonition, suspension from the sacrament of the Lord's Supper for a season; and by excommunication from the Church, according to the nature of the crime, and demerit of the person.

Sec. 1. The Lord Jesus, as King and Head of His Church, hath therein appointed a government, in the hand of Church officers, distinct from the civil magistrate.

One essential characteristic of the true church, according to the Westminster divines, is the presence of a duly established government. This government is designed to promote the purity and peace of the church and to enforce discipline when that is necessary. Section 1 declares that the government of the church has been established by the Head and King of the church, even by the Lord Jesus himself. Just as God has appointed civil magistrates, who are given the power of the sword to protect, maintain, and defend life and liberty, so he has ordained the officers of the church to govern that holy institution. The church is not the state, nor is the state the church. The responsibility to preach the gospel, administer the sacraments, and provide for the spiritual well-being of the people is given to the church, not to the state.

Sec. 2. To these officers the keys of the kingdom of heaven are committed; by virtue whereof, they have power, respectively, to retain, and remit sins; to shut that kingdom against the impenitent, both by the Word, and censures; and to open it unto penitent sinners, by the ministry of the Gospel; and by absolution from censures, as occasion shall require.

Section 2 focuses on the keys of the kingdom of heaven. Christ declared that he would give the keys of the kingdom of heaven to his disciples in Matthew 16:19, and church officers are seen as the heirs of those keys. The keys of the kingdom are central to the Roman Catholic Church's belief in the Treasury of Merits, the granting of indulgences, and the release from purgatory, which in large part provoked the Protestant Reformation. But in that provocation and protest, the Reformers, though they rejected the Roman view of the keys of the kingdom, did not repudiate them, but restored their proper, biblical function.

Here the keys of the kingdom are understood in terms of church discipline. The officers of the church are given the power and authority to retain and remit sins. That is, the church has the power to grant the assurance of pardon to those who repent and to impose censures and discipline on those who remain impenitent. The language of the confession is: **to shut that kingdom against the impenitent.** The shutting of the kingdom is done by removing people from that place where the means of grace are most intensely focused, namely, the church, where the Word of God is preached and the sacraments are celebrated. This follows Paul's injunction to the Corinthian church to impose discipline in the scandalous situation of a man who practiced incest openly, but wasn't disciplined. When the church finally disciplined the incestuous man, Paul required that that man be fully restored to fellowship after he repented. We see in that instance that the purpose of discipline is not merely to remove sinners from the church, but also to rehabilitate and restore those who are repentant. Therefore, the language of the confession involves, not only the shutting of the kingdom, but also the opening of it. It is shut to the impenitent and open to the penitent. This is inseparably linked to the ministry of the gospel, which announces the forgiveness of sins for all who repent.

Sec. 3. Church censures are necessary, for the reclaiming and gaining of offending brethren, for deterring of others from the like offences,

161

for purging out of that leaven which might infect the whole lump, for vindicating the honour of Christ, and the holy profession of the Gospel, and for preventing the wrath of God, which might justly fall upon the Church, if they should suffer His covenant, and the seals thereof, to be profaned by notorious and obstinate offenders.

Section 3 declares that church censures are not only permissible but are indeed necessary **for the reclaiming and gaining of offending brethren.** This means that the goal of church discipline is to bring sinful people to repentance, so that they may be restored to full, active participation in the church. Church discipline is also seen as a deterrent. When discipline is absent from the church, there may be rapid degeneration into worldly vices. Indeed, gross and heinous sin that goes unpunished becomes like that leaven of which Jesus warns, which may **infect the whole lump.** Another purpose for church censures is to vindicate the honor of Christ. The church is first and foremost the body of Christ, and that body is called to bear witness to its Head and King, Jesus himself. When scandalous sin is left unchecked, unbridled, and undisciplined in the visible church, it brings serious dishonor to Christ. It is the duty of Christians, individually and corporately, to make a holy profession of the gospel. Another purpose for church discipline is to prevent the wrath of God, which would justly fall upon the church if sins were left unchecked. But we seek to rescue individuals and the whole body from the corrective wrath of God. The whole of sacred Scripture makes it clear that though God is patient and longsuffering with his people, there comes a point when his church is so profaned by notorious and obstinate sinners that he will no longer permit his covenant community to be so profaned.

Sec. 4. For the better attaining of these ends, the officers of the Church are to proceed by admonition, suspension from the sacrament of the Lord's Supper for a season; and by excommunication from the Church, according to the nature of the crime, and demerit of the person.

Section 4 makes it clear that church discipline is not to be carried out haphazardly in the Christian community, nor is it to be done in a vigilante fashion. The officers of the church are responsible to proceed with church discipline. They must use discretion, for church discipline should not be brought to bear for every transgression. Since "love will cover a multitude of sins" (1 Peter 4:8), every peccadillo or minor slight is not legitimate grounds for bringing a complaint against our neighbor. Rather, church discipline is to be reserved for those sins that are gross and heinous, that are public and scandalous, that bring dishonor to Christ and to his church.

We are also cautioned in section 4 that the ends for which church discipline has been established are better achieved when it proceeds in an orderly and progressive manner. The church does not jump to the final stage of excommunication in the first instance of church discipline, but rather proceeds by degrees, hoping that with each step of the discipline, the desired result of repentance will be achieved, without further discipline being needed. The first step mentioned in section 4 is admonition. When admonition does not cause the offender to repent, the next step is temporary suspension from the Lord's Supper. The length of that suspension is not specified by the confession and is therefore left to the prudence and discretion of the church. The final step is excommunication, in which people are removed from membership and from fellowship within the visible body of Christ. The steps of church discipline to be taken depend upon **the nature of the crime** and the level and severity of the **demerit of the person**.

31

Synods and Councils

The Westminster Confession of Faith
Chapter 31: Of Synods and Councils

Sec. 1. For the better government, and further edification of the Church, there ought to be such assemblies as are commonly called Synods or Councils; and it belongeth to the overseers and other rulers of the particular churches, by virtue of their office, and the power which Christ hath given them for edification and not for destruction, to appoint such assemblies; and to convene together in them, as often as they shall judge it expedient for the good of the Church.

Sec. 2. It belongeth to synods and councils, ministerially to determine controversies of faith, and cases of conscience; to set down rules and directions for the better ordering of the public worship of God, and government of His Church; to receive complaints in cases of maladministration, and authoritatively to determine the same: which decrees and determinations, if consonant to the Word of God, are to be received with reverence and submission; not only for their agreement with the Word, but also for the power whereby they are made, as being an ordinance of God appointed thereunto in His Word.

Sec. 3. All synods or councils, since the Apostles' times, whether general or particular, may err; and many have erred. Therefore they are not to be made the rule of faith, or practice; but to be used as a help in both.

Sec. 4. Synods and councils are to handle, or conclude nothing, but that which is ecclesiastical: and are not to intermeddle with civil affairs which concern the commonwealth, unless by way of humble petition in cases extraordinary; or, by way of advice, for satisfaction of conscience, if they be thereunto required by the civil magistrate.

Sec. 1. For the better government, and further edification of the Church, there ought to be such assemblies as are commonly called Synods or Councils; and it belongeth to the overseers and other rulers of the particular churches, by virtue of their office, and the power which Christ hath given them for edification and not for destruction, to appoint such assemblies; and to convene together in them, as often as they shall judge it expedient for the good of the Church.

Churches should not exist in isolation or be unrelated to each other. Local congregations should be involved with other congregations in the broader church. In the New Testament, we see, for example, the Council of Jerusalem in Acts 15. Representatives from the apostolic community met to deal with issues that related to all of the churches. We also see how Paul appealed to the churches outside of Jerusalem to receive offerings for the saints in Jerusalem. There was an interaction and interrelatedness among the early churches. During church history, different forms of government have developed, each one appealing to the New Testament as the basis for its structure.

In the episcopal form of government, bishops rule the church. The bishop rules over the churches in a geographical area, usually called a diocese. Within the diocese, there may be fifty local churches, led by individual priests. There may be a consistory which governs the local church, but over the local church is the bishop. The bishops meet together regularly in a collegiate way to determine policies that affect the entire church.

There are various forms of episcopal government. There is clear historical evidence that before the first century had ended, an episcopal form of government was in effect in many places. There were bishops in Smyrna, bishops in Rome, and bishops in Ephesus. Gradually the idea developed that certain bishops were higher than others, and eventually the bishop of Rome became the supreme pontiff in the Western Church.

When questions of wide interest needed to be settled, bishops and other delegates met together in ecumenical (church-wide) councils and regional synods. The decisions of the great ecumenical councils of the early church have been received and adopted by most branches of the church. The Trinitarian formulas were established at the Council of Nicaea in 325. Christological formulas, which affect the doctrine of the Lord's Supper, were devised at the Council of Chalcedon in 451. The Roman Catholic Church has had its own councils, particularly the Council of Trent in the sixteenth century. The Council was summoned to respond to the Protestant Reformers, whose distinctive views were condemned as heretical. The next great council was the Vatican Council in 1870, which declared the doctrine of papal infallibility. Vatican Council II was held in the 1960s to come to grips with the modern world.

In addition to episcopal church government, there is a representative form of church government, usually called presbyterian. Ministers and elders meet in regional assemblies, usually called presbyteries or classes (in the Dutch tradition), and representatives from those groups then meet in synods or general assemblies. The presbytery or classis has many of the responsibilities handled by the bishop in an episcopal system. Ecclesiastical and judicial authority is vested in the local church leaders (the session or consistory), subject to review by the higher representative bodies.

Another type of church government is called the congregational form. In this system, all authority is vested in the local congregation. Many congregational or independent churches belong to loose federations, giving them a connectional relationship to similar churches. They meet periodically in assemblies or conventions to share ideas and policies, and to make public statements that are not binding upon particular congregations. But many other independent churches have no such connections. In an independent church, authority is usually vested either in the minister or in a board. In most congregational churches, the congregational meeting is the highest court.

The Westminster Confession favors a presbyterian form of government. Presbyterianism has its roots in Scotland and, to some degree, in the Swiss Reformation. Most of those who developed this form of church government saw it as established in the New Testament.

> Sec. 2. It belongeth to synods and councils, ministerially to determine controversies of faith, and cases of conscience; to set down rules and directions for the better ordering of the public worship of God, and government of His Church; to receive complaints in cases of maladministration, and authoritatively to determine the same: which decrees and determinations, if consonant to the Word of God, are to be received with reverence and submission; not only for their agreement with the Word, but also for the power whereby they are made, as being an ordinance of God appointed thereunto in His Word.

The Westminster Confession affirms that when decisions are made at the local church level with respect to doctrine, behavior, or matters of discipline, there is a court of appeal. If a person is convicted of something in the civil realm, he has the right to appeal to a higher court. Similarly, decisions made in a local congregation can be appealed to a higher court (the presbytery), and then to the highest court (the general assembly). People who are directly involved in a dispute often become so subjective that it helps to have a higher court rule on it.

It belongeth to synods and councils, ministerially to determine controversies of faith. There is a distinction between political power that is vested in the state and the authority that is vested in the church. The church's authority is ministerial, and it deals with controversies of faith, that is, matters of doctrine, cases of conscience, and the public worship of God. The church does not deliver the mail, bear the sword, or raise a standing army. Those are responsibilities that God has given to the civil magistrate. The arena of faith is a matter for the church, and it is a ministerial matter. In matters of faith, Christians are not to go to the civil magistrate to air their grievances with each other. Many Christians believe we are not supposed to go to the civil magistrate for anything. I am not one of those, but certainly, in a theological dispute with a brother, we do not go to the sheriff or to the civil magistrate to have him solve our problem. Likewise, we do not want the civil magistrate interfering in matters of the faith.

The ordering of the public worship of God is and should be under ecclesiastical control. Someone has to order the way in which worship takes place. The denomination from which I withdrew many years ago helped sponsor a national Re-imagining Conference, which trashed every major tenet of the Christian faith and featured the goddess Sofia. That created a controversy that almost broke the church apart. I believe the denomination had a responsibility to regulate that sort of thing. They did not do what should have been done.

How God is to be worshiped is not a matter of personal preference, as we know from the Old Testament. Few things provoked the wrath of God more than people worshiping him in a manner contrary to his instructions. Throughout Israel's history, there was the problem of syncretism. After God established how he was to be worshiped, the

169

people, the clergy, the priests, and the false prophets borrowed elements from their pagan neighbors. They incorporated those pagan or secular elements into the worship of God and provoked his judgment upon the nation.

That did not stop with the Old or New Testament. We can find examples throughout history where the church, to use the late James M. Boice's phrase, "was doing the Lord's work in the world's way." What works in the secular culture may or may not be legitimate within the house of God.

> Sec. 3. All synods or councils, since the Apostles' times, whether general or particular, may err; and many have erred. Therefore they are not to be made the rule of faith, or practice; but to be used as a help in both.

A principle that came out of the Reformation, called *sola Scriptura*, requires that our consciences be bound by the Word of God alone. Luther was shown to be out of line with decisions made by various councils and papal pronouncements, and he said, "My conscience is held captive by the Word of God. Unless you can show me where I am wrong by Scripture, I cannot recant."

A letter came to me from someone who was upset because I had endorsed a book written by one of the members of Ligonier Ministries' staff, Dr. Mathison, on *sola Scriptura*. It is one of the finest works I have ever seen on the subject. The letter writer was irate because Dr. Mathison had appealed to church councils for some of his positions. The letter writer accused me of denying *sola Scriptura* too, in my endorsement of the book, because I cited a historic council against a particular doctrine. However, that particular council was cited because I agreed with their work—not because I believed that the council was infallible. I agree with the Council of Chalcedon and its affirmations about Christology, just as the rest of the Protestant world has agreed with it. We also agree that the fathers of Chalcedon were not infallible, though we think they were right on this matter. If they are wrong, one must be able to demonstrate how they are wrong from Scripture. That is the point of *sola Scriptura.*

Synods and councils, according to section 3, **are not to be made the rule of faith, or practice; but to be used as a help in both.** When I preach from a text of Scripture, I consult commentaries and the historic wisdom of the church. God has gifted the church's great teachers with tremendous insights. To be diligent in studying the Scriptures, I have to examine them, not only from my own twenty-first-century perspective, but from the perspective of the past. As C. S. Lewis once said, "It is helpful to have the winds of the ages blow through your head, lest you be guilty of carrying the contemporary cultural baggage to the text."

Consider, for example, the question of whether Paul in 1 Timothy 3:11 allows for the ordination of women. I don't think we can find a commentator in the history of the church before 1960 who took the position that this passage was intended to be of local application only. It could be argued that the monolithic interpretation of this passage through the centuries was an expression of perpetual male chauvinism. We may think that it wasn't until women's liberation came to the forefront that this error, repeated for two thousand years, was finally exposed. That is possible, but highly unlikely. That is why we look to what church leaders of the first century, the fifth century, and the sixteenth century said and did. It is important to see how the church down through the centuries has understood the Word of God. We don't want simply to depend on tradition, but we want to be helped by the tradition. It is highly unlikely that someone today is going to come up with an insight that will overthrow two thousand years of church history. We use assemblies, councils, and synods of the past as a help to understand the truths of God.

Sec. 4. Synods and councils are to handle, or conclude nothing, but that which is ecclesiastical: and are not to intermeddle with civil affairs

171

which concern the commonwealth, unless by way of humble petition in cases extraordinary; or, by way of advice, for satisfaction of conscience, if they be thereunto required by the civil magistrate.

This statement limits the scope of church councils to ecclesiastical matters. The church ought not to usurp authority that God has given to the civil magistrate. However, there is a debate, within Presbyterian circles, whether the church has the right and/or the responsibility to speak on civil matters. Should the church have had anything to say about whether the American colonists should revolt against England?

We are not allowed by law, as tax-exempt organizations, to preach politics within the church. This is outrageous, because in the Old Testament and in the New, the people of God were called to be engaged in prophetic criticism. When Ahab confiscated Naboth's vineyard, he abused his power as king, and the prophet of God rebuked him. Herod's marriage was against the law of God, and John the Baptist paid with his life for criticizing the king. When the civil government endorses abortion on demand, it is the duty of the church—not only as individuals, but in council—to speak out against those miscarriages of justice and the failure of the church to be what God has called it to be.

When the church speaks out, people say that Christians are trying to take over the government and force their views on others. But we are not calling the state to be the church. We are calling the state to be the state. We are reminding the state of why it was created in the first place and what its responsibility is under God. The state was ordained by God and its primary task is to maintain, protect, and sustain human life. The German church spoke out against Hitler with the Barmen Declaration.

There are divisions within Reformed communities on how section 4 should be applied. Does it mean that the church should never say anything except on ecclesiastical matters, or does the church have the responsibility to be the conscience of the nation? The church is supposed to be the conscience, not the government.

32

THE STATE OF MEN AFTER DEATH, AND THE RESURRECTION OF THE DEAD

The Westminster Confession of Faith
Chapter 32: Of the State of Men after Death, and of the Resurrection of the Dead

Sec. 1. The bodies of men, after death, return to dust, and see corruption: but their souls, which neither die nor sleep, having an immortal subsistence, immediately return to God who gave them: the souls of the righteous, being then made perfect in holiness, are received into the highest heavens, where they behold the face of God, in light and glory, waiting for the full redemption of their bodies. And the souls of the wicked are cast into hell, where they remain in torments and utter darkness, reserved to the judgment of the great day. Beside these two places, for souls separated from their bodies, the Scripture acknowledgeth none.

Sec. 2. At the last day, such as are found alive shall not die, but be changed: and all the dead shall be raised up, with the self-same bodies, and none other (although with different qualities), which shall be united again to their souls for ever.

Sec. 3. The bodies of the unjust shall, by the power of Christ, be raised to dishonour: the bodies of the just, by His Spirit, unto honour; and be made conformable to His own glorious body.

With chapter 32 we enter into that subdivision of theology which is called "eschatology." Eschatology has to do with the future: the return of Jesus, the consummation of the kingdom of God, the state of our existence after death, and the final resurrection. Much information is given about our future state in sacred Scripture. However, there are still many questions about the state of our existence after we die. Will we be old in heaven? Will we be young? Will we show any kind of age? What will our bodies look like? We have hints from the glorified body of Christ, which is the model for us all, but questions remain for which we will not know the answer until we get there.

Sec. 1. The bodies of men, after death, return to dust, and see corruption: but their souls, which neither die nor sleep, having an immortal subsistence, immediately return to God who gave them: the souls of the righteous, being then made perfect in holiness, are received into the highest heavens, where they behold the face of God, in light and glory, waiting for the full redemption of their bodies. And the souls of the wicked are cast into hell, where they remain in torments and utter darkness, reserved to the judgment of the great day. Beside these two places, for souls separated from their bodies, the Scripture acknowledgeth none.

Volumes of theological information about eschatology have been compacted and condensed in this short paragraph. It assumes that the human soul has an **immortal subsistence.** An immortal soul is not mortal and therefore cannot die or be destroyed. Thomas Aquinas, in the *Summa*, gives a cogent argument for affirming the substantive immortality of the human soul because God made it a spiritual substance, not given to corruption. Fundamentally, I agree with his way of articulating the nature of the soul. However, I am troubled by the word *immortal* because of the baggage it carries from ancient Greek philosophy, in which the soul was seen as eternal. As Christians, we believe that human souls are created, not eternal. If we are created, our lives depend on the Creator in whom we live and move and have our being. Our souls are equally dependent upon God for their sustenance and continuity of being. For the Greek, souls have always been and always will be. The Greek notion of the immortality of the soul is that the human soul is inherently and intrinsically immortal. We do not believe that. A human soul cannot survive for five seconds without the sustaining power of God. God will preserve our souls and even the souls of the damned forever, but they are not inherently indestructible. They would perish if God withdrew his providential support from them. He preserves the soul, and in that sense it is immortal extrinsically, but not intrinsically. The perpetual life of the soul rests in the power of God, not in its own power.

The bodies of men, after death, return to dust, and see corruption. Remember the story of Lazarus and his resurrection? He had been in the tomb for four days. His body was already beginning to undergo the natural decomposition of the flesh. When we die, our bodies see corruption. Of course, the notable exception is that God refused to allow his Holy One to see corruption between his death and his resurrection. But all other dead bodies of human beings decay and return to dust. At the funeral service, we say, "Ashes to ashes, dust to dust," but that is not the end of the story. The body that dies will be raised again. It is sown in corruption, but raised in incorruption. It is sown in mortality, but raised in immortality. The curse of corruption that we experience in this body will not be associated with the new body that we will receive at the resurrection.

The confession goes on to say: **The bodies of men, after death, return to dust, and see corruption: but their souls . . . neither die nor sleep.** There are two things that do not happen to us at death. First, our souls do not die. That means that we have the continuity of personal existence beyond the grave. Our personal life, which is currently housed in our physical bodies, does not stop at death. The interim between our birth and our death in this world is an infinitesimal drop in the ocean of the full extent of our life. Second, our souls do not sleep. We sing "Amazing Grace," and in that last verse we acknowledge:

> When we've been there ten thousand years,
> bright shining as the sun,
> We've no less days to sing God's praise
> than when we first begun.

When we join the saints in heaven, even if they died two thousand years ago, they still have as much time left to enjoy life as we do when we get to heaven. It is not that when we go to heaven we get an extra life, or an extra thousand or two thousand years; we live forever.

According to the confession, the soul does not die when the body dies, nor does it go to sleep. According to a popular error called "soul sleep," or *psychopannychia*, the soul goes to sleep when the body dies. It goes into a state of suspended animation until the great resurrection, at which time it will be awakened, so it will seem as if there has been no passage of time. This view is based on the fact that the Bible sometimes speaks of death as sleep. For example, "We shall not all sleep, but we shall all be changed" (1 Cor. 15:51). But this was just a common Jewish figure of speech. It was not meant to describe an intermediate state of suspended animation.

The doctrine of soul sleep is thoroughly demolished in a volume entitled *Psychopannychia*, which is one of the lesser-known works of John Calvin. The Bible teaches that we do not lose consciousness when we die. We will be in heaven, aware of Christ, aware of God, and aware of the other saints who are there. We will not be clothed with our resurrected bodies at that point, but we will be in an intermediate state, in which the soul exists without the body. According to the New Testament, life in this world is a good thing. It is a blessing to be able to live a long life. But the intermediate state is better. Paul said, "For I am hard pressed between the two, having a desire to depart and be with Christ, which is far better. Nevertheless to remain in the flesh is more needful for you" (Phil. 1:23–24). Paul was not in conflict between the good and the bad. It was between the good and the better—and in this case, far better.

Life in the intermediate state is far better than it is now, Paul said, because we are then in the immediate presence of Jesus. However, it is still not the best. The best will come at the final resurrection, when our souls will be united with our glorified bodies. We will live forever in that glorified state. The options for the believer are good, better, and best. But for the unbeliever, they are bad, worse, and unspeakably horrible.

The souls of the deceased **immediately return to God who gave them: the souls of the righteous** are **then made perfect in holiness.** So, as soon as we die, we are perfected. Our sanctification is completed. As we enter into glory, we enter into the state of sinlessness. We may miss our bodies, but we won't miss our sin. There will be no sin there. Immediately, **the souls of the righteous, being then made perfect in holiness, are received into the highest heavens, where they behold the face of God, in light and glory, waiting for the full redemption of their bodies.** The Bible tells us a lot about life after death, but many questions are left unanswered. John wrote, "Behold what manner of love the Father has bestowed on us, that we should be called children of God!" (1 John 3:1). Then he says, "It has not yet been revealed what we shall be, but we know that when He is revealed, we shall be like Him, for we shall see Him as He is" (v. 2). The highest hope of the Christian is the beatific vision of God. We shall see him, John says, as he is.

The promise to *see* God, in the Beatitudes, is given to the pure in heart: "Blessed are the pure in heart, for they shall see God" (Matt. 5:8). They will see him. The vision is described graphically in the last two chapters of the Bible, in the book of Revelation. The saints will behold the unveiled glory of God. One of the hardest things about living the Christian life is that we serve a God whom we have never seen. The culture senses his absence, not his presence, but though we cannot see him, we see the evidence of him, of the work of his hands and his work in history. We have not seen him because it is forbidden for sinners to see him. There is nothing wrong with our eyes. Rather, there is something wrong with our hearts. When our hearts are totally sanctified, when we reach that state of glorification, when we will indeed be altogether pure in heart, then, at last, the beatific vision will flood our soul. We will see him and will continue to see him always.

The confession expresses the hope found in John's epistle. We will see the splendid glory unveiled, the majesty of God. John later described the New Jerusalem coming down from heaven: "There is no moon; there is no sun." There will be no artificial lights in the heavenly Jerusalem, because such modes of illumination will be completely unnecessary. There will be no night there, because the glory of God and of the Son will never be turned off. It radiates and shines forever, and we will live in the midst of that light.

We need to fill our minds with the promises of God and believe them. The martyrs of the first century died singing the praises of God and believing his promises. They believed, and they knew where they were going. They were eager to get there. We will all go in God's time, and we will be in the immediate presence of God.

They behold the face of God, in light and glory, waiting for the full redemption of their bodies. The beatific vision is the ultimate joy and delight for which we were created in the first place. The word *beatitude* comes from the same root as *beatific*. It is the vision that brings with it the supreme state of blessedness.

In the Old Testament, God's promise of blessing stood in stark contrast to the threat of his curse. The curse manifested God's judgment and wrath upon disobedient people, whereas the blessing was his reward for his obedient people. The Mosaic covenant was set up with regard to those dual sanctions. In Deuteronomy 28, God promised the people manifold blessings if they obeyed him, and all manner of curses if they disobeyed him. To be cursed is not only to miss the blessing, but to be cut off from all of the benefits that God has promised to his people.

When Christ died, he took the place of those who were covenant breakers. He took upon himself the curse of God on the cross. "Cursed is everyone who hangs on a tree" (Gal. 3:13). Jesus took the punishment, the curse, that we deserved. Because his righteousness is applied to our account, he wins for us the blessing by his perfect obedience. The supreme level of blessedness that we can hope to experience is the beatific vision.

In the garden of Eden, Adam and Eve were in a state of pure delight, fellowshipping with God as he walked in the cool of the evening. When sin entered into the relationship, Adam and Eve hid from God. God admonished them for their sin, and drove them out of the garden. He cursed the man, the woman, the serpent, and the earth. He prevented anyone from ever entering the garden again.

Because of this breach in intimate fellowship between the Creator and the creature, man could no longer behold the glory of God directly. God did allow his people to come near him. He pitched his tent in their midst, but would not permit his face to be seen. He said to Moses, "You cannot see My face; for no man shall see Me, and live" (Ex. 33:20). The benediction in the Old Testament says, "The Lord bless you and keep you; the Lord make His face shine upon you, and be gracious to you; the Lord lift up His countenance upon you, and give you peace" (Num. 6:24–26). To the Jew, the supreme state of blessedness was not only to experience the nearness of God, but to see the brightness of his countenance.

When the glory of God is manifested in the Scriptures, it is usually accompanied by a cloud that shields people from directly perceiving the face of God. The Shekinah cloud bursts forth with a heavenly radiance, the refulgence of which is so intense that it is blinding to those who see it. Throughout the Scriptures, there are images and metaphors of God as a consuming light. When the risen Christ appeared to Saul on the road to Damascus, he was blinded by a light more intense than the sun. The disciples, on the Mount of Transfiguration, saw the glory of Christ break through the veil of his humanity, and they fell on their faces, blinded by the brilliance. When the Jews prayed, "Make his face shine upon you," they wanted to see the unveiled glory of God.

When I visit Israel, my imagination works overtime. The first time I went to Bethlehem, I slipped away from the group and sat on a stone wall. As far as my eye could see were the fields of Bethlehem. I was sitting near the place where, one night in human history, all heaven broke loose. The glory of God shone brilliantly and filled the shepherds in the fields with terror and fear. They realized they were in the holy presence of God, encountering the supernatural in a brilliant, blinding light. It was every Jew's dream: "Lord, show me your glory." We will see God himself in heaven. That is the beatific vision, to see God unveiled, not as he has been outwardly manifested in a cloud or in a burning bush, but as he really is.

You may say, "But God is invisible, not only because of our sin, but also because he has no physical body. He is a spirit. How will we be able to see that which is invisible?" I don't know the answer to that, and it can be dangerous to speculate. John Calvin commented that, where God closes his holy mouth, we ought to desist from inquiry. But Jonathan Edwards peeled away the layers of Scripture to come up with an idea of how the beatific vision may take place. God is not physical, but neither will we be physical in heaven. We will no longer have a brain, an optic nerve, or eyes. But Edwards said that we won't need them because our soul will have a direct and immediate view of the Being of God. That goes beyond anything we can truly imagine. The perception that we will have of God in heaven, even without our eyes, will be far greater than anything we can perceive right now. If we want to know what is going on in someone's mind, we have to allow that person to tell us. But that person may not want to tell us much about himself. So imagine communication soul to soul, mind to mind, with no barriers. We were made for that kind of communication with the living God, and that is what awaits us in heaven.

Section 1 also describes the souls of the wicked. **And the souls of the wicked are cast into hell, where they remain in torments and utter darkness, reserved to the judgment of the great day. Beside these two places, for souls separated from their bodies, the Scripture acknowledgeth none.** Mark 9:43–48 and Revelation 20:14 describe hell as a lake of fire where the worm never dies and the fire never goes out. I suspect that those are images and symbols of hell. When I say that, I get two different reactions. Some look at me as if I have denied the Bible, and others look at me with relief to hear that I don't think there is a literal lake of fire. Therefore, I hasten to say, "Be careful." When Jesus uses an image, do you suppose that the reality is less intense or more intense than the image? The reason for using images and symbols is that we are not able to bear a more precise picture of reality. That Jesus would choose these terrifying symbols in describing hell indicates to me that the reality will be far worse. The sinner in hell will wish he could be in a lake of fire, rather than the reality to which it points.

Some define hell as the absence of God. But I understand the Bible to teach that the most tormenting thing for the sinner in hell is not the absence of God, but his presence. In Matthew 7:21–23, Jesus says: "Not everyone who says to Me, 'Lord, Lord,' shall enter the kingdom of heaven. . . . Many will say to Me in that day, 'Lord, Lord, have we not prophesied in Your name, cast out demons in Your name, and done many wonders in Your name?'" His reply will be: "I will declare to them, 'I never knew you; depart from Me, you who practice lawlessness!'" In hell the sinner will want to say, "Get out of here, please, God." There is no place where God is not. Therefore, the presence of God extends to the depths of hell.

It is not just his presence that is so troubling, but what he is doing. He is manifesting his judgment. He is pouring out his wrath upon those who are in hell. The two great errors we hear about hell are that God is not there and that the sinner is not there.

Sec. 2. At the last day, such as are found alive shall not die, but be changed: and all the dead shall be raised up, with the self-same bodies, and none other (although with different qualities), which shall be united again to their souls for ever.

All the dead shall be raised up. At the final trumpet, according to the New Testament, those who are still alive on this earth will not die, but will be instantly changed. At the same time, all of the dead will be raised. This refers to what we call the general resurrection. And those who are raised from the dead will be raised with the same bodies in which they perished. Their bodies will be transformed in the resurrection and will not be affected by the manner in which they died. Some people are concerned that those who have lost limbs or have had other physical harm to their body will somehow be lacking in the resurrection. By no means. When God, who has the power of life and the power of resurrection, gives to his people a resurrected body, his power to do so will hardly be limited by our physical condition at death. In the general resurrection, we will reach the final state, for our resurrected bodies will be united with our souls and will remain like that forever.

Sec. 3. The bodies of the unjust shall, by the power of Christ, be raised to dishonour: the bodies of the just, by His Spirit, unto honour; and be made conformable to His own glorious body.

The bodies of the unjust shall . . . be raised to dishonour. Here is the affirmation that the resurrection of the body is not limited to the redeemed, but that the resurrection of the body applies to all who die. All people will have their bodies raised in the last judgment. The redeemed will have their bodies raised so that they may enjoy the glorious, honorable resurrection for all eternity. The bodies of the unjust will also be raised by Christ, but to dishonor.

In recent decades, annihilationism has gained some adherents within the evangelical world. The annihilation of the wicked has been the position of some sects and cults, but it has not been considered an orthodox view of hell over the centuries of church history. However, some evangelical leaders have taken an interest in it. John Stott, for example, has taken a position in which he at least holds out the possibility of annihilation for the unjust. A similar position was taken by the late Philip Edgcumbe Hughes, a formidable New Testament scholar and theologian.

The Christian view of immortality differs from the Greek view of immortality. The Greek view teaches that the soul is by its very nature indestructible and eternal. Hughes argued that the idea of the eternal damnation and punishment of the soul was based upon the Greek view of the soul's indestructibility. As we mentioned above, the proper Christian view is that the soul is extrinsically, not intrinsically, immortal. Souls continue after death because God preserves them. The souls of human beings are mortal in the sense that they could be destroyed, were it not for God, who sustains their ongoing existence.

According to the confession, Christ raises the bodies of the damned and preserves them to endure everlasting punishment. That is difficult to fathom or even to contemplate. One of the metaphors used in the New Testament is that hell is the place where the worm does not die. That suggests the possibility of a parasite that lives off the flesh of another creature. If the flesh is completely consumed, the parasite dies. The ghastly image is that in hell the worm always has more flesh to eat. That means that the body of the damned has to be preserved by the power of God in order to endure the punishment that it is to receive.

Some years ago, I heard Dr. John Gerstner giving a series of lectures on hell. He presented a careful study of what the New Testament teaches about hell. He observed, first of all, that Jesus talked more about hell than about heaven. Almost everything that we know about hell comes from the lips of Jesus. Jesus warns that there will be a last judgment and that every human being will appear before the throne of God and be held accountable for his or her life. God will judge each one of us according to the standard of his own righteousness. Every idle word that we have spoken will be brought up. In Romans 2:5–6, the apostle Paul warns people that they are heaping up wrath that will come upon them in the day of wrath.

We know of people who, no matter how godless their lives were, suddenly seem to become saints at their funerals. It is a dreadful thought, of course, that someone who has just died has gone to that awful place of judgment. But the apostle Paul warns us that every sin of the impenitent will be judged by a holy and just God. "But in accordance with your hardness and your impenitent heart you are treasuring up for yourself wrath in the day of wrath and revelation of the righteous judgment of God, who 'will render to each one according to his deeds'" (Rom. 2:5–6).

The Evangelism Explosion program asks diagnostic questions. The first question is: Have you come to the place in your thinking that you know for sure that when you die you are going to heaven? Many people say they don't know. And then the second question is: If you were to die tonight, and stand before God, and God said to you, "Why should I let you into my heaven?" what would you say? Ninety percent of the people answer that question by saying, "I tried to live a good life," or words to that effect, rather than fleeing to the gospel of Christ. I once asked these questions to a man, whose face turned white as he replied, "I know when I die I'm going to hell." But most unbelievers either do not believe in hell or think that they will be able to escape it.

The doctrine of evolution has sparked controversy and debate between scientists and theologians. Many people in our culture have embraced macroevolution with a smile. Why would they be happy to find out that they are a cosmic accident and that their final destiny is annihilation? I can only think of one answer: evolution offers people an escape from accountability. When we die, it is over. We don't have to worry about facing a holy and righteous Creator. If someone convinced me that macroevolution were in fact true, I would be in utter despair. I would have to recognize that I am utterly insignificant and that my life and labor are meaningless. People like Jean-Paul Sartre, the pessimistic existentialist, considered life to be "a useless passion." Even so, people would rather have their life be a useless passion than for death to bring them before a just and holy God. Perhaps that accounts for the great hostility that the world has toward the church. Christians are often accused of being "holier than thou." People assume that we think we will get to heaven because of our holiness. The hostility is there because people do not want to confront the thought that they will someday have to face God and his judgment.

33

THE LAST JUDGMENT

The Westminster Confession of Faith
Chapter 33: Of the Last Judgment

Sec. 1. God hath appointed a day, wherein He will judge the world, in righteousness, by Jesus Christ, to whom all power and judgment is given of the Father. In which day, not only the apostate angels shall be judged, but likewise all persons that have lived upon earth shall appear before the tribunal of Christ, to give an account of their thoughts, words, and deeds; and to receive according to what they have done in the body, whether good or evil.

Sec. 2. The end of God's appointing this day is for the manifestation of the glory of His mercy, in the eternal salvation of the elect; and of His justice, in the damnation of the reprobate, who are wicked and disobedient. For then shall the righteous go into everlasting life, and receive that fulness of joy and refreshing, which shall come from the presence of the Lord: but the wicked, who know not God, and obey not the Gospel of Jesus Christ, shall be cast into eternal torments, and be punished with everlasting destruction from the presence of the Lord, and from the glory of His power.

Sec. 3. As Christ would have us to be certainly persuaded that there shall be a day of judgment, both to deter all men from sin; and for the greater consolation of the godly in their adversity: so will He have that day unknown to men, that they may shake off all carnal security, and be always watchful, because they know not at what hour the Lord will come; and may be ever prepared to say, Come Lord Jesus, come quickly. Amen.

Sec. 1. God hath appointed a day, wherein He will judge the world, in righteousness, by Jesus Christ, to whom all power and judgment is given of the Father. In which day, not only the apostate angels shall be judged, but likewise all persons that have lived upon earth shall appear before the tribunal of Christ, to give an account of their thoughts, words, and deeds; and to receive according to what they have done in the body, whether good or evil.

The language in this section was taken directly from the pages of the New Testament. When the apostle Paul was at Athens, he confronted the Stoic and Epicurean philosophers. Although the Stoics and the Epicureans differed sharply in their cosmology, they agreed that ultimate truth cannot really be known. They were the relativists of their day. They taught that since we cannot know ultimate truth, we should only be concerned with how we live out our days in this world. The Stoics faced the ultimate meaninglessness of their existence by trying to be imperturbable. Even today we describe such people as being stoical, as having a stiff upper lip. Stoics recognize that they have no control over what happens, and can control only their feelings about what happens to them. Stoicism was a philosophical escapism from the grim realty of a meaningless life.

188

The Epicureans developed a sophisticated philosophy of hedonism. They defined the good as the maximum enjoyment of pleasure and the minimum amount of pain. They sought their meaning through physical pleasure.

Paul met with the Greeks at the Areopagus and saw that they had an altar to an unknown god. "The One whom you worship without knowing, Him I proclaim to you," said Paul (Acts 17:23). He explained that the God in whom they lived and moved and had their being was the God who had made them. He cautioned that the former days of ignorance, when God overlooked people's sins, were over, and that now all men everywhere are commanded to repent (v. 30). That is the universal mandate of God.

We soften the gospel in our day. In modern forms of mass evangelism, part of the strategy is called the invitation. People are "invited" to come to Christ. That was not how the apostles did it. An invitation is something that can be politely declined with impunity. But a command cannot be declined with impunity. Paul said that God commands everyone, everywhere, to repent. We decline that command at our own peril.

Paul went on to say that God has appointed a day in which he will judge the world (v. 31). In God's calendar, there is already a fixed date for the day of judgment. Each one of us will be brought before God to be judged by Christ on that date. Those who are Christ's will have him not only as their judge but also as their defense attorney. We will be garbed in his righteousness, which alone can meet the requirements of God. Those who are not in Christ will also appear before him, standing there on their own, as their every idle word is judged. The description in the New Testament of the response of the unbeliever on that day is always the same. Their response will be silence. When God reads the indictment and makes the charge against them, it will be so clear, so irrefutable, that every mouth will be stopped. People will see the utter futility of arguing with God about the record.

I once had a brilliant student in a course on modern philosophy. After graduation, he attended Harvard Medical School and specialized in psychiatry and neurobiology. After he had completed his postdoctoral work, he told me, "We are doing cutting-edge research and study into the function of the brain, brain synapses, the different ways in which the brain deals with data. You know, R.C., every single bit of your life and your experience is recorded in your brain." Then he added, "You know what terrifies me? I have a mental image of how God may judge us at the end of our lives. Perhaps he will take our brains out of our heads, put them on a table, plug them in, and listen to the playback. There will be incontrovertible evidence to us of what we have done."

Jesus says that the last judgment will be the end of secrets. Nothing will any longer be hidden. If the world knew everything we had ever done or thought, we would be ruined.

In the last judgment, there will be nowhere to flee. The things we have done in darkness will be brought to the light. People do not want to believe that there will, in fact, be a last judgment. But if Jesus of Nazareth taught anything as a teacher, he taught that there will be a final judgment. Paul echoed that teaching. There is a day coming that nobody will be able to erase.

Sec. 2. The end of God's appointing this day is for the manifestation of the glory of His mercy, in the eternal salvation of the elect; and of His justice, in the damnation of the reprobate, who are wicked and disobedient. For then shall the righteous go into everlasting life, and receive that fulness of joy and refreshing, which shall come from the presence of the Lord: but the wicked, who know not God, and obey not the Gospel of Jesus Christ, shall be cast into eternal torments, and be punished with everlasting destruction from the presence of the Lord, and from the glory of His power.

The opening phrase, **the end of**, means "the purpose of." The confession is stating the purpose for the last judgment. Both heaven and hell have the same ultimate purpose: to glorify God.

People argue for and against capital punishment. Those who argue against it insist it does no good, and will not deter anyone. Nor will it bring back the one who was killed. The only real justification for capital punishment is to satisfy the demands of justice. God instituted capital punishment in the Old Testament because life is sacred. He taught in the Noachic covenant that because people are made in the image of God, they are so precious that if someone willfully takes another person's life, he forfeits his own. God has placed his image on human beings, and he manifests the importance of that image by protecting individual lives. When the murderer is executed and justice prevails, the sanctity of human life is honored.

God created people who are in rebellion against him and who daily disobey his law, insult his dignity, and deny his glory. Yet he graciously saves some of us through Jesus Christ, and he manifests the glory of his grace in the salvation of the saints. But he also displays the glory of his righteousness by condemning the unsaved for their wickedness. Heaven declares the glory of God's grace. Hell declares the glory of God's justice. In both cases, the glory of God is made manifest.

No one will be able to say, when God dispenses a verdict at the last judgment, "That is not fair." Jonathan Edwards, in his famous sermon, "Sinners in the Hands of an Angry God," says that the only reason we do not fall into the fire is the grace of God. His hand has held us back. Edwards says, "Oh, sinner, you can give no reason why, since you got out of your bed this morning, God hasn't thrown you into that fire." His sermon is about grace, about the hand of God's mercy, which keeps his people from what they deserve.

Some people think that a good God would never actually punish anyone. But just the reverse is true. A judge who never punishes the wicked is not a good judge. And God is the perfect judge, whose judgment is good.

Sec. 3. As Christ would have us to be certainly persuaded that there shall be a day of judgment, both to deter all men from sin; and for the greater consolation of the godly in their adversity: so will He have that day unknown to men, that they may shake off all carnal security, and be always watchful, because they know not at what hour the Lord will come; and may be ever prepared to say, Come Lord Jesus, come quickly. Amen.

It is important that we understand the teaching of Christ with respect to the last judgment. This section tells us that **Christ would have us to be certainly persuaded that there shall be a day of judgment.** His reason is **both to deter all men from sin; and for the greater consolation of the godly in their adversity.** If people are persuaded that they will be held accountable by God for their behavior, they will be restrained in their evil, if only out of fear and enlightened self-interest. Even if they never come to full repentance and faith in Christ, they can, to some degree, ameliorate their punishment in hell. Scripture is clear that both in heaven and in hell there are degrees. There are degrees of blessedness in heaven, for each person will be rewarded according to his or her works. Their works are not meritorious, but God, in his grace, has determined to reward people according to their measure of service and obedience. There are at least twenty-five texts in the New Testament that speak of degrees of reward for godliness. We are encouraged to work out our salvation with fear and trembling. That does not mean that we can earn our way into heaven, because even the obedience we offer to Christ is rendered in his strength and by his grace. In the final analysis, we would still, by a strict standard of justice, be unprofitable servants, unable to claim any reward. Nevertheless, God graciously saves us on the grounds of Christ's righteousness, and also, in his grace, gives extra rewards to those who are obedient and diligent in serving Christ. We are given incentives to work for that reward, to store up for ourselves treasures in heaven. Augustine, in explaining the gracious aspect of God's rewards—not "because of" our works, but "according to" them—said that God will simply be crowning his own works.

192

In like manner, Paul warns against heaping up wrath for the day of wrath because, at the final judgment, those who are not believers will have to give an account before God for every single sin. They will receive a just punishment for their transgressions. God will judge them according to his perfect standard of righteousness. Jonathan Edwards encouraged the people of Northampton who were not certain of their salvation to be present at the preaching of the Word. Even if the gospel did not bring forth the fruit of salvation in their hearts, he said, at least they would have the benefit of restraint on their evil inclinations, making their punishment in hell less severe.

It is not just unbelievers who will face the judgment of God, but also believers. Many Christians seem to think that being saved means not having to stand before the judgment seat of Christ. It is true that we will not face condemnation, but we will still undergo an evaluation. Christ will examine our lives and determine our degree of obedience and sanctification. The knowledge that that examination awaits us at the last judgment should motivate us to be more diligent in our obedience and desire to please him, so that when we appear before him, he will say to us, "Well done, good and faithful servant."

The second advantage to knowing that the last judgment is coming is that it provides consolation to believers as they are mistreated in the world. This was of great importance to the early church and is certainly important to any Christian today who has suffered persecution. Our Lord tells us that if we are faithful to him in this life, we will encounter tribulation. The Christian can reasonably expect to be a victim of injustice in this world. Indeed, if we are not, it indicates that we have distanced ourselves from Christ. When we embrace him fully, we are called to participate in his humiliation, as well as in his exaltation. Christians are often downcast, but never bereft of hope. We need the comfort of God's promise that there will come a time when we will experience his vindication.

In his parable of the persistent widow, in Luke 18:1–8, Jesus describes a judge who has no regard either for people or for God. Luke tells us that Jesus taught this parable to encourage us always to pray and never to give up. In the parable, an importunate widow, a victim of injustice, goes before the judge for her vindication. The judge won't hear her case because he is corrupt and unjust. But the woman persists in her plea to the judge. Finally, to rid himself of this woman, he hears her case. The point of Jesus' parable is seen at the end: "And shall God not avenge His own elect who cry out day and night to Him? . . . Nevertheless, when the Son of Man comes, will He really find faith on the earth?" If a corrupt, insensitive human judge will on some occasions administer justice, how much more will the Judge of heaven and earth, who is perfectly righteous, make sure that those who have suffered unjustly for the name of Christ are vindicated in the end?

But then Jesus asks, "When I come, will I find anybody who needs to be vindicated?" He is speaking to us. Though the world despises Christ's people, and though we may never receive vindication or justice in this world, we have the absolute promise of God that he will vindicate his people who cry unto him day and night. Paul repeats the biblical teaching, "'Vengeance is Mine, I will repay,' says the Lord" (Rom. 12:19). When God pays the debt, he does it justly. We may be so blinded by our pain that we inflict more damage on the person who hurts us than justice requires. Vengeance is to be God's own activity, and we are to take heart that he will repay. The last judgment is part of the consolation that God provides.

Jonathan Edwards served the people of Northampton for many years. A member of his congregation opposed him and spread false rumors that attacked his character. People fed on the rumors, and a major crisis developed at the church. The church elders begged Edwards to speak to the matters and defend himself. Edwards didn't want to respond publicly to the false charges. The elders inquired, "Dr. Edwards, don't you want to be vindicated?" He replied that he did, but he thought that if he defended himself, that would be the extent of his defense. He believed that if he suffered those things in silence, then God himself would move heaven and earth to vindicate him, and Edwards preferred to have the vindication that God brings to bear, rather than anything that Edwards could accomplish on his own.

As a direct result of the slander, Edwards was removed from his church's pulpit, and he became a missionary to the Indians in Stockbridge, where he wrote *Freedom of the Will*. About ten years later, the man who had falsely accused him was so guilt-stricken about what he had done that he confessed publicly that he had lied. Edwards was completely vindicated, but in the meantime he had suffered the slander in silence. I'm not sure that we should always do that. I think there are times when we need to respond to slander. But we need to learn to expect it as part of the way of this world. When we are plunged into misery by unfair and unjust charges or other experiences, we are not to be as people without hope. We have God's promise that there will be a last judgment.

Edwards's final sermon at Northampton had no bitterness in it. He displayed his concern for his congregation. He told them that it wasn't the last time that they would meet together as pastor and congregation, because they would meet at least one more time—at the judgment throne of God. He commended the blessing of God on the people and left. When we feel that we have been wronged and that justice has not been served, we know that there will be the last judgment.

Section 3 continues: **So will He have that day unknown to men, that they may shake off all carnal security, and be always watchful, because they know not at what hour the Lord will come.** The Lord has told us that he will come. God has appointed a day. It is fixed. Nothing will cause it to be postponed.

The reason why God doesn't reveal the day is to keep us alert and ready. We are to flee from **carnal security**. The longer God delays judgment, the more people begin to assume that there will be no judgment. They think they will continue to get away with their sin with impunity. That is carnal security, the security of the flesh, the security of the hardened heart and of the stiff-necked person. It is a false security. We are to remind people that there will be a time of judgment, and that we do not know when it will be. It could be tonight; it could be tomorrow. It could be a thousand years from now.

There is a story about Dwight L. Moody, who preached an intense, fiery, evangelistic service one night in Chicago. At the close of the service, he told the people to go home and think about his admonition, and that the following week they would be called to make a decision. That very night, after the service, came the Great Chicago Fire. Many of those who had attended his service died. Moody said after that experience that he would never again postpone the calling of people to commit their lives to Christ. You never know if you have more time.

The confession ends with these words: **That they may . . . be always watchful, because they know not at what hour the Lord will come; and may be ever prepared to say, Come Lord Jesus [maranatha], come quickly. Amen.** These are the same words with which the New Testament ends, praying that Jesus will return quickly.

Are we prepared to say, "Lord, come"? Augustine said, "Lord, change me, but not yet." We should be in such a state of reconciliation with Christ that we earnestly desire that he not delay another day, but come right now. Do we instead say, "Lord, we want you to come, but give us a little bit of time to get our house in order or to take care of some things that we would like to accomplish." The prayer of the godly heart is "Lord come, and come quickly."

At the beginning of our study, I said that the Westminster Confession of Faith is a creedal statement, written by uninspired men. The confession is not sacred Scripture. It is not absolutely binding on our conscience. It was designed in the seventeenth century by Puritan divines to set forth the system of doctrine that is found in sacred Scripture. From my perspective as a professional theologian, I am convinced that in the history of Christendom there has never been written a more precise, more accurate, more thorough, and more comprehensive confession of faith. The Lord raised up bright and godly men to write this document. More than half of them were eventually excommunicated from the church by those who could not bear this doctrine. Those divines ended up saying, **Come Lord Jesus, come quickly.**

Appendix A

THE WESTMINSTER
LARGER CATECHISM

Q. 1. *What is the chief and highest end of man?*
A. Man's chief and highest end is to glorify God, and fully to enjoy him forever.

Q. 2. *How doth it appear that there is a God?*
A. The very light of nature in man, and the works of God, declare plainly that there is a God; but his word and Spirit only do sufficiently and effectually reveal him unto men for their salvation.

Q. 3. *What is the Word of God?*
A. The holy Scriptures of the Old and New Testament are the Word of God, the only rule of faith and obedience.

Q. 4. *How doth it appear that the Scriptures are the Word of God?*
A. The Scriptures manifest themselves to be the Word of God, by their majesty and purity; by the consent of all the parts, and the scope of the whole, which is to give all glory to God; by their light and power to convince and convert sinners, to comfort and build up believers unto salvation: but the Spirit of God bearing witness by and with the Scriptures in

199

the heart of man, is alone able fully to persuade it that they are the very Word of God.

Q. 5. *What do the Scriptures principally teach?*
A. The Scriptures principally teach what man is to believe concerning God, and what duty God requires of man.

WHAT MAN OUGHT TO BELIEVE CONCERNING GOD.

Q. 6. *What do the Scriptures make known of God?*
A. The Scriptures make known what God is, the persons in the Godhead, his decrees, and the execution of his decrees.

Q. 7. *What is God?*
A. God is a Spirit, in and of himself infinite in being, glory, blessedness, and perfection; all-sufficient, eternal, unchangeable, incomprehensible, every-where present, almighty, knowing all things, most wise, most holy, most just, most merciful and gracious, longsuffering, and abundant in goodness and truth.

Q. 8. *Are there more Gods than one?*
A. There is but one only, the living and true God.

Q. 9. *How many persons are there in the Godhead?*
A. There be three persons in the Godhead, the Father, the Son, and the Holy Ghost; and these three are one true, eternal God, the same in substance, equal in power and glory; although distinguished by their personal properties.

Q. 10. *What are the personal properties of the three persons in the Godhead?*
A. It is proper to the Father to beget the Son, and to the Son to be begotten of the Father, and to the Holy Ghost to proceed from the Father and the Son from all eternity.

Q. 11. *How doth it appear that the Son and the Holy Ghost are God equal with the Father?*

200

A. The Scriptures manifest that the Son and the Holy Ghost are God equal with the Father, ascribing unto them such names, attributes, works, and worship, as are proper to God only.

Q. 12. *What are the decrees of God?*
A. God's decrees are the wise, free, and holy acts of the counsel of his will, whereby, from all eternity, he hath, for his own glory, unchangeably foreordained whatsoever comes to pass in time, especially concerning angels and men.

Q. 13. *What hath God especially decreed concerning angels and men?*
A. God, by an eternal and immutable decree, out of his mere love, for the praise of his glorious grace, to be manifested in due time, hath elected some angels to glory; and in Christ hath chosen some men to eternal life, and the means thereof: and also, according to his sovereign power, and the unsearchable counsel of his own will (whereby he extendeth or withholdeth favor as he pleaseth), hath passed by and foreordained the rest to dishonor and wrath, to be for their sin inflicted, to the praise of the glory of his justice.

Q. 14. *How doth God execute his decrees?*
A. God executeth his decrees in the works of creation and providence, according to his infallible foreknowledge, and the free and immutable counsel of his own will.

Q. 15. *What is the work of creation?*
A. The work of creation is that wherein God did in the beginning, by the word of his power, make of nothing the world, and all things therein, for himself, within the space of six days, and all very good.

Q. 16. *How did God create angels?*
A. God created all the angels spirits, immortal, holy, excelling in knowledge, mighty in power, to execute his commandments, and to praise his name, yet subject to change.

Q. 17. *How did God create man?*
A. After God had made all other creatures, he created man male and female;

formed the body of the man of the dust of the ground, and the woman of the rib of the man, endued them with living, reasonable, and immortal souls; made them after his own image, in knowledge, righteousness, and holiness; having the law of God written in their hearts, and power to fulfill it, and dominion over the creatures; yet subject to fall.

Q. 18. *What are God's works of providence?*
A. God's works of providence are his most holy, wise, and powerful preserving and governing all his creatures; ordering them, and all their actions, to his own glory.

Q. 19. *What is God's providence towards the angels?*
A. God by his providence permitted some of the angels, willfully and irrecoverably, to fall into sin and damnation, limiting and ordering that, and all their sins, to his own glory; and established the rest in holiness and happiness; employing them all, at his pleasure, in the administrations of his power, mercy, and justice.

Q. 20. *What was the providence of God toward man in the estate in which he was created?*
A. The providence of God toward man in the estate in which he was created, was the placing him in paradise, appointing him to dress it, giving him liberty to eat of the fruit of the earth; putting the creatures under his dominion, and ordaining marriage for his help; affording him communion with himself; instituting the Sabbath; entering into a covenant of life with him, upon condition of personal, perfect, and perpetual obedience, of which the tree of life was a pledge; and forbidding to eat of the tree of the knowledge of good and evil, upon the pain of death.

Q. 21. *Did man continue in that estate wherein God at first created him?*
A. Our first parents being left to the freedom of their own will, through the temptation of Satan, transgressed the commandment of God in eating the forbidden fruit; and thereby fell from the estate of innocency wherein they were created.

Q. 22. *Did all mankind fall in that first transgression?*
A. The covenant being made with Adam as a public person, not for himself

202

only, but for his posterity, all mankind descending from him by ordinary generation, sinned in him, and fell with him in that first transgression.

Q. 23. *Into what estate did the fall bring mankind?*
A. The fall brought mankind into an estate of sin and misery.

Q. 24. *What is sin?*
A. Sin is any want of conformity unto, or transgression of, any law of God, given as a rule to the reasonable creature.

Q. 25. *Wherein consisteth the sinfulness of that estate whereinto man fell?*
A. The sinfulness of that estate whereinto man fell, consisteth in the guilt of Adam's first sin, the want of that righteousness wherein he was created, and the corruption of his nature, whereby he is utterly indisposed, disabled, and made opposite unto all that is spiritually good, and wholly inclined to all evil, and that continually; which is commonly called original sin, and from which do proceed all actual transgressions.

Q. 26. *How is original sin conveyed from our first parents unto their posterity?*
A. Original sin is conveyed from our first parents unto their posterity by natural generation, so as all that proceed from them in that way are conceived and born in sin.

Q. 27. *What misery did the fall bring upon mankind?*
A. The fall brought upon mankind the loss of communion with God, his displeasure and curse; so as we are by nature children of wrath, bond slaves to Satan, and justly liable to all punishments in this world, and that which is to come.

Q. 28. *What are the punishments of sin in this world?*
A. The punishments of sin in this world are either inward, as blindness of mind, a reprobate sense, strong delusions, hardness of heart, horror of conscience, and vile affections; or outward, as the curse of God upon the creatures for our sakes, and all other evils that befall us in our bodies, names, estates, relations, and employments; together with death itself.

Q. 29. *What are the punishments of sin in the world to come?*
A. The punishments of sin in the world to come, are everlasting separation from the comfortable presence of God, and most grievous torments in soul and body, without intermission, in hell-fire forever.

Q. 30. *Doth God leave all mankind to perish in the estate of sin and misery?*
A. God doth not leave all men to perish in the estate of sin and misery, into which they fell by the breach of the first covenant, commonly called the covenant of works; but of his mere love and mercy delivereth his elect out of it, and bringeth them into an estate of salvation by the second covenant, commonly called the covenant of grace.

Q. 31. *With whom was the covenant of grace made?*
A. The covenant of grace was made with Christ as the second Adam, and in him with all the elect as his seed.

Q. 32. *How is the grace of God manifested in the second covenant?*
A. The grace of God is manifested in the second covenant, in that he freely provideth and offereth to sinners a mediator, and life and salvation by him; and requiring faith as the condition to interest them in him, promiseth and giveth his Holy Spirit to all his elect, to work in them that faith, with all other saving graces; and to enable them unto all holy obedience, as the evidence of the truth of their faith and thankfulness to God, and as the way which he hath appointed them to salvation.

Q. 33. *Was the covenant of grace always administered after one and the same manner?*
A. The covenant of grace was not always administered after the same manner, but the administrations of it under the Old Testament were different from those under the New.

Q. 34. *How was the covenant of grace administered under the Old Testament?*
A. The covenant of grace was administered under the Old Testament, by promises, prophecies, sacrifices, circumcision, the passover, and other types and ordinances, which did all foresignify Christ then to come, and were for

that time sufficient to build up the elect in faith in the promised messiah, by whom they then had full remission of sin, and eternal salvation.

Q. 35. *How is the covenant of grace administered under the New Testament?*
A. Under the New Testament, when Christ the substance was exhibited, the same covenant of grace was and still is to be administered in the preaching of the word, and the administration of the sacraments of baptism and the Lord's supper; in which grace and salvation are held forth in more fullness, evidence, and efficacy, to all nations.

Q. 36. *Who is the mediator of the covenant of grace?*
A. The only mediator of the covenant of grace is the Lord Jesus Christ, who, being the eternal Son of God, of one substance and equal with the Father, in the fullness of time became man, and so was and continues to be God and man, in two entire distinct natures, and one person, forever.

Q. 37. *How did Christ, being the Son of God, become man?*
A. Christ the Son of God became man, by taking to himself a true body, and a reasonable soul, being conceived by the power of the Holy Ghost in the womb of the virgin Mary, of her substance, and born of her, yet without sin.

Q. 38. *Why was it requisite that the mediator should be God?*
A. It was requisite that the mediator should be God, that he might sustain and keep the human nature from sinking under the infinite wrath of God, and the power of death; give worth and efficacy to his sufferings, obedience, and intercession; and to satisfy God's justice, procure his favor, purchase a peculiar people, give his Spirit to them, conquer all their enemies, and bring them to everlasting salvation.

Q. 39. *Why was it requisite that the mediator should be man?*
A. It was requisite that the mediator should be man, that he might advance our nature, perform obedience to the law, suffer and make intercession for us in our nature, have a fellow-feeling of our infirmities; that we might receive the adoption of sons, and have comfort and access with boldness unto the throne of grace.

Q. 40. *Why was it requisite that the mediator should be God and man in one person?*
A. It was requisite that the mediator, who was to reconcile God and man, should himself be both God and man, and this in one person, that the proper works of each nature might be accepted of God for us, and relied on by us, as the works of the whole person.

Q. 41. *Why was our mediator called Jesus?*
A. Our mediator was called Jesus, because he saveth his people from their sins.

Q. 42. *Why was our mediator called Christ?*
A. Our mediator was called Christ, because he was anointed with the Holy Ghost above measure; and so set apart, and fully furnished with all authority and ability, to execute the offices of prophet, priest, and king of his church, in the estate both of his humiliation and exaltation.

Q. 43. *How doth Christ execute the office of a prophet?*
A. Christ executeth the office of a prophet, in his revealing to the church, in all ages, by his Spirit and word, in divers ways of administration, the whole will of God, in all things concerning their edification and salvation.

Q. 44. *How doth Christ execute the office of a priest?*
A. Christ executeth the office of a priest, in his once offering himself a sacrifice without spot to God, to be a reconciliation for the sins of the people; and in making continual intercession for them.

Q. 45. *How doth Christ execute the office of a king?*
A. Christ executeth the office of a king, in calling out of the world a people to himself, and giving them officers, laws, and censures, by which he visibly governs them; in bestowing saving grace upon his elect, rewarding their obedience, and correcting them for their sins, preserving and supporting them under all their temptations and sufferings, restraining and overcoming all their enemies, and powerfully ordering all things for his own glory, and their good; and also in taking vengeance on the rest, who know not God, and obey not the gospel.

206

Q. 46. *What was the estate of Christ's humiliation?*

A. The estate of Christ's humiliation was that low condition, wherein he for our sakes, emptying himself of his glory, took upon him the form of a servant, in his conception and birth, life, death, and after his death, until his resurrection.

Q. 47. *How did Christ humble himself in his conception and birth?*

A. Christ humbled himself in his conception and birth, in that, being from all eternity the Son of God, in the bosom of the Father, he was pleased in the fullness of time to become the son of man, made of a woman of low estate, and to be born of her; with divers circumstances of more than ordinary abasement.

Q. 48. *How did Christ humble himself in his life?*

A. Christ humbled himself in his life, by subjecting himself to the law, which he perfectly fulfilled; and by conflicting with the indignities of the world, temptations of Satan, and infirmities in his flesh, whether common to the nature of man, or particularly accompanying that his low condition.

Q. 49. *How did Christ humble himself in his death?*

A. Christ humbled himself in his death, in that having been betrayed by Judas, forsaken by his disciples, scorned and rejected by the world, condemned by Pilate, and tormented by his persecutors; having also conflicted with the terrors of death, and the powers of darkness, felt and borne the weight of God's wrath, he laid down his life an offering for sin, enduring the painful, shameful, and cursed death of the cross.

Q. 50. *Wherein consisted Christ's humiliation after his death?*

A. Christ's humiliation after his death consisted in his being buried, and continuing in the state of the dead, and under the power of death till the third day; which hath been otherwise expressed in these words, *He descended into hell.*

Q. 51. *What was the estate of Christ's exaltation?*

A. The estate of Christ's exaltation comprehendeth his resurrection, ascension, sitting at the right hand of the Father, and his coming again to judge the world.

Q. 52. *How was Christ exalted in his resurrection?*
A. Christ was exalted in his resurrection, in that, not having seen corruption in death (of which it was not possible for him to be held), and having the very same body in which he suffered, with the essential properties thereof (but without mortality, and other common infirmities belonging to this life), really united to his soul, he rose again from the dead the third day by his own power; whereby he declared himself to be the Son of God, to have satisfied divine justice, to have vanquished death, and him that had power of it, and to be Lord of quick and dead: all which he did as a public person, the head of his church, for the justification, quickening in grace, support against enemies, and to assure them of their resurrection from the dead at the last day.

Q. 53. *How was Christ exalted in his ascension?*
A. Christ was exalted in his ascension, in that having after his resurrection often appeared unto and conversed with his apostles, speaking to them of the things pertaining to the kingdom of God, and giving them commission to preach the gospel to all nations, forty days after his resurrection, he, in our nature, and as our head, triumphing over enemies, visibly went up into the highest heavens, there to receive gifts for men, to raise up our affections thither, and to prepare a place for us, where himself is, and shall continue till his second coming at the end of the world.

Q. 54. *How is Christ exalted in his sitting at the right hand of God?*
A. Christ is exalted in his sitting at the right hand of God, in that as God-man he is advanced to the highest favor with God the Father, with all fullness of joy, glory, and power over all things in heaven and earth; and doth gather and defend his church, and subdue their enemies; furnisheth his ministers and people with gifts and graces, and maketh intercession for them.

Q. 55. *How doth Christ make intercession?*
A. Christ maketh intercession, by his appearing in our nature continually before the Father in heaven, in the merit of his obedience and sacrifice on earth, declaring his will to have it applied to all believers; answering all accusa-

tions against them, and procuring for them quiet of conscience, notwith-standing daily failings, access with boldness to the throne of grace, and acceptance of their persons and services.

Q. 56. *How is Christ to be exalted in his coming again to judge the world?*
A. Christ is to be exalted in his coming again to judge the world, in that he, who was unjustly judged and condemned by wicked men, shall come again at the last day in great power, and in the full manifestation of his own glory, and of his Father's, with all his holy angels, with a shout, with the voice of the archangel, and with the trumpet of God, to judge the world in righteousness.

Q. 57. *What benefits hath Christ procured by his mediation?*
A. Christ, by his mediation, hath procured redemption, with all other benefits of the covenant of grace.

Q. 58. *How do we come to be made partakers of the benefits which Christ hath procured?*
A. We are made partakers of the benefits which Christ hath procured, by the application of them unto us, which is the work especially of God the Holy Ghost.

Q. 59. *Who are made partakers of redemption through Christ?*
A. Redemption is certainly applied, and effectually communicated, to all those for whom Christ hath purchased it; who are in time by the Holy Ghost enabled to believe in Christ according to the gospel. .

Q. 60. *Can they who have never heard the gospel, and so know not Jesus Christ, nor believe in him, be saved by their living according to the light of nature?*
A. They who, having never heard the gospel, know not Jesus Christ, and believe not in him, cannot be saved, be they never so diligent to frame their lives according to the light of nature, or the laws of that religion which they profess; neither is there salvation in any other, but in Christ alone, who is the Savior only of his body the church.

Q. 61. *Are all they saved who hear the gospel, and live in the church?*
A. All that hear the gospel, and live in the visible church, are not saved; but they only who are true members of the church invisible.

Q. 62. *What is the visible church?*
A. The visible church is a society made up of all such as in all ages and places of the world do profess the true religion, and of their children.

Q. 63. *What are the special privileges of the visible church?*
A. The visible church hath the privilege of being under God's special care and government; of being protected and preserved in all ages, notwithstanding the opposition of all enemies; and of enjoying the communion of saints, the ordinary means of salvation, and offers of grace by Christ to all the members of it in the ministry of the gospel, testifying, that whosoever believes in him shall be saved, and excluding none that will come unto him.

Q. 64. *What is the invisible church?*
A. The invisible church is the whole number of the elect, that have been, are, or shall be gathered into one under Christ the head.

Q. 65. *What special benefits do the members of the invisible church enjoy by Christ?*
A. The members of the invisible church by Christ enjoy union and communion with him in grace and glory.

Q. 66. *What is that union which the elect have with Christ?*
A. The union which the elect have with Christ is the work of God's grace, whereby they are spiritually and mystically, yet really and inseparably, joined to Christ as their head and husband; which is done in their effectual calling.

Q. 67. *What is effectual calling?*
A. Effectual calling is the work of God's almighty power and grace, whereby (out of his free and special love to his elect, and from nothing in them moving him thereunto) he doth, in his accepted time, invite and draw them to Jesus Christ, by his word and Spirit; savingly enlightening their minds, re-

newing and powerfully determining their wills, so as they (although in themselves dead in sin) are hereby made willing and able freely to answer his call, and to accept and embrace the grace offered and conveyed therein.

Q. 68. *Are the elect only effectually called?*
A. All the elect, and they only, are effectually called; although others may be, and often are, outwardly called by the ministry of the word, and have some common operations of the Spirit; who, for their willful neglect and contempt of the grace offered to them, being justly left in their unbelief, do never truly come to Jesus Christ.

Q. 69. *What is the communion in grace which the members of the invisible church have with Christ?*
A. The communion in grace which the members of the invisible church have with Christ, is their partaking of the virtue of his mediation, in their justification, adoption, sanctification, and whatever else, in this life, manifests their union with him.

Q. 70. *What is justification?*
A. Justification is an act of God's free grace unto sinners, in which he pardoneth all their sins, accepteth and accounteth their persons righteous in his sight; not for anything wrought in them, or done by them, but only for the perfect obedience and full satisfaction of Christ, by God imputed to them, and received by faith alone.

Q. 71. *How is justification an act of God's free grace?*
A. Although Christ, by his obedience and death, did make a proper, real, and full satisfaction to God's justice in the behalf of them that are justified; yet inasmuch as God accepteth the satisfaction from a surety, which he might have demanded of them, and did provide this surety, his own only Son, imputing his righteousness to them, and requiring nothing of them for their justification but faith, which also is his gift, their justification is to them of free grace.

Q. 72. *What is justifying faith?*
A. Justifying faith is a saving grace, wrought in the heart of a sinner by the

Spirit and Word of God, whereby he, being convinced of his sin and misery, and of the disability in himself and all other creatures to recover him out of his lost condition, not only assenteth to the truth of the promise of the gospel, but receiveth and resteth upon Christ and his righteousness, therein held forth, for pardon of sin, and for the accepting and accounting of his person righteous in the sight of God for salvation.

Q. 73. *How doth faith justify a sinner in the sight of God?*
A. Faith justifies a sinner in the sight of God, not because of those other graces which do always accompany it, or of good works that are the fruits of it, nor as if the grace of faith, or any act thereof, were imputed to him for his justification; but only as it is an instrument by which he receiveth and applieth Christ and his righteousness.

Q. 74. *What is adoption?*
A. Adoption is an act of the free grace of God, in and for his only Son Jesus Christ, whereby all those that are justified are received into the number of his children, have his name put upon them, the Spirit of his Son given to them, are under his fatherly care and dispensations, admitted to all the liberties and privileges of the sons of God, made heirs of all the promises, and fellow-heirs with Christ in glory.

Q. 75. *What is sanctification?*
A. Sanctification is a work of God's grace, whereby they whom God hath, before the foundation of the world, chosen to be holy, are in time, through the powerful operation of his Spirit applying the death and resurrection of Christ unto them, renewed in their whole man after the image of God; having the seeds of repentance unto life, and all other saving graces, put into their hearts, and those graces so stirred up, increased, and strengthened, as that they more and more die unto sin, and rise unto newness of life.

Q. 76. *What is repentance unto life?*
A. Repentance unto life is a saving grace, wrought in the heart of a sinner by the Spirit and Word of God, whereby, out of the sight and sense, not only of the danger, but also of the filthiness and odiousness of his sins, and

upon the apprehension of God's mercy in Christ to such as are penitent, he so grieves for and hates his sins, as that he turns from them all to God, purposing and endeavoring constantly to walk with him in all the ways of new obedience.

Q. 77. *Wherein do justification and sanctification differ?*
A. Although sanctification be inseparably joined with justification, yet they differ, in that God in justification imputeth the righteousness of Christ; in sanctification his Spirit infuseth grace, and enableth to the exercise thereof; in the former, sin is pardoned; in the other, it is subdued: the one doth equally free all believers from the revenging wrath of God, and that perfectly in this life, that they never fall into condemnation; the other is neither equal in all, nor in this life perfect in any, but growing up to perfection.

Q. 78. *Whence ariseth the imperfection of sanctification in believers?*
A. The imperfection of sanctification in believers ariseth from the remnants of sin abiding in every part of them, and the perpetual lustings of the flesh against the spirit; whereby they are often foiled with temptations, and fall into many sins, are hindered in all their spiritual services, and their best works are imperfect and defiled in the sight of God.

Q. 79. *May not true believers, by reason of their imperfections, and the many temptations and sins they are overtaken with, fall away from the state of grace?*
A. True believers, by reason of the unchangeable love of God, and his decree and covenant to give them perseverance, their inseparable union with Christ, his continual intercession for them, and the Spirit and seed of God abiding in them, can neither totally nor finally fall away from the state of grace, but are kept by the power of God through faith unto salvation.

Q. 80. *Can true believers be infallibly assured that they are in the estate of grace, and that they shall persevere therein unto salvation?*
A. Such as truly believe in Christ, and endeavor to walk in all good conscience before him, may, without extraordinary revelation, by faith grounded upon the truth of God's promises, and by the Spirit enabling them to discern in themselves those graces to which the promises of life are made, and

bearing witness with their spirits that they are the children of God, be infallibly assured that they are in the estate of grace, and shall persevere therein unto salvation.

Q. 81. *Are all true believers at all times assured of their present being in the estate of grace, and that they shall be saved?*
A. Assurance of grace and salvation not being of the essence of faith, true believers may wait long before they obtain it; and, after the enjoyment thereof, may have it weakened and intermitted, through manifold distempers, sins, temptations, and desertions; yet are they never left without such a presence and support of the Spirit of God as keeps them from sinking into utter despair.

Q. 82. *What is the communion in glory which the members of the invisible church have with Christ?*
A. The communion in glory which the members of the invisible church have with Christ, is in this life, immediately after death, and at last perfected at the resurrection and day of judgment.

Q. 83. *What is the communion in glory with Christ which the members of the invisible church enjoy in this life?*
A. The members of the invisible church have communicated to them in this life the firstfruits of glory with Christ, as they are members of him their head, and so in him are interested in that glory which he is fully possessed of; and, as an earnest thereof, enjoy the sense of God's love, peace of conscience, joy in the Holy Ghost, and hope of glory; as, on the contrary, sense of God's revenging wrath, horror of conscience, and a fearful expectation of judgment, are to the wicked the beginning of their torments which they shall endure after death.

Q. 84. *Shall all men die?*
A. Death being threatened as the wages of sin, it is appointed unto all men once to die; for that all have sinned.

Q. 85. *Death being the wages of sin, why are not the righteous delivered from death, seeing all their sins are forgiven in Christ?*

214

A. The righteous shall be delivered from death itself at the last day, and even in death are delivered from the sting and curse of it; so that, although they die, yet it is out of God's love, to free them perfectly from sin and misery, and to make them capable of further communion with Christ in glory, which they then enter upon.

Q. 86. *What is the communion in glory with Christ which the members of the invisible church enjoy immediately after death?*
A. The communion in glory with Christ which the members of the invisible church enjoy immediately after death, is, in that their souls are then made perfect in holiness, and received into the highest heavens, where they behold the face of God in light and glory, waiting for the full redemption of their bodies, which even in death continue united to Christ, and rest in their graves as in their beds, till at the last day they be again united to their souls. Whereas the souls of the wicked are at their death cast into hell, where they remain in torments and utter darkness, and their bodies kept in their graves, as in their prisons, till the resurrection and judgment of the great day.

Q. 87. *What are we to believe concerning the resurrection?*
A. We are to believe that at the last day there shall be a general resurrection of the dead, both of the just and unjust: when they that are then found alive shall in a moment be changed; and the selfsame bodies of the dead which were laid in the grave, being then again united to their souls forever, shall be raised up by the power of Christ. The bodies of the just, by the Spirit of Christ, and by virtue of his resurrection as their head, shall be raised in power, spiritual, incorruptible, and made like to his glorious body; and the bodies of the wicked shall be raised up in dishonor by him, as an offended judge.

Q. 88. *What shall immediately follow after the resurrection?*
A. Immediately after the resurrection shall follow the general and final judgment of angels and men; the day and hour whereof no man knoweth, that all may watch and pray, and be ever ready for the coming of the Lord.

Q. 89. *What shall be done to the wicked at the day of judgment?*
A. At the day of judgment, the wicked shall be set on Christ's left hand, and,

215

upon clear evidence, and full conviction of their own consciences, shall have the fearful but just sentence of condemnation pronounced against them; and thereupon shall be cast out from the favorable presence of God, and the glorious fellowship with Christ, his saints, and all his holy angels, into hell, to be punished with unspeakable torments, both of body and soul, with the devil and his angels forever.

Q. 90. *What shall be done to the righteous at the day of judgment?*
A. At the day of judgment, the righteous, being caught up to Christ in the clouds, shall be set on his right hand, and there openly acknowledged and acquitted, shall join with him in the judging of reprobate angels and men, and shall be received into heaven, where they shall be fully and forever freed from all sin and misery; filled with inconceivable joys, made perfectly holy and happy both in body and soul, in the company of innumerable saints and holy angels, but especially in the immediate vision and fruition of God the Father, of our Lord Jesus Christ, and of the Holy Spirit, to all eternity. And this is the perfect and full communion which the members of the invisible church shall enjoy with Christ in glory, at the resurrection and day of judgment.

HAVING SEEN WHAT THE SCRIPTURES PRINCIPALLY TEACH US TO BELIEVE CONCERNING GOD, IT FOLLOWS TO CONSIDER WHAT THEY REQUIRE AS THE DUTY OF MAN.

Q. 91. *What is the duty which God requireth of man?*
A. The duty which God requireth of man, is obedience to his revealed will.

Q. 92. *What did God first reveal unto man as the rule of his obedience?*
A. The rule of obedience revealed to Adam in the estate of innocence, and to all mankind in him, besides a special command not to eat of the fruit of the tree of the knowledge of good and evil, was the moral law.

Q. 93. *What is the moral law?*
A. The moral law is the declaration of the will of God to mankind, directing and binding every one to personal, perfect, and perpetual conformity and obedience thereunto, in the frame and disposition of the whole man, soul,

and body, and in performance of all those duties of holiness and righteousness which he oweth to God and man: promising life upon the fulfilling, and threatening death upon the breach of it.

Q. 94. *Is there any use of the moral law since the fall?*
A. Although no man, since the fall, can attain to righteousness and life by the moral law; yet there is great use thereof, as well common to all men, as peculiar either to the unregenerate, or the regenerate.

Q. 95. *Of what use is the moral law to all men?*
A. The moral law is of use to all men, to inform them of the holy nature and will of God, and of their duty, binding them to walk accordingly; to convince them of their disability to keep it, and of the sinful pollution of their nature, hearts, and lives: to humble them in the sense of their sin and misery, and thereby help them to a clearer sight of the need they have of Christ, and of the perfection of his obedience.

Q. 96. *What particular use is there of the moral law to unregenerate men?*
A. The moral law is of use to unregenerate men, to awaken their consciences to flee from the wrath to come, and to drive them to Christ; or, upon the continuance in the estate and way of sin, to leave them inexcusable, and under the curse thereof.

Q. 97. *What special use is there of the moral law to the regenerate?*
A. Although they that are regenerate, and believe in Christ, be delivered from the moral law as a covenant of works, so as thereby they are neither justified nor condemned; yet besides the general uses thereof common to them with all men, it is of special use, to show them how much they are bound to Christ for his fulfilling it, and enduring the curse thereof in their stead, and for their good; and thereby to provoke them to more thankfulness, and to express the same in their greater care to conform themselves thereunto as the rule of their obedience.

Q. 98. *Where is the moral law summarily comprehended?*
A. The moral law is summarily comprehended in the Ten Commandments,

which were delivered by the voice of God upon mount Sinai, and written by him in two tables of stone; and are recorded in the twentieth chapter of Exodus; the four first commandments containing our duty to God, and the other six our duty to man.

Q. 99. *What rules are to be observed for the right understanding of the Ten Commandments?*
A. For the right understanding of the Ten Commandments, these rules are to be observed:
1. That the law is perfect, and bindeth every one to full conformity in the whole man unto the righteousness thereof, and unto entire obedience forever; so as to require the utmost perfection of every duty, and to forbid the least degree of every sin.
2. That it is spiritual, and so reacheth the understanding, will, affections, and all other powers of the soul; as well as words, works, and gestures.
3. That one and the same thing, in divers respects, is required or forbidden in several commandments.
4. That as, where a duty is commanded, the contrary sin is forbidden; and, where a sin is forbidden, the contrary duty is commanded: so, where a promise is annexed, the contrary threatening is included; and, where a threatening is annexed, the contrary promise is included.
5. That what God forbids, is at no time to be done; what he commands, is always our duty; and yet every particular duty is not to be done at all times.
6. That under one sin or duty, all of the same kind are forbidden or commanded; together with all the causes, means, occasions, and appearances thereof, and provocations thereunto.
7. That what is forbidden or commanded to ourselves, we are bound, according to our places, to endeavor that it may be avoided or performed by others, according to the duty of their places.
8. That in what is commanded to others, we are bound, according to our places and callings, to be helpful to them; and to take heed of partaking with others in what is forbidden them.

Q. 100. *What special things are we to consider in the Ten Commandments?*
A. We are to consider, in the Ten Commandments, the preface, the substance

of the commandments themselves, and several reasons annexed to some of them, the more to enforce them.

Q. 101. *What is the preface to the Ten Commandments?*
A. The preface to the Ten Commandments is contained in these words, *I am the LORD thy God, which have brought thee out of the land of Egypt, out of the house of bondage.* Wherein God manifesteth his sovereignty, as being JEHOVAH, the eternal, immutable, and almighty God; having his being in and of himself, and giving being to all his words and works: and that he is a God in covenant, as with Israel of old, so with all his people; who, as he brought them out of their bondage in Egypt, so he delivereth us from our spiritual thraldom; and that therefore we are bound to take him for our God alone, and to keep all his commandments.

Q. 102. *What is the sum of the four commandments which contain our duty to God?*
A. The sum of the four commandments containing our duty to God, is, to love the Lord our God with all our heart, and with all our soul, and with all our strength, and with all our mind.

Q. 103. *Which is the first commandment?*
A. The first commandment is, *Thou shalt have no other gods before me.*

Q. 104. *What are the duties required in the first commandment?*
A. The duties required in the first commandment are, the knowing and acknowledging of God to be the only true God, and our God; and to worship and glorify him accordingly, by thinking, meditating, remembering, highly esteeming, honoring, adoring, choosing, loving, desiring, fearing of him; believing him; trusting, hoping, delighting, rejoicing in him; being zealous for him; calling upon him, giving all praise and thanks, and yielding all obedience and submission to him with the whole man; being careful in all things to please him, and sorrowful when in anything he is offended; and walking humbly with him.

Q. 105. *What are the sins forbidden in the first commandment?*
A. The sins forbidden in the first commandment, are, atheism, in denying or

219

not having a God; idolatry, in having or worshiping more gods than one, or any with or instead of the true God; the not having and avouching him for God, and our God; the omission or neglect of anything due to him, required in this commandment; ignorance, forgetfulness, misapprehensions, false opinions, unworthy and wicked thoughts of him; bold and curious searching into his secrets; all profaneness, hatred of God; self-love, self-seeking, and all other inordinate and immoderate setting of our mind, will, or affections upon other things, and taking them off from him in whole or in part; vain credulity, unbelief, heresy, misbelief, distrust, despair, incorrigibleness, and insensibleness under judgments, hardness of heart, pride, presumption, carnal security, tempting of God; using unlawful means, and trusting in lawful means; carnal delights and joys; corrupt, blind, and indiscreet zeal; lukewarmness, and deadness in the things of God; estranging ourselves, and apostatizing from God; praying, or giving any religious worship, to saints, angels, or any other creatures; all compacts and consulting with the devil, and hearkening to his suggestions; making men the lords of our faith and conscience; slighting and despising God and his commands; resisting and grieving of his Spirit, discontent and impatience at his dispensations, charging him foolishly for the evils he inflicts on us; and ascribing the praise of any good we either are, have, or can do, to fortune, idols, ourselves, or any other creature.

Q. 106. *What are we specially taught by these words, before me, in the first commandment?*
A. These words, *before me*, or before my face, in the first commandment, teach us, that God, who seeth all things, taketh special notice of, and is much displeased with, the sin of having any other God: that so it may be an argument to dissuade from it, and to aggravate it as a most impudent provocation: as also to persuade us to do as in his sight, whatever we do in his service.

Q. 107. *Which is the second commandment?*
A. The second commandment is, *Thou shalt not make unto thee any graven image, or any likeness of anything that is in heaven above, or that is in the earth beneath, or that is in the water under the earth. Thou shalt not bow down thyself to them, nor serve them: for I the* LORD *thy God am a jealous God, visiting the iniquity of the fathers upon the children unto the third and*

fourth generation of them that hate me; and shewing mercy unto thousands of them that love me, and keep my commandments.

Q. 108. *What are the duties required in the second commandment?*
A. The duties required in the second commandment are, the receiving, observing, and keeping pure and entire, all such religious worship and ordinances as God hath instituted in his word; particularly prayer and thanksgiving in the name of Christ; the reading, preaching, and hearing of the word; the administration and receiving of the sacraments; church government and discipline; the ministry and maintenance thereof; religious fasting; swearing by the name of God, and vowing unto him: as also the disapproving, detesting, opposing, all false worship; and, according to each one's place and calling, removing it, and all monuments of idolatry.

Q. 109. *What sins are forbidden in the second commandment?*
A. The sins forbidden in the second commandment are, all devising, counseling, commanding, using, and any wise approving, any religious worship not instituted by God himself; the making any representation of God, of all or of any of the three persons, either inwardly in our mind, or outwardly in any kind of image or likeness of any creature whatsoever; all worshiping of it, or God in it or by it; the making of any representation of feigned deities, and all worship of them, or service belonging to them; all superstitious devices, corrupting the worship of God, adding to it, or taking from it, whether invented and taken up of ourselves, or received by tradition from others, though under the title of antiquity, custom, devotion, good intent, or any other pretense whatsoever; simony; sacrilege; all neglect, contempt, hindering, and opposing the worship and ordinances which God hath appointed.

Q. 110. *What are the reasons annexed to the second commandment, the more to enforce it?*
A. The reasons annexed to the second commandment, the more to enforce it, contained in these words, *For I the LORD thy God am a jealous God, visiting the iniquity of the fathers upon the children unto the third and fourth generation of them that hate me; and shewing mercy unto thousands of them that love me, and keep my commandments*; are, besides God's sovereignty

221

over us, and propriety in us, his fervent zeal for his own worship, and his revengeful indignation against all false worship, as being a spiritual whoredom; accounting the breakers of this commandment such as hate him, and threatening to punish them unto divers generations; and esteeming the observers of it such as love him and keep his commandments, and promising mercy to them unto many generations.

Q. 111. *Which is the third commandment?*
A. The third commandment is, *Thou shalt not take the name of the Lord thy God in vain: for the Lord will not hold him guiltless that taketh his name in vain.*

Q. 112. *What is required in the third commandment?*
A. The third commandment requires, that the name of God, his titles, attributes, ordinances, the word, sacraments, prayer, oaths, vows, lots, his works, and whatsoever else there is whereby he makes himself known, be holily and reverently used in thought, meditation, word, and writing; by an holy profession, and answerable conversation, to the glory of God, and the good of ourselves, and others.

Q. 113. *What are the sins forbidden in the third commandment?*
A. The sins forbidden in the third commandment are, the not using of God's name as is required; and the abuse of it in an ignorant, vain, irreverent, profane, superstitious, or wicked mentioning or otherwise using his titles, attributes, ordinances, or works, by blasphemy, perjury; all sinful cursings, oaths, vows, and lots; violating of our oaths and vows, if lawful; and fulfilling them, if of things unlawful; murmuring and quarreling at, curious prying into, and misapplying of God's decrees and providences; misinterpreting, misapplying, or any way perverting the word, or any part of it, to profane jests, curious or unprofitable questions, vain janglings, or the maintaining of false doctrines; abusing it, the creatures, or anything contained under the name of God, to charms, or sinful lusts and practices; the maligning, scorning, reviling, or any wise opposing of God's truth, grace, and ways; making profession of religion in hypocrisy, or for sinister ends; being ashamed of it, or a shame to it, by unconformable, unwise, unfruitful, and offensive walking, or backsliding from it.

Q. 114. *What reasons are annexed to the third commandment?*
A. The reasons annexed to the third commandment, in these words, *The LORD thy God*, and, *For the LORD will not hold him guiltless that taketh his name in vain*, are, because he is the Lord and our God, therefore his name is not to be profaned, or any way abused by us; especially because he will be so far from acquitting and sparing the transgressors of this commandment, as that he will not suffer them to escape his righteous judgment, albeit many such escape the censures and punishments of men.

Q. 115. *Which is the fourth commandment?*
A. The fourth commandment is, *Remember the sabbath day, to keep it holy. Six days shalt thou labor, and do all thy work; but the seventh day is the sabbath of the LORD thy God: in it thou shalt not do any work, thou, nor thy son, nor thy daughter, thy manservant, nor thy maidservant, nor thy cattle, nor thy stranger that is within thy gates. For in six days the LORD made heaven and earth, the sea, and all that in them is, and rested the seventh day: wherefore the LORD blessed the sabbath day, and hallowed it.*

Q. 116. *What is required in the fourth commandment?*
A. The fourth commandment requireth of all men the sanctifying or keeping holy to God such set times as he hath appointed in his word, expressly one whole day in seven; which was the seventh from the beginning of the world to the resurrection of Christ, and the first day of the week ever since, and so to continue to the end of the world; which is the Christian sabbath, and in the New Testament called *The Lord's Day*.

Q. 117. *How is the sabbath or the Lord's day to be sanctified?*
A. The sabbath or Lord's day is to be sanctified by an holy resting all the day, not only from such works as are at all times sinful, but even from such worldly employments and recreations as are on other days lawful; and making it our delight to spend the whole time (except so much of it as is to be taken up in works of necessity and mercy) in the public and private exercises of God's worship: and, to that end, we are to prepare our hearts, and with such foresight, diligence, and moderation, to dispose and seasonably dispatch our worldly business, that we may be the more free and fit for the duties of that day.

223

Q. 118. *Why is the charge of keeping the sabbath more specially directed to governors of families, and other superiors?*
A. The charge of keeping the sabbath is more specially directed to governors of families, and other superiors, because they are bound not only to keep it themselves, but to see that it be observed by all those that are under their charge; and because they are prone ofttimes to hinder them by employments of their own.

Q. 119. *What are the sins forbidden in the fourth commandment?*
A. The sins forbidden in the fourth commandment are, all omissions of the duties required, all careless, negligent, and unprofitable performing of them, and being weary of them; all profaning the day by idleness, and doing that which is in itself sinful; and by all needless works, words, and thoughts, about our worldly employments and recreations.

Q. 120. *What are the reasons annexed to the fourth commandment, the more to enforce it?*
A. The reasons annexed to the fourth commandment, the more to enforce it, are taken from the equity of it, God allowing us six days of seven for our own affairs, and reserving but one for himself, in these words, *Six days shalt thou labor, and do all thy work*: from God's challenging a special propriety in that day, *The seventh day is the sabbath of the LORD thy God*: from the example of God, who *in six days . . . made heaven and earth, the sea, and all that in them is, and rested the seventh day*: and from that blessing which God put upon that day, not only in sanctifying it to be a day for his service, but in ordaining it to be a means of blessing to us in our sanctifying it; *Wherefore the LORD blessed the sabbath day, and hallowed it.*

Q. 121. *Why is the word* Remember *set in the beginning of the fourth commandment?*
A. The word *Remember* is set in the beginning of the fourth commandment, partly, because of the great benefit of remembering it, we being thereby helped in our preparation to keep it, and, in keeping it, better to keep all the rest of the commandments, and to continue a thankful remembrance of the two great benefits of creation and redemption, which contain a short abridgment of re-

224

ligion; and partly, because we are very ready to forget it, for that there is less light of nature for it, and yet it restraineth our natural liberty in things at other times lawful; that it cometh but once in seven days, and many worldly businesses come between, and too often take off our minds from thinking of it, either to prepare for it, or to sanctify it; and that Satan with his instruments much labor to blot out the glory, and even the memory of it, to bring in all irreligion and impiety.

Q. 122. *What is the sum of the six commandments which contain our duty to man?*
A. The sum of the six commandments which contain our duty to man, is, to love our neighbor as ourselves, and to do to others what we would have them do to us.

Q. 123. *Which is the fifth commandment?*
A. The fifth commandment is, *Honour thy father and thy mother: that thy days may be long upon the land which the Lord thy God giveth thee.*

Q. 124. *Who are meant by* father *and* mother *in the fifth commandment?*
A. By *father* and *mother*, in the fifth commandment, are meant, not only natural parents, but all superiors in age and gifts; and especially such as, by God's ordinance, are over us in place of authority, whether in family, church, or commonwealth.

Q. 125. *Why are superiors styled* Father *and* Mother?
A. Superiors are styled *Father* and *Mother*, both to teach them in all duties toward their inferiors, like natural parents, to express love and tenderness to them, according to their several relations; and to work inferiors to a greater willingness and cheerfulness in performing their duties to their superiors, as to their parents.

Q. 126. *What is the general scope of the fifth commandment?*
A. The general scope of the fifth commandment is, the performance of those duties which we mutually owe in our several relations, as inferiors, superiors or equals.

Q. 127. *What is the honor that inferiors owe to their superiors?*
A. The honor which inferiors owe to their superiors is, all due reverence in heart, word, and behavior; prayer and thanksgiving for them; imitation of their virtues and graces; willing obedience to their lawful commands and counsels; due submission to their corrections; fidelity to, defense, and maintenance of their persons and authority, according to their several ranks, and the nature of their places; bearing with their infirmities, and covering them in love, that so they may be an honor to them and to their government.

Q. 128. *What are the sins of inferiors against their superiors?*
A. The sins of inferiors against their superiors are, all neglect of the duties required toward them; envying at, contempt of, and rebellion against their persons and places, in their lawful counsels, commands, and corrections; cursing, mocking, and all such refractory and scandalous carriage, as proves a shame and dishonor to them and their government.

Q. 129. *What is required of superiors towards their inferiors?*
A. It is required of superiors, according to that power they receive from God, and that relation wherein they stand, to love, pray for, and bless their inferiors; to instruct, counsel, and admonish them; countenancing, commending, and rewarding such as do well; and discountenancing, reproving, and chastising such as do ill; protecting, and providing for them all things necessary for soul and body: and by grave, wise, holy, and exemplary carriage, to procure glory to God, honor to themselves, and so to preserve that authority which God hath put upon them.

Q. 130. *What are the sins of superiors?*
A. The sins of superiors are, besides the neglect of the duties required of them, an inordinate seeking of themselves, their own glory, ease, profit, or pleasure; commanding things unlawful, or not in the power of inferiors to perform; counseling, encouraging, or favoring them in that which is evil; dissuading, discouraging, or discountenancing them in that which is good; correcting them unduly; careless exposing, or leaving them to wrong, temptation, and danger; provoking them to wrath; or any way dishonoring themselves, or lessening their authority, by an unjust, indiscreet, rigorous, or remiss behavior.

Q. 131. *What are the duties of equals?*
A. The duties of equals are, to regard the dignity and worth of each other, in giving honor to go one before another; and to rejoice in each others' gifts and advancement, as their own.

Q. 132. *What are the sins of equals?*
A. The sins of equals are, besides the neglect of the duties required, the undervaluing of the worth, envying the gifts, grieving at the advancement or prosperity one of another; and usurping preeminence one over another.

Q. 133. *What is the reason annexed to the fifth commandment, the more to enforce it?*
A. The reason annexed to the fifth commandment, in these words, *That thy days may be long upon the land which the LORD thy God giveth thee*, is an express promise of long life and prosperity, as far as it shall serve for God's glory and their own good, to all such as keep this commandment.

Q. 134. *Which is the sixth commandment?*
A. The sixth commandment is, *Thou shalt not kill.*

Q. 135. *What are the duties required in the sixth commandment?*
A. The duties required in the sixth commandment are, all careful studies, and lawful endeavors, to preserve the life of ourselves and others by resisting all thoughts and purposes, subduing all passions, and avoiding all occasions, temptations, and practices, which tend to the unjust taking away the life of any; by just defense thereof against violence, patient bearing of the hand of God, quietness of mind, cheerfulness of spirit; a sober use of meat, drink, physic, sleep, labor, and recreations; by charitable thoughts, love, compassion, meekness, gentleness, kindness; peaceable, mild and courteous speeches and behavior; forbearance, readiness to be reconciled, patient bearing and forgiving of injuries, and requiting good for evil; comforting and succoring the distressed, and protecting and defending the innocent.

Q. 136. *What are the sins forbidden in the sixth commandment?*
A. The sins forbidden in the sixth commandment are, all taking away the

life of ourselves, or of others, except in case of public justice, lawful war, or necessary defense; the neglecting or withdrawing the lawful and necessary means of preservation of life; sinful anger, hatred, envy, desire of revenge; all excessive passions, distracting cares; immoderate use of meat, drink, labor, and recreations; provoking words, oppression, quarreling, striking, wounding, and whatsoever else tends to the destruction of the life of any.

Q. 137. *Which is the seventh commandment?*
A. The seventh commandment is, *Thou shalt not commit adultery.*

Q. 138. *What are the duties required in the seventh commandment?*
A. The duties required in the seventh commandment are, chastity in body, mind, affections, words, and behavior; and the preservation of it in ourselves and others; watchfulness over the eyes and all the senses; temperance, keeping of chaste company, modesty in apparel; marriage by those that have not the gift of continency, conjugal love, and cohabitation; diligent labor in our callings; shunning all occasions of uncleanness, and resisting temptations thereunto.

Q. 139. *What are the sins forbidden in the seventh commandment?*
A. The sins forbidden in the seventh commandment, besides the neglect of the duties required, are, adultery, fornication, rape, incest, sodomy, and all unnatural lusts; all unclean imaginations, thoughts, purposes, and affections; all corrupt or filthy communications, or listening thereunto; wanton looks, impudent or light behavior, immodest apparel; prohibiting of lawful, and dispensing with unlawful marriages; allowing, tolerating, keeping of stews, and resorting to them; entangling vows of single life, undue delay of marriage; having more wives or husbands than one at the same time; unjust divorce, or desertion; idleness, gluttony, drunkenness, unchaste company; lascivious songs, books, pictures, dancings, stage plays; and all other provocations to, or acts of uncleanness, either in ourselves or others.

Q. 140. *Which is the eighth commandment?*
A. The eighth commandment is, *Thou shalt not steal.*

Q. 141. *What are the duties required in the eighth commandment?*
A. The duties required in the eighth commandment are, truth, faithfulness, and justice in contracts and commerce between man and man; rendering to every one his due; restitution of goods unlawfully detained from the right owners thereof; giving and lending freely, according to our abilities, and the necessities of others; moderation of our judgments, wills, and affections concerning worldly goods; a provident care and study to get, keep, use, and dispose these things which are necessary and convenient for the sustentation of our nature, and suitable to our condition; a lawful calling, and diligence in it; frugality; avoiding unnecessary lawsuits, and suretiship, or other like engagements; and an endeavor, by all just and lawful means, to procure, preserve, and further the wealth and outward estate of others, as well as our own.

Q. 142. *What are the sins forbidden in the eighth commandment?*
A. The sins forbidden in the eighth commandment, besides the neglect of the duties required, are, theft, robbery, man-stealing, and receiving anything that is stolen; fraudulent dealing, false weights and measures, removing landmarks, injustice and unfaithfulness in contracts between man and man, or in matters of trust; oppression, extortion, usury, bribery, vexatious lawsuits, unjust enclosures and depredation; engrossing commodities to enhance the price; unlawful callings, and all other unjust or sinful ways of taking or withholding from our neighbor what belongs to him, or of enriching ourselves; covetousness; inordinate prizing and affecting worldly goods; distrustful and distracting cares and studies in getting, keeping, and using them; envying at the prosperity of others; as likewise idleness, prodigality, wasteful gaming; and all other ways whereby we do unduly prejudice our own outward estate, and defrauding ourselves of the due use and comfort of that estate which God hath given us.

Q. 143. *Which is the ninth commandment?*
A. The ninth commandment is, *Thou shalt not bear false witness against thy neighbour.*

Q. 144. *What are the duties required in the ninth commandment?*
A. The duties required in the ninth commandment are, the preserving and promoting of truth between man and man, and the good name of our

neighbor, as well as our own; appearing and standing for the truth; and from the heart, sincerely, freely, clearly, and fully, speaking the truth, and only the truth, in matters of judgment and justice, and in all other things whatsoever; a charitable esteem of our neighbors; loving, desiring, and rejoicing in their good name; sorrowing for and covering of their infirmities; freely acknowledging of their gifts and graces, defending their innocency; a ready receiving of a good report, and unwillingness to admit of an evil report, concerning them; discouraging talebearers, flatterers, and slanderers; love and care of our own good name, and defending it when need requireth; keeping of lawful promises; studying and practicing of whatsoever things are true, honest, lovely, and of good report.

Q. 145. *What are the sins forbidden in the ninth commandment?*
A. The sins forbidden in the ninth commandment are, all prejudicing the truth, and the good name of our neighbors, as well as our own, especially in public judicature; giving false evidence, suborning false witnesses, wittingly appearing and pleading for an evil cause, outfacing and overbearing the truth; passing unjust sentence, calling evil good, and good evil; rewarding the wicked according to the work of the righteous, and the righteous according to the work of the wicked; forgery, concealing the truth, undue silence in a just cause, and holding our peace when iniquity calleth for either a reproof from ourselves, or complaint to others; speaking the truth unseasonably, or maliciously to a wrong end, or perverting it to a wrong meaning, or in doubtful or equivocal expressions, to the prejudice of the truth or justice; speaking untruth, lying, slandering, backbiting, detracting, talebearing, whispering, scoffing, reviling, rash, harsh, and partial censuring; misconstructing intentions, words, and actions; flattering, vainglorious boasting, thinking or speaking too highly or too meanly of ourselves or others; denying the gifts and graces of God; aggravating smaller faults; hiding, excusing, or extenuating of sins, when called to a free confession; unnecessary discovering of infirmities; raising false rumors, receiving and countenancing evil reports, and stopping our ears against just defense; evil suspicion; envying or grieving at the deserved credit of any; endeavoring or desiring to impair it, rejoicing in their disgrace and infamy; scornful contempt, fond admiration; breach of lawful promises; neglecting such things as are of good report, and practicing, or not avoiding ourselves, or not hindering what we can in others, such things as procure an ill name.

230

Q. 146. *Which is the tenth commandment?*
A. The tenth commandment is, *Thou shalt not covet thy neighbour's house, thou shalt not covet thy neighbor's wife, nor his manservant, nor his maidservant, nor his ox, nor his ass, nor anything that is thy neighbour's.*

Q. 147. *What are the duties required in the tenth commandment?*
A. The duties required in the tenth commandment are, such a full contentment with our own condition, and such a charitable frame of the whole soul toward our neighbor, as that all our inward motions and affections touching him, tend unto, and further all that good which is his.

Q. 148. *What are the sins forbidden in the tenth commandment?*
A. The sins forbidden in the tenth commandment are, discontentment with our own estate; envying and grieving at the good of our neighbor, together with all inordinate motions and affections to anything that is his.

Q. 149. *Is any man able perfectly to keep the commandments of God?*
A. No man is able, either of himself, or by any grace received in this life, perfectly to keep the commandments of God; but doth daily break them in thought, word, and deed,

Q. 150. *Are all transgressions of the law of God equally heinous in themselves, and in the sight of God?*
A. All transgressions of the law are not equally heinous; but some sins in themselves, and by reason of several aggravations, are more heinous in the sight of God than others.

Q. 151. *What are those aggravations that make some sins more heinous than others?*
A. Sins receive their aggravations,
1. From the persons offending; if they be of riper age, greater experience or grace, eminent for profession, gifts, place, office, guides to others, and whose example is likely to be followed by others.
2. From the parties offended: if immediately against God, his attributes, and worship; against Christ, and his grace; the Holy Spirit, his witness, and work-

ings; against superiors, men of eminency, and such as we stand especially related and engaged unto; against any of the saints, particularly weak brethren, the souls of them, or any other, and the common good of all or many.

3. From the nature and quality of the offence: if it be against the express letter of the law, break many commandments, contain in it many sins: if not only conceived in the heart, but breaks forth in words and actions, scandalize others, and admit of no reparation: if against means, mercies, judgments, light of nature, conviction of conscience, public or private admonition, censures of the church, civil punishments; and our prayers, purposes, promises, vows, covenants, and engagements to God or men: if done deliberately, willfully, presumptuously, impudently, boastingly, maliciously, frequently, obstinately, with delight, continuance, or relapsing after repentance.

4. From circumstances of time, and place: if on the Lord's day, or other times of divine worship; or immediately before or after these, or other helps to prevent or remedy such miscarriages: if in public, or in the presence of others, who are thereby likely to be provoked or defiled.

Q. 152. *What doth every sin deserve at the hands of God?*
A. Every sin, even the least, being against the sovereignty, goodness, and holiness of God, and against his righteous law, deserveth his wrath and curse, both in this life, and that which is to come; and cannot be expiated but by the blood of Christ.

Q. 153. *What doth God require of us, that we may escape his wrath and curse due to us by reason of the transgression of the law?*
A. That we may escape the wrath and curse of God due to us by reason of the transgression of the law, he requireth of us repentance toward God, and faith toward our Lord Jesus Christ, and the diligent use of the outward means whereby Christ communicates to us the benefits of his mediation.

Q. 154. *What are the outward means whereby Christ communicates to us the benefits of his mediation?*
A. The outward and ordinary means whereby Christ communicates to his church the benefits of his mediation, are all his ordinances; especially the word, sacraments, and prayer; all which are made effectual to the elect for their salvation.

Q. 155. *How is the word made effectual to salvation?*
A. The Spirit of God maketh the reading, but especially the preaching of the word, an effectual means of enlightening, convincing, and humbling sinners; of driving them out of themselves, and drawing them unto Christ; of conforming them to his image, and subduing them to his will; of strengthening them against temptations and corruptions; or building them up in grace, and establishing their hearts in holiness and comfort through faith unto salvation.

Q. 156. *Is the Word of God to be read by all?*
A. Although all are not to be permitted to read the word publicly to the congregation, yet all sorts of people are bound to read it apart by themselves, and with their families: to which end, the holy Scriptures are to be translated out of the original into vulgar languages.

Q. 157. *How is the Word of God to be read?*
A. The holy Scriptures are to be read with an high and reverent esteem of them; with a firm persuasion that they are the very Word of God, and that he only can enable us to understand them; with desire to know, believe, and obey the will of God revealed in them; with diligence, and attention to the matter and scope of them; with meditation, application, self-denial, and prayer.

Q. 158. *By whom is the Word of God to be preached?*
A. The Word of God is to be preached only by such as are sufficiently gifted, and also duly approved and called to that office.

Q. 159. *How is the Word of God to be preached by those that are called thereunto?*
A. They that are called to labor in the ministry of the word, are to preach sound doctrine, diligently, in season and out of season; plainly, not in the enticing words of man's wisdom, but in demonstration of the Spirit, and of power; faithfully, making known the whole counsel of God; wisely, applying themselves to the necessities and capacities of the hearers; zealously, with fervent love to God and the souls of his people; sincerely, aiming at his glory, and their conversion, edification, and salvation.

233

Q. 160. *What is required of those that hear the word preached?*
A. It is required of those that hear the word preached, that they attend upon it with diligence, preparation, and prayer; examine what they hear by the Scriptures; receive the truth with faith, love, meekness, and readiness of mind, as the Word of God; meditate, and confer of it; hide it in their hearts, and bring forth the fruit of it in their lives.

Q. 161. *How do the sacraments become effectual means of salvation?*
A. The sacraments become effectual means of salvation, not by any power in themselves, or any virtue derived from the piety or intention of him by whom they are administered, but only by the working of the Holy Ghost, and the blessing of Christ, by whom they are instituted.

Q. 162. *What is a sacrament?*
A. A sacrament is an holy ordinance instituted by Christ in his church, to signify, seal, and exhibit unto those that are within the covenant of grace, the benefits of his mediation; to strengthen and increase their faith, and all other graces; to oblige them to obedience; to testify and cherish their love and communion one with another; and to distinguish them from those that are without.

Q. 163. *What are the parts of a sacrament?*
A. The parts of a sacrament are two; the one an outward and sensible sign, used according to Christ's own appointment; the other an inward and spiritual grace thereby signified.

Q. 164. *How many sacraments hath Christ instituted in his church under the New Testament?*
A. Under the New Testament Christ hath instituted in his church only two sacraments, baptism and the Lord's supper.

Q. 165. *What is baptism?*
A. Baptism is a sacrament of the New Testament, wherein Christ hath ordained the washing with water in the name of the Father, and of the Son, and of the Holy Ghost, to be a sign and seal of ingrafting into himself, of remis-

sion of sins by his blood, and regeneration by his Spirit; of adoption, and resurrection unto everlasting life; and whereby the parties baptized are solemnly admitted into the visible church, and enter into an open and professed engagement to be wholly and only the Lord's.

Q. 166. *Unto whom is baptism to be administered?*

A. Baptism is not to be administered to any that are out of the visible church, and so strangers from the covenant of promise, till they profess their faith in Christ, and obedience to him, but infants descending from parents, either both, or but one of them, professing faith in Christ, and obedience to him, are in that respect within the covenant, and to be baptized.

Q. 167. *How is baptism to be improved by us?*

A. The needful but much neglected duty of improving our baptism, is to be performed by us all our life long, especially in the time of temptation, and when we are present at the administration of it to others; by serious and thankful consideration of the nature of it, and of the ends for which Christ instituted it, the privileges and benefits conferred and sealed thereby, and our solemn vow made therein; by being humbled for our sinful defilement, our falling short of, and walking contrary to, the grace of baptism, and our engagements; by growing up to assurance of pardon of sin, and of all other blessings sealed to us in that sacrament; by drawing strength from the death and resurrection of Christ, into whom we are baptized, for the mortifying of sin, and quickening of grace; and by endeavoring to live by faith, to have our conversation in holiness and righteousness, as those that have therein given up their names to Christ; and to walk in brotherly love, as being baptized by the same Spirit into one body.

Q. 168. *What is the Lord's supper?*

A. The Lord's supper is a sacrament of the New Testament, wherein, by giving and receiving bread and wine according to the appointment of Jesus Christ, his death is showed forth; and they that worthily communicate feed upon his body and blood, to their spiritual nourishment and growth in grace; have their union and communion with him confirmed; testify and renew their thankfulness, and engagement to God, and their mutual love and fellowship each with other, as members of the same mystical body.

Q. 169. *How hath Christ appointed bread and wine to be given and received in the sacrament of the Lord's supper?*

A. Christ hath appointed the ministers of his word, in the administration of this sacrament of the Lord's supper, to set apart the bread and wine from common use, by the word of institution, thanksgiving, and prayer; to take and break the bread, and to give both the bread and the wine to the communicants: who are, by the same appointment, to take and eat the bread, and to drink the wine, in thankful remembrance that the body of Christ was broken and given, and his blood shed, for them.

Q. 170. *How do they that worthily communicate in the Lord's supper feed upon the body and blood of Christ therein?*

A. As the body and blood of Christ are not corporally or carnally present in, with, or under the bread and wine in the Lord's supper, and yet are spiritually present to the faith of the receiver, no less truly and really than the elements themselves are to their outward senses; so they that worthily communicate in the sacrament of the Lord's supper, do therein feed upon the body and blood of Christ, not after a corporal and carnal, but in a spiritual manner; yet truly and really, while by faith they receive and apply unto themselves Christ crucified, and all the benefits of his death.

Q. 171. *How are they that receive the sacrament of the Lord's supper to prepare themselves before they come unto it?*

A. They that receive the sacrament of the Lord's supper are, before they come, to prepare themselves thereunto, by examining themselves of their being in Christ, of their sins and wants; of the truth and measure of their knowledge, faith, repentance; love to God and the brethren, charity to all men, forgiving those that have done them wrong; of their desires after Christ, and of their new obedience; and by renewing the exercise of these graces, by serious meditation, and fervent prayer.

Q. 172. *May one who doubteth of his being in Christ, or of his due preparation, come to the Lord's supper?*

A. One who doubteth of his being in Christ, or of his due preparation to the sacrament of the Lord's supper, may have true interest in Christ, though he

236

be not yet assured thereof; and in God's account hath it, if he be duly affected with the apprehension of the want of it, and unfeignedly desires to be found in Christ, and to depart from iniquity: in which case (because promises are made, and this sacrament is appointed, for the relief even of weak and doubting Christians) he is to bewail his unbelief, and labor to have his doubts resolved; and, so doing, he may and ought to come to the Lord's supper, that he may be further strengthened.

Q. 173. *May any who profess the faith, and desire to come to the Lord's supper, be kept from it?*
A. Such as are found to be ignorant or scandalous, notwithstanding their profession of the faith, and desire to come to the Lord's supper, may and ought to be kept from that sacrament, by the power which Christ hath left in his church, until they receive instruction, and manifest their reformation.

Q. 174. *What is required of them that receive the sacrament of the Lord's supper in the time of the administration of it?*
A. It is required of them that receive the sacrament of the Lord's supper, that, during the time of the administration of it, with all holy reverence and attention they wait upon God in that ordinance, diligently observe the sacramental elements and actions, heedfully discern the Lord's body, and affectionately meditate on his death and sufferings, and thereby stir up themselves to a vigorous exercise of their graces; in judging themselves, and sorrowing for sin; in earnest hungering and thirsting after Christ, feeding on him by faith, receiving of his fullness, trusting in his merits, rejoicing in his love, giving thanks for his grace; in renewing of their covenant with God, and love to all the saints.

Q. 175. *What is the duty of Christians, after they have received the sacrament of the Lord's supper?*
A. The duty of Christians, after they have received the sacrament of the Lord's supper, is seriously to consider how they have behaved themselves therein, and with what success; if they find quickening and comfort, to bless God for it, beg the continuance of it, watch against relapses, fulfill their vows, and encourage themselves to a frequent attendance on that ordinance: but if they find no present benefit, more exactly to review their preparation to, and

237

carriage at, the sacrament; in both which, if they can approve themselves to God and their own consciences, they are to wait for the fruit of it in due time: but, if they see they have failed in either, they are to be humbled, and to attend upon it afterwards with more care and diligence.

Q. 176. *Wherein do the sacraments of baptism and the Lord's supper agree?*
A. The sacraments of baptism and the Lord's supper agree, in that the author of both is God; the spiritual part of both is Christ and his benefits; both are seals of the same covenant, are to be dispensed by ministers of the gospel, and by none other; and to be continued in the church of Christ until his second coming.

Q. 177. *Wherein do the sacraments of baptism and the Lord's supper differ?*
A. The sacraments of baptism and the Lord's supper differ, in that baptism is to be administered but once, with water, to be a sign and seal of our regeneration and ingrafting into Christ, and that even to infants; whereas the Lord's supper is to be administered often, in the elements of bread and wine, to represent and exhibit Christ as spiritual nourishment to the soul, and to confirm our continuance and growth in him, and that only to such as are of years and ability to examine themselves.

Q. 178. *What is prayer?*
A. Prayer is an offering up of our desires unto God, in the name of Christ, by the help of his Spirit; with confession of our sins, and thankful acknowledgement of his mercies.

Q. 179. *Are we to pray unto God only?*
A. God only being able to search the hearts, hear the requests, pardon the sins, and fulfill the desires of all; and only to be believed in, and worshiped with religious worship; prayer, which is a special part thereof, is to be made by all to him alone, and to none other.

Q. 180. *What is it to pray in the name of Christ?*
A. To pray in the name of Christ is, in obedience to his command, and in confidence on his promises, to ask mercy for his sake; not by bare mentioning of

his name, but by drawing our encouragement to pray, and our boldness, strength, and hope of acceptance in prayer, from Christ and his mediation.

Q. 181. *Why are we to pray in the name of Christ?*
A. The sinfulness of man, and his distance from God by reason thereof, being so great, as that we can have no access into his presence without a mediator; and there being none in heaven or earth appointed to, or fit for, that glorious work but Christ alone, we are to pray in no other name but his only.

Q. 182. *How doth the Spirit help us to pray?*
A. We not knowing what to pray for as we ought, the Spirit helpeth our infirmities, by enabling us to understand both for whom, and what, and how prayer is to be made; and by working and quickening in our hearts (although not in all persons, nor at all times, in the same measure) those apprehensions, affections, and graces which are requisite for the right performance of that duty.

Q. 183. *For whom are we to pray?*
A. We are to pray for the whole church of Christ upon earth; for magistrates, and ministers; for ourselves, our brethren, yea, our enemies; and for all sorts of men living, or that shall live hereafter; but not for the dead, nor for those that are known to have sinned the sin unto death.

Q. 184. *For what things are we to pray?*
A. We are to pray for all things tending to the glory of God, the welfare of the church, our own or others' good; but not for anything that is unlawful.

Q. 185. *How are we to pray?*
A. We are to pray with an awful apprehension of the majesty of God, and deep sense of our own unworthiness, necessities, and sins; with penitent, thankful, and enlarged hearts; with understanding, faith, sincerity, fervency, love, and perseverance, waiting upon him, with humble submission to his will.

Q. 186. *What rule hath God given for our direction in the duty of prayer?*
A. The whole Word of God is of use to direct us in the duty of prayer; but the

special rule of direction is that form of prayer which our Savior Christ taught his disciples, commonly called *The Lord's prayer.*

Q. 187. *How is the Lord's prayer to be used?*
A. The Lord's prayer is not only for direction, as a pattern, according to which we are to make other prayers; but may also be used as a prayer, so that it be done with understanding, faith, reverence, and other graces necessary to the right performance of the duty of prayer.

Q. 188. *Of how many parts doth the Lord's prayer consist?*
A. The Lord's prayer consists of three parts; a preface, petitions, and a conclusion.

Q. 189. *What doth the preface of the Lord's prayer teach us?*
A. The preface of the Lord's prayer (contained in these words, *Our Father which art in heaven*) teacheth us, when we pray, to draw near to God with confidence of his fatherly goodness, and our interest therein; with reverence, and all other childlike dispositions, heavenly affections, and due apprehensions of his sovereign power, majesty, and gracious condescension: as also, to pray with and for others.

Q. 190. *What do we pray for in the first petition?*
A. In the first petition (which is, *Hallowed be thy name*), acknowledging the utter inability and indisposition that is in ourselves and all men to honor God aright, we pray, that God would by his grace enable and incline us and others to know, to acknowledge, and highly to esteem him, his titles, attributes, ordinances, word, works, and whatsoever he is pleased to make himself known by; and to glorify him in thought, word, and deed: that he would prevent and remove atheism, ignorance, idolatry, profaneness, and whatsoever is dishonorable to him; and, by his overruling providence, direct and dispose of all things to his own glory.

Q. 191. *What do we pray for in the second petition?*
A. In the second petition (which is, *Thy kingdom come*), acknowledging ourselves and all mankind to be by nature under the dominion of sin and Satan,

we pray, that the kingdom of sin and Satan may be destroyed, the gospel propagated throughout the world, the Jews called, the fullness of the Gentiles brought in; the church furnished with all gospel officers and ordinances, purged from corruption, countenanced and maintained by the civil magistrate; that the ordinances of Christ may be purely dispensed, and made effectual to the converting of those that are yet in their sins, and the confirming, comforting, and building up of those that are already converted: that Christ would rule in our hearts here, and hasten the time of his second coming, and our reigning with him forever: and that he would be pleased so to exercise the kingdom of his power in all the world, as may best conduce to these ends.

Q. 192. *What do we pray for in the third petition?*
A. In the third petition (which is, *Thy will be done in earth, as it is in heaven*), acknowledging that by nature we and all men are not only utterly unable and unwilling to know and to do the will of God, but prone to rebel against his word, to repine and murmur against his providence, and wholly inclined to do the will of the flesh, and of the devil: we pray, that God would by his Spirit take away from ourselves and others all blindness, weakness, indisposedness, and perverseness of heart; and by his grace make us able and willing to know, do, and submit to his will in all things, with the like humility, cheerfulness, faithfulness, diligence, zeal, sincerity, and constancy, as the angels do in heaven.

Q. 193. *What do we pray for in the fourth petition?*
A. In the fourth petition (which is, *Give us this day our daily bread*), acknowledging that in Adam, and by our own sin, we have forfeited our right to all the outward blessings of this life, and deserve to be wholly deprived of them by God, and to have them cursed to us in the use of them; and that neither they of themselves are able to sustain us, nor we to merit, or by our own industry to procure them; but prone to desire, get, and use them unlawfully: we pray for ourselves and others, that both they and we, waiting upon the providence of God from day to day in the use of lawful means, may, of his free gift, and as to his fatherly wisdom shall seem best, enjoy a competent portion of them; and have the same continued and blessed unto us in our

holy and comfortable use of them, and contentment in them; and be kept from all things that are contrary to our temporal support and comfort.

Q. 194. *What do we pray for in the fifth petition?*
A. In the fifth petition (which is, *Forgive us our debts, as we forgive our debtors*), acknowledging that we and all others are guilty both of original and actual sin, and thereby become debtors to the justice of God; and that nei-ther we, nor any other creature, can make the least satisfaction for that debt: we pray for ourselves and others, that God of his free grace would, through the obedience and satisfaction of Christ, apprehended and applied by faith, acquit us both from the guilt and punishment of sin, accept us in his Beloved; continue his favor and grace to us, pardon our daily failings, and fill us with peace and joy, in giving us daily more and more assurance of forgiveness; which we are the rather emboldened to ask, and encouraged to expect, when we have this testimony in ourselves, that we from the heart forgive others their offenses.

Q. 195. *What do we pray for in the sixth petition?*
A. In the sixth petition (which is, *And lead us not into temptation, but de-liver us from evil*), acknowledging that the most wise, righteous, and gra-cious God, for divers holy and just ends, may so order things, that we may be assaulted, foiled, and for a time led captive by temptations; that Satan, the world, and the flesh, are ready powerfully to draw us aside, and ensnare us; and that we, even after the pardon of our sins, by reason of our corrup-tion, weakness, and want of watchfulness, are not only subject to be tempted, and forward to expose ourselves unto temptations, but also of ourselves un-able and unwilling to resist them, to recover out of them, and to improve them; and worthy to be left under the power of them; we pray, that God would so overrule the world and all in it, subdue the flesh, and restrain Satan, order all things, bestow and bless all means of grace, and quicken us to watchfulness in the use of them, that we and all his people may by his prov-idence be kept from being tempted to sin; or, if tempted, that by his Spirit we may be powerfully supported and enabled to stand in the hour of temp-tation; or when fallen, raised again and recovered out of it, and have a sanc-tified use and improvement thereof: that our sanctification and salvation may

be perfected, Satan trodden under our feet, and we fully freed from sin, temptation, and all evil, forever.

Q. 196. *What doth the conclusion of the Lord's prayer teach us?*
A. The conclusion of the Lord's prayer (which is, *For thine is the kingdom, and the power, and the glory, forever. Amen.*) teacheth us to enforce our petitions with arguments, which are to be taken, not from any worthiness in ourselves, or in any other creature, but from God; and with our prayers to join praises, ascribing to God alone eternal sovereignty, omnipotency, and glorious excellency; in regard whereof, as he is able and willing to help us, so we by faith are emboldened to plead with him that he would, and quietly to rely upon him, that he will fulfill our requests. And, to testify this our desire and assurance, we say, *Amen.*

Appendix B

THE WESTMINSTER SHORTER CATECHISM

Q. 1. *What is the chief end of man?*
A. Man's chief end is to glorify God, and to enjoy him forever.

Q. 2. *What rule hath God given to direct us how we may glorify and enjoy him?*
A. The word of God, which is contained in the scriptures of the Old and New Testaments, is the only rule to direct us how we may glorify and enjoy him.

Q. 3. *What do the scriptures principally teach?*
A. The scriptures principally teach what man is to believe concerning God, and what duty God requires of man.

Q. 4. *What is God?*
A. God is a spirit, infinite, eternal, and unchangeable, in his being, wisdom, power, holiness, justice, goodness and truth.

Q. 5. *Are there more Gods than one?*
A. There is but one only, the living and true God.

Q. 6. *How many persons are there in the godhead?*

A. There are three persons in the Godhead; the Father, the Son, and the Holy Ghost; and these three are one God, the same in substance, equal in power and glory.

Q. 7. *What are the decrees of God?*

A. The decrees of God are his eternal purpose, according to the counsel of his will, whereby, for his own glory, he hath foreordained whatsoever comes to pass.

Q. 8. *How doth God execute his decrees?*

A. God executeth his decrees in the works of creation and providence.

Q. 9. *What is the work of creation?*

A. The work of creation is God's making all things of nothing, by the word of his power, in the space of six days, and all very good.

Q. 10. *How did God create man?*

A. God created man male and female, after his own image, in knowledge, righteousness and holiness, with dominion over the creatures.

Q. 11. *What are God's works of providence?*

A. God's works of providence are his most holy, wise and powerful preserving and governing all his creatures, and all their actions.

Q. 12. *What special act of providence did God exercise toward man in the estate wherein he was created?*

A. When God had created man, he entered into a covenant of life with him, upon condition of perfect obedience; forbidding him to eat of the tree of the knowledge of good and evil, upon the pain of death.

Q. 13. *Did our first parents continue in the estate wherein they were created?*

A. Our first parents, being left to the freedom of their own will, fell from the estate wherein they were created, by sinning against God.

Q. 14. *What is sin?*

A. Sin is any want of conformity unto, or transgression of, the law of God.

Q. 15. *What was the sin whereby our first parents fell from the estate wherein they were created?*
A. The sin whereby our first parents fell from the estate wherein they were created was their eating the forbidden fruit.

Q. 16. *Did all mankind fall in Adam's first transgression?*
A. The covenant being made with Adam, not only for himself, but for his posterity; all mankind, descending from him by ordinary generation, sinned in him, and fell with him, in his first transgression.

Q. 17. *Into what estate did the fall bring mankind?*
A. The fall brought mankind into an estate of sin and misery.

Q. 18. *Wherein consists the sinfulness of that estate whereinto man fell?*
A. The sinfulness of that estate whereinto man fell consists in the guilt of Adam's first sin, the want of original righteousness, and the corruption of his whole nature, which is commonly called original sin; together with all actual transgressions which proceed from it.

Q. 19. *What is the misery of that estate whereinto man fell?*
A. All mankind by their fall lost communion with God, are under his wrath and curse, and so made liable to all miseries in this life, to death itself, and to the pains of hell forever.

Q. 20. *Did God leave all mankind to perish in the estate of sin and misery?*
A. God having, out of his mere good pleasure, from all eternity, elected some to everlasting life, did enter into a covenant of grace, to deliver them out of the estate of sin and misery, and to bring them into an estate of salvation by a redeemer.

Q. 21. *Who is the redeemer of God's elect?*
A. The only redeemer of God's elect is the Lord Jesus Christ, who, being the eternal Son of God, became man, and so was, and continueth to be, God and man in two distinct natures, and one person, forever.

Q. 22. *How did Christ, being the Son of God, become man?*
A. Christ, the Son of God, became man, by taking to himself a true body and a reasonable soul, being conceived by the power of the Holy Ghost in the womb of the virgin Mary, and born of her, yet without sin.

Q. 23. *What offices doth Christ execute as our redeemer?*
A. Christ, as our redeemer, executeth the offices of a prophet, of a priest, and of a king, both in his estate of humiliation and exaltation.

Q. 24. *How doth Christ execute the office of a prophet?*
A. Christ executeth the office of a prophet, in revealing to us, by his word and Spirit, the will of God for our salvation.

Q. 25. *How doth Christ execute the office of a priest?*
A. Christ executeth the office of a priest, in his once offering up of himself a sacrifice to satisfy divine justice, and reconcile us to God; and in making continual intercession for us.

Q. 26. *How doth Christ execute the office of a king?*
A. Christ executeth the office of a king, in subduing us to himself, in ruling and defending us, and in restraining and conquering all his and our enemies.

Q. 27. *Wherein did Christ's humiliation consist?*
A. Christ's humiliation consisted in his being born, and that in a low condition, made under the law, undergoing the miseries of this life, the wrath of God, and the cursed death of the cross; in being buried, and continuing under the power of death for a time.

Q. 28. *Wherein consisteth Christ's exaltation?*
A. Christ's exaltation consisteth in his rising again from the dead on the third day, in ascending up into heaven, in sitting at the right hand of God the Father, and in coming to judge the world at the last day.

Q. 29. *How are we made partakers of the redemption purchased by Christ?*

248

A. We are made partakers of the redemption purchased by Christ, by the effectual application of it to us by his Holy Spirit.

Q. 30. *How doth the Spirit apply to us the redemption purchased by Christ?*
A. The Spirit applieth to us the redemption purchased by Christ, by working faith in us, and thereby uniting us to Christ in our effectual calling.

Q. 31. *What is effectual calling?*
A. Effectual calling is the work of God's Spirit, whereby, convincing us of our sin and misery, enlightening our minds in the knowledge of Christ, and renewing our wills, he doth persuade and enable us to embrace Jesus Christ, freely offered to us in the gospel.

Q. 32. *What benefits do they that are effectually called partake of in this life?*
A. They that are effectually called do in this life partake of justification, adoption and sanctification, and the several benefits which in this life do either accompany or flow from them.

Q. 33. *What is justification?*
A. Justification is an act of God's free grace, wherein he pardoneth all our sins, and accepteth us as righteous in his sight, only for the righteousness of Christ imputed to us, and received by faith alone.

Q. 34. *What is adoption?*
A. Adoption is an act of God's free grace, whereby we are received into the number, and have a right to all the privileges of, the sons of God.

Q. 35. *What is sanctification?*
A. Sanctification is the work of God's free grace, whereby we are renewed in the whole man after the image of God, and are enabled more and more to die unto sin, and live unto righteousness.

Q. 36. *What are the benefits which in this life do accompany or flow from justification, adoption and sanctification?*
A. The benefits which in this life do accompany or flow from justification,

adoption and sanctification, are, assurance of God's love, peace of conscience, joy in the Holy Ghost, increase of grace, and perseverance therein to the end.

Q. 37. *What benefits do believers receive from Christ at death?*
A. The souls of believers are at their death made perfect in holiness, and do immediately pass into glory; and their bodies, being still united to Christ, do rest in their graves till the resurrection.

Q. 38. *What benefits do believers receive from Christ at the resurrection?*
A. At the resurrection, believers being raised up in glory, shall be openly acknowledged and acquitted in the day of judgment, and made perfectly blessed in the full enjoying of God to all eternity.

Q. 39. *What is the duty which God requireth of man?*
A. The duty which God requireth of man is obedience to his revealed will.

Q. 40. *What did God at first reveal to man for the rule of his obedience?*
A. The rule which God at first revealed to man for his obedience was the moral law.

Q. 41. *Where is the moral law summarily comprehended?*
A. The moral law is summarily comprehended in the ten commandments.

Q. 42. *What is the sum of the ten commandments?*
A. The sum of the ten commandments is to love the Lord our God with all our heart, with all our soul, with all our strength, and with all our mind; and our neighbor as ourselves.

Q. 43. *What is the preface to the ten commandments?*
A. The preface to the ten commandments is in these words, *I am the Lord thy God, which have brought thee out of the land of Egypt, out of the house of bondage.*

Q. 44. *What doth the preface to the ten commandments teach us?*

A. The preface to the ten commandments teacheth us that because God is the Lord, and our God, and redeemer, therefore we are bound to keep all his commandments.

Q. 45. *Which is the first commandment?*
A. The first commandment is, *Thou shalt have no other gods before me.*

Q. 46. *What is required in the first commandment?*
A. The first commandment requireth us to know and acknowledge God to be the only true God, and our God; and to worship and glorify him accordingly.

Q. 47. *What is forbidden in the first commandment?*
A. The first commandment forbiddeth the denying, or not worshiping and glorifying the true God as God, and our God; and the giving of that worship and glory to any other, which is due to him alone.

Q. 48. *What are we specially taught by these words* before me *in the first commandment?*
A. These words *before me* in the first commandment teach us that God, who seeth all things, taketh notice of, and is much displeased with, the sin of having any other god.

Q. 49. *Which is the second commandment?*
A. The second commandment is, *Thou shalt not make unto thee any graven image, or any likeness of anything that is in heaven above, or that is in the earth beneath, or that is in the water under the earth: thou shalt not bow down thyself to them, nor serve them: for I the Lord thy God am a jealous God, visiting the iniquity of the fathers upon the children unto the third and fourth generation of them that hate me; and showing mercy unto thousands of them that love me, and keep my commandments.*

Q. 50. *What is required in the second commandment?*
A. The second commandment requireth the receiving, observing, and keeping pure and entire, all such religious worship and ordinances as God hath appointed in his word.

Q. 51. *What is forbidden in the second commandment?*
A. The second commandment forbiddeth the worshiping of God by images, or any other way not appointed in his word.

Q. 52. *What are the reasons annexed to the second commandment?*
A. The reasons annexed to the second commandment are, God's sovereignty over us, his propriety in us, and the zeal he hath to his own worship.

Q. 53. *Which is the third commandment?*
A. The third commandment is, *Thou shalt not take the name of the Lord thy God in vain: for the Lord will not hold him guiltless that taketh his name in vain.*

Q. 54. *What is required in the third commandment?*
A. The third commandment requireth the holy and reverent use of God's names, titles, attributes, ordinances, word and works.

Q. 55. *What is forbidden in the third commandment?*
A. The third commandment forbiddeth all profaning or abusing of anything whereby God maketh himself known.

Q. 56. *What is the reason annexed to the third commandment?*
A. The reason annexed to the third commandment is that however the breakers of this commandment may escape punishment from men, yet the Lord our God will not suffer them to escape his righteous judgment.

Q. 57. *Which is the fourth commandment?*
A. The fourth commandment is, *Remember the sabbath day, to keep it holy. Six days shalt thou labor, and do all thy work: but the seventh day is the sabbath of the Lord thy God: in it thou shalt not do any work, thou, nor thy son, nor thy daughter, thy manservant, nor thy maidservant, nor thy cattle, nor thy stranger that is within thy gates: for in six days the Lord made heaven and earth, the sea, and all that in them is, and rested the seventh day: wherefore the Lord blessed the sabbath day, and hallowed it.*

Q. 58. *What is required in the fourth commandment?*

A. The fourth commandment requireth the keeping holy to God such set times as he hath appointed in his word; expressly one whole day in seven, to be a holy sabbath to himself.

Q. 59. *Which day of the seven hath God appointed to be the weekly sabbath?*
A. From the beginning of the world to the resurrection of Christ, God appointed the seventh day of the week to be the weekly sabbath; and the first day of the week ever since, to continue to the end of the world, which is the Christian sabbath.

Q. 60. *How is the sabbath to be sanctified?*
A. The sabbath is to be sanctified by a holy resting all that day, even from such worldly employments and recreations as are lawful on other days; and spending the whole time in the public and private exercises of God's worship, except so much as is to be taken up in the works of necessity and mercy.

Q. 61. *What is forbidden in the fourth commandment?*
A. The fourth commandment forbiddeth the omission or careless performance of the duties required, and the profaning the day by idleness, or doing that which is in itself sinful, or by unnecessary thoughts, words or works, about our worldly employments or recreations.

Q. 62. *What are the reasons annexed to the fourth commandment?*
A. The reasons annexed to the fourth commandment are, God's allowing us six days of the week for our own employments, his challenging a special propriety in the seventh, his own example, and his blessing the sabbath day.

Q. 63. *Which is the fifth commandment?*
A. The fifth commandment is, *Honor thy father and thy mother; that thy days may be long upon the land which the Lord thy God giveth thee.*

Q. 64. *What is required in the fifth commandment?*

A. The fifth commandment requireth the preserving the honor, and performing the duties, belonging to every one in their several places and relations, as superiors, inferiors or equals.

Q. 65. *What is forbidden in the fifth commandment?*
A. The fifth commandment forbiddeth the neglecting of, or doing anything against, the honor and duty which belongeth to every one in their several places and relations.

Q. 66. *What is the reason annexed to the fifth commandment?*
A. The reason annexed to the fifth commandment is a promise of long life and prosperity (as far as it shall serve for God's glory and their own good) to all such as keep this commandment.

Q. 67. *Which is the sixth commandment?*
A. The sixth commandment is, *Thou shalt not kill.*

Q. 68. *What is required in the sixth commandment?*
A. The sixth commandment requireth all lawful endeavors to preserve our own life, and the life of others.

Q. 69. *What is forbidden in the sixth commandment?*
A. The sixth commandment forbiddeth the taking away of our own life, or the life of our neighbor unjustly, or whatsoever tendeth thereunto.

Q. 70. *Which is the seventh commandment?*
A. The seventh commandment is, *Thou shalt not commit adultery.*

Q. 71. *What is required in the seventh commandment?*
A. The seventh commandment requireth the preservation of our own and our neighbor's chastity, in heart, speech and behavior.

Q. 72. *What is forbidden in the seventh commandment?*
A. The seventh commandment forbiddeth all unchaste thoughts, words and actions.

254

Q. 73. *Which is the eighth commandment?*
A. The eighth commandment is, *Thou shalt not steal.*

Q. 74. *What is required in the eighth commandment?*
A. The eighth commandment requireth the lawful procuring and furthering the wealth and outward estate of ourselves and others.

Q. 75. *What is forbidden in the eighth commandment?*
A. The eighth commandment forbiddeth whatsoever doth or may unjustly hinder our own or our neighbor's wealth or outward estate.

Q. 76. *Which is the ninth commandment?*
A. The ninth commandment is, *Thou shalt not bear false witness against thy neighbor.*

Q. 77. *What is required in the ninth commandment?*
A. The ninth commandment requireth the maintaining and promoting of truth between man and man, and of our own and our neighbor's good name, especially in witness-bearing.

Q. 78. *What is forbidden in the ninth commandment?*
A. The ninth commandment forbiddeth whatsoever is prejudicial to truth, or injurious to our own or our neighbor's good name.

Q. 79. *Which is the tenth commandment?*
A. The tenth commandment is, *Thou shalt not covet thy neighbor's house, thou shalt not covet thy neighbor's wife, nor his manservant, nor his maidservant, nor his ox, nor his ass, nor anything that is thy neighbor's.*

Q. 80. *What is required in the tenth commandment?*
A. The tenth commandment requireth full contentment with our own condition, with a right and charitable frame of spirit toward our neighbor, and all that is his.

Q. 81. *What is forbidden in the tenth commandment?*

A. The tenth commandment forbiddeth all discontentment with our own estate, envying or grieving at the good of our neighbor, and all inordinate motions and affections to anything that is his.

Q. 82. *Is any man able perfectly to keep the commandments of God?*
A. No mere man since the fall is able in this life perfectly to keep the commandments of God, but doth daily break them in thought, word and deed.

Q. 83. *Are all transgressions of the law equally heinous?*
A. Some sins in themselves, and by reason of several aggravations, are more heinous in the sight of God than others.

Q. 84. *What doth every sin deserve?*
A. Every sin deserveth God's wrath and curse, both in this life, and that which is to come.

Q. 85. *What doth God require of us that we may escape his wrath and curse due to us for sin?*
A. To escape the wrath and curse of God due to us for sin, God requireth of us faith in Jesus Christ, repentance unto life, with the diligent use of all the outward means whereby Christ communicateth to us the benefits of redemption.

Q. 86. *What is faith in Jesus Christ?*
A. Faith in Jesus Christ is a saving grace, whereby we receive and rest upon him alone for salvation, as he is offered to us in the gospel.

Q. 87. *What is repentance unto life?*
A. Repentance unto life is a saving grace, whereby a sinner, out of a true sense of his sin, and apprehension of the mercy of God in Christ, doth, with grief and hatred of his sin, turn from it unto God, with full purpose of, and endeavor after, new obedience.

Q. 88. *What are the outward means whereby Christ communicateth to us the benefits of redemption?*
A. The outward and ordinary means whereby Christ communicateth to us the

benefits of redemption, are his ordinances, especially the word, sacraments, and prayer; all which are made effectual to the elect for salvation.

Q. 89. *How is the word made effectual to salvation?*
A. The Spirit of God maketh the reading, but especially the preaching, of the word, an effectual means of convincing and converting sinners, and of building them up in holiness and comfort, through faith, unto salvation.

Q. 90. *How is the word to be read and heard, that it may become effectual to salvation?*
A. That the word may become effectual to salvation, we must attend thereunto with diligence, preparation and prayer; receive it with faith and love, lay it up in our hearts, and practice it in our lives.

Q. 91. *How do the sacraments become effectual means of salvation?*
A. The sacraments become effectual means of salvation, not from any virtue in them, or in him that doth administer them; but only by the blessing of Christ, and the working of his Spirit in them that by faith receive them.

Q. 92. *What is a sacrament?*
A. A sacrament is an holy ordinance instituted by Christ; wherein, by sensible signs, Christ, and the benefits of the new covenant, are represented, sealed, and applied to believers.

Q. 93. *Which are the sacraments of the New Testament?*
A. The sacraments of the New Testament are baptism and the Lord's supper.

Q. 94. *What is baptism?*
A. Baptism is a sacrament, wherein the washing with water in the name of the Father, and of the Son, and of the Holy Ghost, doth signify and seal our ingrafting into Christ, and partaking of the benefits of the covenant of grace, and our engagement to be the Lord's.

Q. 95. *To whom is baptism to be administered?*
A. Baptism is not to be administered to any that are out of the visible church,

till they profess their faith in Christ, and obedience to him; but the infants of such as are members of the visible church are to be baptized.

Q. 96. *What is the Lord's supper?*
A. The Lord's supper is a sacrament, wherein, by giving and receiving bread and wine according to Christ's appointment, his death is showed forth; and the worthy receivers are, not after a corporal and carnal manner, but by faith, made partakers of his body and blood, with all his benefits, to their spiritual nourishment and growth in grace.

Q. 97. *What is required to the worthy receiving of the Lord's supper?*
A. It is required of them that would worthily partake of the Lord's supper, that they examine themselves of their knowledge to discern the Lord's body, of their faith to feed upon him, of their repentance, love, and new obedience; lest, coming unworthily, they eat and drink judgment to themselves.

Q. 98. *What is prayer?*
A. Prayer is an offering up of our desires unto God, for things agreeable to his will, in the name of Christ, with confession of our sins, and thankful acknowledgment of his mercies.

Q. 99. *What rule hath God given for our direction in prayer?*
A. The whole word of God is of use to direct us in prayer; but the special rule of direction is that form of prayer which Christ taught his disciples, commonly called the Lord's prayer.

Q. 100. *What doth the preface of the Lord's prayer teach us?*
A. The preface of the Lord's prayer, which is, *Our Father which art in heaven,* teacheth us to draw near to God with all holy reverence and confidence, as children to a father able and ready to help us; and that we should pray with and for others.

Q. 101. *What do we pray for in the first petition?*
A. In the first petition, which is, *Hallowed be thy name,* we pray that God would enable us and others to glorify him in all that whereby he maketh

himself known; and that he would dispose all things to his own glory.

Q. 102. *What do we pray for in the second petition?*
A. In the second petition, which is, *Thy kingdom come*, we pray that Satan's kingdom may be destroyed; and that the kingdom of grace may be advanced, ourselves and others brought into it, and kept in it; and that the kingdom of glory may be hastened.

Q. 103. *What do we pray for in the third petition?*
A. In the third petition, which is, *Thy will be done in earth, as it is in heaven*, we pray that God, by his grace, would make us able and willing to know, obey and submit to his will in all things, as the angels do in heaven.

Q. 104. *What do we pray for in the fourth petition?*
A. In the fourth petition, which is, *Give us this day our daily bread*, we pray that of God's free gift we may receive a competent portion of the good things of this life, and enjoy his blessing with them.

Q. 105. *What do we pray for in the fifth petition?*
A. In the fifth petition, which is, *And forgive us our debts, as we forgive our debtors*, we pray that God, for Christ's sake, would freely pardon all our sins; which we are the rather encouraged to ask, because by his grace we are enabled from the heart to forgive others.

Q. 106. *What do we pray for in the sixth petition?*
A. In the sixth petition, which is, *And lead us not into temptation, but deliver us from evil*, we pray that God would either keep us from being tempted to sin, or support and deliver us when we are tempted.

Q. 107. *What doth the conclusion of the Lord's prayer teach us?*
A. The conclusion of the Lord's prayer, which is, *For thine is the kingdom, and the power, and the glory, forever, Amen*, teacheth us to take our encouragement in prayer from God only, and in our prayers to praise him, ascribing kingdom, power and glory to him. And in testimony of our desire, and assurance to be heard, we say, *Amen*.

INDEX OF SCRIPTURE

INDEX OF SUBJECTS
AND NAMES

blasphemy against, **2**:155–56,
   3:156–57
and death, **1**:248, 253, 270, **2**:156
deity of, **2**:58, 235–36, **3**:124
and fulfilling the law, **1**:251–52,
   2:267–70
as head of the church, **1**:238–39, **3**:60
   (*see also* church, as body of Christ)
humiliation of, **2**:72, **3**:193
and institution of sacraments,
   3:80–81, 92, 97, 112, 134–39
kingdom of, **3**:45–49, 161, 174
as Logos, **3**:87
as Mediator, **1**:60, 213, 231–79,
   2:271, 286, 317–20
nature of, **1**:243–50, 269, **2**:19,
   3:149–55
obedience of, **1**:218–19, 252, 260–61,
   2:45–46, 62, 119, **3**:179
offices of, **1**:236–39, 273
as only begotten Son, **1**:71–72, 236,
   241
person of, **1**:254–59, **3**:135–36
presence in Lord's Supper, **3**:148–49,
   151–52, 155–56
suffering with, **3**:65–67
work of, **1**:260–79, **2**:46–48, 50,
   122–23, 195, 247–48, **3**:95,
   142–43
See also obedience, to Jesus Christ
joy, **2**:241, 345–46
Judaism, **1**:33, **2**:69, 317, **3**:113
Judas, **2**:200–201
judgment, **1**:85, 160, 165–66, 239,
   2:38–39, 192–93, 221, **3**:107, 179,
   182–85, 187–97
just war theory, **3**:13–14

justice, **1**:65–66, 85, 105–6, 149–51, 183,
   2:37, 255, **3**:8, 14, 143
justification
   and baptism, **3**:94, 117
   and crucifixion of Christ, **1**:253–54
   by faith alone, **1**:217–18, 266–67,
      2:121–22, 125, 224, 236, **3**:58–59,
      82, 90, 95–96
   and good works, **1**:219, **2**:113,
      119–20, 151, 170
   and order of salvation, **1**:100–103
   and sanctification, **1**:161, **2**:77–79, 85
   understanding doctrine of, **2**:35–66,
      223
Justin Martyr, **2**:259

kenotic heresy, **1**:37
Keswick movement, **2**:82
"keys to the kingdom," **3**:18, 161
King James Version, **1**:26
kings, **1**:234, 237, **3**:85–86
Kline, Meredith, **1**:127, 206, 212–13
Knox, John, **2**:342
Küng, Hans, **1**:215–16

last rites, **2**:149, **3**:101
law
   blessings and curses of, **2**:283–84
   and the bounds of God, **1**:50, 157–58
   casuistic, **2**:255–56
   ceremonial, **2**:260–65, 337
   civil, **2**:183, 358, **3**:7, 22, 24
   conformity to, **1**:188–91, **2**:183, 194
   as defining goodness/badness,
      2:170–72
   dietary, **2**:337
   divine, **1**:194–95, 210, **2**:96–97, 103,
      245–76, **3**:191